Equality and Economy

❦

February 2005

To Martin Kafka:

with thanks for
your help in getting
this book done &
with hopes that
...ill enjoy it!

FOUNDATIONS OF CULTURAL THOUGHT SERIES

Series Editors
Donald Brenneis and Daniel Segal

Series Description

Continued challenges to theory and ethnographic method have led scholars to explore new definitions and dimensions of anthropological inquiry, even to redraw the contours of the field. As scholars seek to further redefine anthropology they also face the challenge of conveying the importance and creativity of this new work to future generations of students. Designed to meet this challenge, *Foundations of Cultural Thought* offers learned, concise, and accessible works on topics at the heart of anthropology's future. Each book will be written by an author of distinctive accomplishment and will build upon the field's best writing and research, providing a prospective essay on transformations taking place in anthropological and cultural theory.

Series Editors

Donald Brenneis, Anthropology Board, Social Sciences 1, University of California-Santa Cruz, Santa Cruz, CA 95064, brenneis@cats.ucsc.edu

Daniel Segal, Dept. of Anthropology, Pitzer College, Claremont CA 91711, dsegal@pitzer.edu

Books in the Series

Equality and Economy

The Global Challenge

Michael Blim

A Division of
ROWMAN & LITTLEFIELD PUBLISHERS, INC.
Walnut Creek • Lanham • New York • Toronto • Oxford

To

Donald Di Salvo

Compassionate and Patient Partner

ALTAMIRA PRESS
A division of Rowman & Littlefield Publishers, Inc.
1630 North Main Street, #367
Walnut Creek, CA 94596
www.altamirapress.com

Rowman & Littlefield Publishers, Inc.
A wholly owned subsidiary of The Rowman & Littlefield Publishing Group, Inc.
4501 Forbes Boulevard, Suite 200
Lanham, MD 20706

PO Box 317
Oxford
OX2 9RU, UK

Copyright © 2005 by AltaMira Press

British Library Cataloguing in Publication Information Available

Library of Congress Cataloging-in-Publication Data

Blim, Michael.
  Equality and economy : the global challenge / Michael Blim.
    p. cm. — (Foundations of cultural thought series ; 1)
  Includes bibliographical references and index.
  ISBN 0-7591-0687-8 (cloth : alk. paper) — ISBN 0-7591-0688-6 (pbk. : alk. paper)
  1. Equality. 2. Poverty. 3. Income distribution. 4. Globalization. I. Title. II. Series.

  HM821.B56 2004
  305.5—dc22   2004011839

Printed in the United States of America

∞™ The paper used in this publication meets the minimum requirements of
American National Standard for Information Sciences—Permanence of Paper for
Printed Library Materials, ANSI/NISO Z39.48-1992.

Contents

Acknowledgments

I want to thank Donald Brenneis, Daniel Segal, and Dean Birkenkamp for initiating this series and for giving me the chance to write the book I needed to write. Thanks, too, to Rosalie Robertson and Brian Richards for seeing the manuscript through production.

I owe a profound debt to friends and colleagues who have encouraged this project and provided valuable feedback throughout its execution. Thanks to Kalman Applbaum, Julian Brash, Vincent Crapanzano, Gerald Creed, David Harvey, Magali Sarfatti Larson, Louise Lennihan, Michael Miller, Frances Fox Piven, Donald Robotham, Frances Rothstein, Jane Schneider, Peter Schneider, Alan Smart, Neil Smith, Mary Taylor, and Nathan Woods.

A special thanks to Douglas Porpora, for twenty-five years the wisest of friends and counselors.

Finally, this book is dedicated to Donald Di Salvo, who did more than he knows to help me get to the end of what turned out to be a terrific adventure.

MB

CHAPTER ONE

The World We Live In

Anna Melnic was sold for $1,000. She was hustled out of her native Moldova on a train. She woke up in Romania. She was beaten, raped, and driven across Yugoslavia. In the foothills of Albania, she was passed to a pimp, ending up in Vlora, where she jumped off a fourth-floor balcony trying to escape her next fate, a smuggler's boat bound for Italy.[1]

The slavery in the charcoal camps of Mato Grosso do Sul, Brazil, is just one example of many, many kinds of bondage in the country. Slaves cut down the Amazon rain forests and harvest the sugarcane. They mine gold and precious stones or work as prostitutes. The rubber industry relies on slavery, as does cattle and timber. Indians are especially likely to be enslaved, but all poor Brazilians run the risk of bondage.[2]

In 1999, the remuneration of the average chief executive of a big U.S. corporation was 475 times greater than that of the average non-managerial worker. . . . That is six times more than he or she made a decade ago.[3]

Ours is a world of contrasts—often obscene contrasts. How does one value a human life? Almost half of the world's 6 billion people live on less than $2 a day. About 1.5 billion live on less than $1 a day.[4] An awkward, ethnocentric measure, at best, of personal income, the dollar. But can someone's life really be worth four to eight cents an hour?

Perhaps it is possible in a world where the poor are falling further behind the rich.[5] The average family in the United States is now seventy-two times richer than the average family in Ethiopia, a dramatic change from the 3:1 ratio at the beginning of the nineteenth century.[6] Can someone's life be seventy-two times more valuable than that of another? Further, what has occurred to the world economy to so drastically increase economic inequality?

To mitigate the degree to which this gap reveals a high level of human suffering felt around the world, one could argue that standards of living are relative. Even at a sliver of a fraction of the wealth held by a U.S. citizen, an Ethiopian might conspire to survive. But deprivation is absolute, local ways notwithstanding. Otherwise, how does one explain that in poor countries, one out of twelve children dies before age five, and one of every six children under age five is malnourished?[7] How does one rationalize the facts that among the 4.4 billion people living in developing countries, three-fifths have no sanitation, one-third have no access to clean water, and one-quarter lack adequate housing?[8] How does one rationalize the fact that the average citizen in rich countries has a life expectancy of seventy-four while those in poor countries can hope on average for no more than sixty-two years of life? In sub-Saharan Africa, only forty-seven years of life?[9]

What is the price of a human life? Experts estimate that some 27 million people around the world live in a condition of slavery. Some, as in northern and western Africa, are born into servitude. Others in South Asia become bonded labor by "giving" themselves into slavery as security against a loan or an inherited debt. Still others are abducted into a life of involuntary servitude, and they may be found in domestic, sexual, and industrial labor throughout the world.[10]

Many of these caught in the web of servitude are children. Human Rights Watch, for instance, estimates that of the 60 to 115 million estimated child workers in India, 15 million of these children work as bonded laborers. They begin their account of bonded labor in India with the description of one child's life. He is Lakshmi, a nine-year-old cigarette roller in Tamil Nadu:

> My sister is ten years old. Every morning at seven she goes to the bonded labor man, and every night at nine she comes home. He treats her badly; he hits her if he thinks she is working slowly or if she talks to other children, he yells at her, he comes looking for her if she is sick and cannot go to work. . . . I don't care about school or playing. All I want is to bring my sister home from the bonded labor man. For 600 rupees (US$17), I can bring her home. We don't have 600 rupees . . . we will never have 600 rupees.[11]

As discouraging as these facts are, some improvements in the human condition have occurred since 1980. Although, as we noted, one in twelve children dies before age five, child mortality rates have dropped in every country save three in sub-Saharan Africa since 1980.[12] Though famines are often encountered between the Sahara and equatorial Africa, and hunger is a chronic problem in areas throughout the world, food production has doubled in the last twenty-five years.[13] Although a person living in Western Europe, Japan, or North America will live twenty years longer than a person in sub-Saharan Africa, a person born in a poor country in 1995 will live ten years longer than one born in 1970.[14] Since the 1970s, illiteracy in poor countries has been cut from 47 percent to 25 percent of all adults.[15] These are important achievements.

Yet the overall picture remains disheartening, and every effort to improve the human condition through economic development, it seems, carries the cost of greater environmental degradation and increased global warming.[16] Greenhouse gases from industrialization have increased world surface temperature half a degree since 1975, which puts us at the highest average temperature level in 1,000 years. New and highly reputable studies estimate that global average temperature could rise between 1.5 degrees and 6 degrees by the year 2100. Estimates, not including possible polar meltdowns, are that mean sea level could rise 15–95 centimeters by 2100, swamping large cities like New York and Bombay, not to mention low-lying countries like the Maldives and Bangladesh.[17]

There is sufficient wealth in the world. As astonishing as it may seem, if one divided the wealth of the world by the number of its inhabitants, there would be the equivalent of US$5,000 for every man, woman, and child on the planet. Ideally distributed, there is enough wealth worldwide to support a standard of living equivalent to that enjoyed by the people of Uruguay.[18] Yet look at the world's present distribution of income. The World Bank reports that the top 1 percent of the world's people, some 50 million people worldwide, earns as much as the poorest 57 percent on the planet. Put into numbers, this means that the richest 50 million people in the world earn as much as 2.7 billion of the world's poorest.[19]

There is starvation and malnourishment amid abundance. If all of the world's food were divided equally, every person on the planet could consume 2,700 calories a day—700 calories more than the minimum daily requirement, according to the Food and Agricultural Organization. Instead, 800 million persons are chronically undernourished, and famine watches by international organizations for vast areas of Africa are common.[20]

One hears discussion of greater economic growth. Often the refrain is to let the poor people of the world pull harder, and they too can taste the benefits of prosperity. But there is precious little talk of worldwide income redistribution. This is because our moral imaginations, if not some of our pocketbooks, are impoverished. The sheer quantity of poverty and economic and social inequality inures us. Our acceptance of capitalism as the only real possibly successful economy prevents us from imagining others—or even modifications of capitalism. Instead, there is an unspoken conviction that the chaos and suffering that arises with capitalism must be borne as a cost of partaking in its spoils.

This is not only the belief of conservative politicians and ideologues, but there is something of a general consensus that people in poor countries need to suffer in order to succeed economically. Take, for example, the case of Nicholas Kristof and Sheryl WuDunn, two Pulitzer Prize–winning reporters of the *New York Times*. In an article entitled "Two Cheers for Sweatshops," they argue, almost in the form of testimony, for the value of exploitation:

> Fourteen years ago, we moved to Asia and began reporting there. Like most Westerners, we arrived in the region outraged at sweatshops. In time, though, we came to accept the view supported by most Asians: that the campaign against sweatshops risks harming the very people it is intended to help. For beneath their grime, sweatshops are a clear sign of the industrial revolution that is beginning to reshape Asia. . . . For all the misery they can engender, sweatshops at least offer a precarious escape from the poverty that is the developing world's greatest problem.[21]

The cost of escaping poverty is apparently more misery. The underlying belief is that capitalism requires this further degradation as the price of progress. Must we, like the authors, resign others to this fate? Are there no alternatives?

In capitalism, profit is the measure of all things. On the one hand, it is an end in itself. "To be rich is glorious," the post-Mao Chinese adage goes. On the other hand, it is a means to an end. People pursuing profit, Adam Smith argued, unwittingly provide for us all. Each of us serves the other by serving ourselves.

After decades of "development," in which poor nations since the 1960s have tried one formula after another to increase their economic well-being through profit-making in the world economy, the results have been less than salutary. One can name the short number of successes easily. In the first wave after World War II, the defeated powers of Japan, Germany, and Italy recovered their industrial prowess. A second wave of development in southern Europe lifted the economic prospects of Spain, Portugal, and Greece. Close behind, a third wave hit the East Asian Pacific coast, carrying upward the economies of Hong Kong, Singapore, Taiwan, Malaysia, Thailand, Indonesia, and South Korea. Behind them China floated its huge coastal economy with the aid of its enormous internal market and its unprecedented access to foreign capital.

For the great majority of other societies in Central and Latin America, South Asia, Africa, Eastern Europe, and the Middle East, the periods of world economic growth in the 1980s and 1990s have passed them by. Fully eighty countries, according to the United Nations Development Programme, find themselves with lower per capita incomes than they had a decade or more ago.[22] This disconcerting finding is true, notwithstanding the fact that since about 1980, a major proportion of world manufacturing capacity moved out of rich countries into poor countries. Industrialization, once thought of as the engine of economic development for the poor, has not narrowed the enormous disparities between the "haves" and the "have-nots" worldwide.[23]

Nor has globalization, if what we mean by the term is the increased integration of world markets for labor, goods, and capital. Globalization, following Manuel Castells, means more than just a faster world economy: It is an economy "with the capacity to work as a unit in real time on a planetary scale."[24] The ability of a producer like the Ford Motor Company to calculate worldwide demand for a product like the Ford Taurus, to secure financing from international credit markets for the car's manufacture, and to produce and distribute the car from facilities coordinated worldwide by a single corporate "mastermind" in Detroit is a quantum leap over Henry Ford's efforts to put a Model A in European and Latin American, as well as U.S., garages. The planet has become one market, its populations one mass consumer, and its workers one mass producer.

But just as telephone and Internet connections put the world in continuous contact, the globalization of world markets more successfully links the world's "haves" than it does its "have-nots." As the writer Arundhati Roy says of India, the world is dividing into two populations—a minority consisting of a rising class "on its way to a glittering destination somewhere near the top of the world," and a vast majority composed of classes that are sinking into a morass of poverty and unspeakable degradation. She describes the process with a succinct starkness:

> In the lane behind my house [in New Delhi, India], every night I walk past road gangs of emaciated laborers digging a trench to lay fiber-optic cables to speed up our digital revolution. In the bitter winter cold, they work by the light of a few candles.[25]

The pursuit of profit, then, even in its global guise, has not brought us a better world. Despite the gargantuan growth of the world economy since the

1980s, the social inequalities we have described persist. If we imagine that the goal of our global economy is to provide universal well-being, we have failed. The yawning deficits in human provisioning become by virtue of globalization our collective problems rather than those that are visited upon others.

Human Values, Human Lives

Universal well-being is a concept difficult to pin down. In many ways, we have an intuition of what it means. It includes the absence of things such as deprivation, poverty, pain, and exploitation. It involves a sense of satisfaction in our contact with others and ourselves in our world. It consists of enjoyment of a measure of happiness. As Aristotle asserted long ago, happiness is perhaps the one human virtue above honor, reason, and pleasure that we select for its own sake alone. Happiness, he believed, is the one end we would choose if we could.[26]

Aristotle also asserted that happiness derives from the completeness of life. For instance, a child may not be judged completely happy, as she has not yet had the fullest of opportunities to exercise her talents. On the other hand, someone, as Aristotle says, who ends his life with the misfortunes of King Priam, the victim of ancient Greek revenge who loses all in the Trojan Wars, can hardly said to be happy in some lasting or stable sense either. Happiness refers to a state wherein like a shoemaker, we make best shoes out of the leather we find before us. Thus Aristotle reasons in ways similar to our intuition that happiness has to do with optimizing fulfillment of our human potential.[27]

If happiness is an ultimate goal of human life, and well-being enables us to work toward it, how do we assess a person's well-being? We need to acknowledge immediately that every person's capacity for well-being differs. Even in a day when experiments in human cloning hold out the prospect that making a superhuman is just within our grasp, a more homely account of human life suggests that each of us is born with and acquires different cognitive, emotional, and physical capabilities that influence what we can do with our bodies and minds. At the same time, each of us receives a set of social designations: We are differentiated by gender, race, and ethnic markers to which we adapt and through which we act. Our family backgrounds and socioeconomic statuses count too in enabling or limiting us in achieving our human potential. The measure of each of us, then, is what kind of person we fashion out of the very facets with which we are composed. Clearly, even though we may be compared with others and constantly compare ourselves with others, each of our lives is unique, no less in part because we make ourselves unique. Following Aristotle here, too, we are like his shoemaker: Living becomes a skilled accomplishment and we the pursuers and users of craft.

Moreover, there is an important sense in which an awareness of self-fulfillment, once thought to be a goal fitting only for or available to the privileged few, is becoming a universal human aspiration. People feel "called" to a vocation or a path of life, judging, as Charles Taylor observes, that their lives would be somehow wasted or deeply mistaken if they didn't pursue a particular course of action or way of being.[28] Each of us discovers in ourselves what Douglas Porpora calls "a human vocation."[29]

Well-being itself connotes more than minimal human functioning. It implies a more robust expectation that a person can function normally in the world without a particular characteristic of her being diminishing her capabilities. "Some functionings," writes Amartya Sen, the principal theorist of a capabilities approach to human happiness:

> are elementary, such as being adequately nourished, being in good health, etc., and these may be strongly valued for all, for obvious reasons. Others may be more complex, but still widely valued, such as achieving self-respect or being socially integrated. Individuals may, however, differ a good deal from each in the weights they attach to these different functionings—valuable though they may all be—and the assessment of individual and social advantages must be alive to these variations.[30]

Sen thus challenges us to ask some fundamental questions about the ways we determine well-being. Can a person go about her life undertaking the normal challenges of existence without the burden of disadvantage dulling or reducing her basic human capabilities? Second, and no less important, what does *she* think she needs to function fully in the society in which she lives?

If we ask these questions, we find that many people are in predicaments where the simple satisfaction of needs is not enough to create or restore well-being. For instance, let us take up physical disadvantage. A person disabled physically at birth will likely need more than an average share of available resources to attain adequate functioning. She may need compensatory education, prostheses, mobility aids, adjunct therapies, adapted workplaces—many things, in short, that the unaffected do not need. A person with HIV or AIDS, given current medical knowledge, needs a battery of medications designed to restore physical equilibrium and thus facilitate normal functioning.

Social disadvantage, too, weighs heavily upon its holders. A woman in the world, but especially in poor countries, finds herself less well nourished, less well educated, and less wealthy than her male counterparts. Her basic capabilities and even her physical movements are more restricted than are those of men. She may need compensatory access to more or to specifically targeted additional resources if she is to achieve a normal level of functioning. A person of color in rich and in poor countries often finds herself stigmatized and deprived of the resources she needs to function adequately in the world. Her situation, too, usually cries out for compensation, so that she can experience well-being at levels to which others are accustomed. Even a child, by virtue of her tender age, requires special attention and greater access to resources. In each case of social disadvantage we encounter, something other than the "average" access to resources is required, because giving both an advantaged and disadvantaged person equal access will result in disadvantage anew for the disadvantaged person.

To be sure, averages matter. They tell us how far above or below our peers we are in our experiences of well-being. They become important measures by which we estimate the degree to which social policies and programs that seek to improve well-being are in fact working. Further, they identify social characteristics some persons possess that may disadvantage them in achieving well-being.

But a person does not experience well-being as an "average" experience. She may encounter feelings of fullness, satisfaction, and realization, or their opposites, among many others. As Sen alerts us in the quotation above, it is important to consider what each person considers adequate for her state of well-being. For finally, happiness is something an individual feels or she doesn't; something she has or she lacks. Her understanding of the self and its satisfactions is an important indication of just how far we can move toward universal well-being, our common human vocation.

Norms—that is, what we expect and what is typically the case in human settings—help guide policy. What set of norms, those that connote minimal functioning or those that imply maximal functioning, should apply to the goal of universal well-being? Though the human species has changed little over the past 100,000 years, the human condition has changed a great deal. The norms of rich countries as they pertain to standard of living and survivability are clearly superior to those characteristic of poor countries. For instance, a century ago, a life expectancy of sixty years seemed for its time an adequate test of a person's presumed lifetime viability. Today, rich societies have added fifteen years to the average life span, thus signifying an expansion in the range of human potential that could serve as a benchmark for all.[31] Likewise, an infant mortality rate of 8 percent was normal worldwide in 1980; as of 2004 the rate hovers at 5 percent. In rich countries the infant mortality rate drops to less than 1 percent.[32] As the human condition improves, so do the norms, and so do our expectations as well as our experience of what humans should be able to achieve.

Consequently, I think we should choose the more optimal norms for human well-being that are found in rich countries as the best available measures of human well-being. First, all things being equal, it is reasonable to assume that the more favorable rates also signify a higher state of well-being for the population as a whole. While old age can bring hardship and suffering, especially in societies without pensions for the elderly, an increase in longer life chances would constitute an additional benefit for people around the world. Parenthetically, one could imagine that if people could choose, they would choose a longer rather than a shorter life.

Second, I think it is important to avoid the invidious distinction that one state of well-being, while inferior to the optimal functioning of another, could be "adequate" for another society. People in rich countries tend to believe, for instance, that it costs "less" to live in poor countries. Armed with First World money and circumnavigating the globe on tourist jaunts, they assume that as they find things "cheap" in poor countries, so do the local residents. This is an illusion. Hunger, deprivation, disease, and shortened life spans are the rewards of their lower standard of living. Thus, pursuing for a subsistence floor something we might call a worldwide "average" state of well-being still entails human costs that reflect the economic inequalities among peoples. If others, notably people in rich societies, are functioning at a higher level of human potential, how does one justify not seeking the same for all others?

Living with Capitalism

As one looks around the world today, there is no practical use in denying that capitalism plays the dominant role in the world economy. Instead, it is probably more accurate to say that capitalism's entrance into former socialist countries signifies its arrival at the final frontiers of the planet's economy. Some countries, particularly those that are rich, find themselves closely guided by the capitalist rules of the game and more tightly integrated into the world economy where those rules are coercive. In others, particularly poor countries, the daily preoccupations with subsistence on the part of a majority of their citizens, obscure or disguise the role of capitalism in ordering their economic lives. Their ultimate involvement is signified by the fact that most poor countries find themselves international debtors to more powerful capitalist countries or to international lending agents such as the International Monetary Fund, the World Bank, or various regional economic development banks that act as the rich countries' surrogates. Thus, whether in the beginning and throughout the moves, or only at its final accounting, all countries are caught up in the capitalist game.

And capitalism does create in our lived experience the sensation of a game, of endless competition in endless arenas in our lives and in the lives of those over whose shoulders we peer via the media. Not far from our experience of life's surfaces is the constant fear and occasional insight that the game is not "win-win" but "zero-sum." We either lose or win over and over, in a succession of moments that ends only with the grave. It feels as if capitalism is an uncontrollable chain reaction and we merely reagents in its seemingly infinite combinations and recombinations. Constantly changing, it feels changeless. There seems to be no exit from the game and no respite from its toils.

It may seem counterintuitive, but it is true all the same, that capitalist economies, albeit jiggered increasingly into one global system, are nonetheless subject to our will and reliant upon our consent. And it is within our powers to bring about some changes in capitalism that will enhance human well-being worldwide. By understanding and acting on our experience of capitalism, there is some prospect that we can change it for the better.

To envision changing capitalism is not as utopian as it might seem at first blush. The most obvious alternative to capitalism, the communist experiments of the twentieth century, countenanced revolutionary changes in the relationship of societies with their economies. Their stories ended badly, as state-administered economies were unable to compete successfully with capitalist economies in the provision of goods or in the satisfaction of people's needs. Yet their example can be instructive, if only to indicate the possible outer limits of what reforms of capitalism are achievable without killing it as a viable economic mechanism.

On the other hand, Western industrialized societies over the past century established welfare states that took some of the pain out of the exploitation and dislocations chronic to capitalism's operations. Old-age and disability pensions, unemployment insurance, jobs programs, free public education and medical assistance produced important improvements in the well-being of peoples whose societies undertook these tasks. During the course of our discussion in this book, we evaluate the degree to which welfare measures undertaken in rich societies have a wider applicability of use in poorer societies. We also explore how the rich societies, no less than poor societies, need to strengthen and support the people's provisioning needs rather than simply keep capitalism's masters happy.

Reconstructing our economies requires two complementary activities. First, we need to change our orientation to capitalism by recognizing it as something that brings both harms and benefits. This means exploring the degree to which the application of values other than those associated conventionally with capitalism might yield a better life trajectory for people around the globe. Second, we should engage in the kind of social experimentation that can lead us to new solutions to economic problems that lie beyond capitalism's limited repertoire of means for the satisfaction of our needs and wants. This implies that efforts be undertaken to mitigate its ill effects through regulation and redistribution of wealth and opportunities.

As Sen argues,[33] the ultimate measure of well-being is whether we can acquire and exercise fundamental human capabilities that enable us to function effectively in our environments. Can we use the nourishment, education, shelter, and medical care available to us in our environments to live active, enlightened lives, or do we find our lives limited by early death, chronic disease, educational deprivation, and gender and racial discrimination?

As I have suggested above, the metric for a flourishing human life is imprecise, but not impossible to calculate. Consider the virtues of being able to enjoy one's seventies tending a garden, hiking, reading a book, telling stories to a child or a loved one, or cooking a meal, in contrast to finding one's life at an end at age fifty. The lives of children could be better served more by learning skills than being used up as unskilled child labor. The quality of women's lives could improve if they had increased prospects of surviving childbearing years and if they could develop their capabilities to the extent that men do. These are illustrations of how we might extend a concept of well-being to include the more practical (and measurable) aspects of provisioning. In this way, we can begin to reimagine what an economy should be for.

How to Read This Book

In *How to Read Donald Duck*, the writer and human rights advocate Ariel Dorfman suggests that one can read in the adventures of the Disney denizen how American imperialism works, and how Americans as an imperial people think. There is a message in the cartoon of the feckless and luckless duck that can help a reader explain what Americans intend in the world, even if they think they are only having harmless fun at his expense.[34]

I have not intentionally hidden any message in this book. It is written to reveal rather than disguise the fullness of the reality in which we live. It is explicitly written to persuade the reader that she should adopt a different orientation in regard to our shared economic lives. Further, I assume the reader is much like me. That is, she is a resident of the United States, and thus has at least minimal access to its economic advantages, as considered against the plight of poor people around the world. This means that she shares in a vision of the world very much influenced by her position in it, as a resident of a nation at the center of the world's economy, generating some 30 percent of global goods and services. I mean to awaken in the reader both her sense of the difficulty of "seeing" the enormity of the world's problems from a position of comparative affluence, as well her sense of her expanded capabilities to do something about the world as she can come to see it. It is not guilt I seek to stimulate, but responsibility and engagement.

Having said that, let me make it clear that accepting the reorientation that I advocate does not commit the reader, or the writer, for that matter, to a particular theory of how the globe got into its contemporary sorry state. Do the world's rich get richer at the expense of the world's poor? Certainly, in some ways, yes. Have the rich been luckier, either by birth, place, or commercial advantage? Probably so. Yet writer and reader can disagree as to the nature and extent of the culpability—or the cupidity—of the rich in the making of the modern world while still agreeing on a more just basis for human existence. Wouldn't greater equality in its many dimensions be better than what we have now?

Yet let's not forget about Donald Duck. We need to listen to how others read and reflect critically on the stories we tell about ourselves. It can reveal to us what our collective myopia cannot about the role our mentality and our actions as a world power play in making the world tragically what it is. It can help us see what we must overcome in our own bearing and actions in helping create what the world might in a more humane sense become. It can also help us realize that a new stance is both necessary and possible.

I write this book out of my experience and training as an anthropologist—a fact that may seem initially strange to a reader accustomed to associating anthropology with stones, bones, and the analysis of the quaint and curious customs of non-Western peoples. Yet from its foundation, anthropology has sought to fulfill a larger human purpose: namely, to be the science of the species. It also has tried to provide people with a humane reflection upon human life, its history, and dimensions. Put simply, we explore how human beings are different, and how they are the same. This seems almost a task of naive description: We find this group of natives one way and that group another way. We find certain things that human groups have in common, or the different ways that they handle common problems. But these descriptions imply another reflection. They obligate the writer, and by extension the reader who has learned with the writer, to look at and act in the world differently as a consequence of this fuller knowledge.

Anthropology also investigates on a grand scale the universal possibilities and limits to our human natures, while examining in minute detail the particularities of people's lives. Thus, even as we help sort out the global human battle against the HIV virus, others among us investigate the treatment of AIDS patients on a street corner, in a clinic, in a hospital, in some corner of the world. Even as we try to account for the role of violence in human affairs, anthropologists in the field try to understand how genocide broke out among ordinary people in Bosnian and Rwandan hamlets during the 1990s. The large and the small, the universal as well as the particular, vitally concern us.

Anthropology, thus, is a human activity embracing the fullness of human dimensions—from the global to the local, the systemic to the idiosyncratic, the collective to the individual. Its unique value lies in its ability to speak creatively about the human condition in all of its manifestations. In some sense, to be good anthropology, our work must reflect a concern for the species as universal beings and as individual living beings. This book undertakes this obligation.

Let the study of race in anthropology be our guide. On the one hand, anthropology has long been involved in investigating human origins, trying to explain with the fossil record and nutritional studies our anatomical and physiological development as a species. Much of its evidence suggests that race itself accounts for no significant variation in human capacities. Our observable differences in body shape and hue reflect a short-term adaptation to temperature and light extremes on a post–Ice Age planet. On the other hand, anthropologists in a variety of settings have tried to show how we come to define social differences as racial ones, thus casting a dangerous shadow over the affairs of everyday life. Both planes of investigation are helpful and necessary in determining who we are and who we are becoming.

So, too, with this book. I evaluate remedies with worldwide as well as local consequences. I offer arguments for the development of universal welfare remedies, believing that there are fundamental problems of human existence that can only be solved by utilizing the full resources of the planet. I examine attempts by regions, communities, and social movements around the world to improve the human condition, and point to some that can serve as exemplars for other regions, communities, and movements striving to do the same. I offer these outlines of remedies in the name of redirecting our economic efforts according to the value of equality. I show why acting with equality in mind can substantially improve the human condition for all as well as for each ordinary person.

The next chapters discuss some of the economic and social consequences of the contemporary capitalist world economy. I then suggest that we orient our economic action around the value of equality in its several dimensions, and subsequently argue the superiority of equality over other possible values that can guide our actions. The second half of the book is devoted to examining economic alternatives from the point of view of how they advance equality.

This is a book that is founded in hope—not for some great millenarian revival but for a rediscovery of moral-practical problem solving that can greatly improve human well-being. Though many political and intellectual figures oppose globalization and the capitalist economy that motors it, I see globalization via capitalism as part and parcel of our world reality for some time to come, regardless of how one feels about it. I ask how we can in any event construct a new world where all human beings can live decently with dignity and grace. This is the most fundamental challenge we in this world face.

Notes

1. *Philadelphia Inquirer*, May 10, 2000, 1. According to the United Nations Development Programme's *Human Development Report 1999* (New York: Oxford University Press, 1999), 5, the traffic in exploitation of women and girls in Western Europe is estimated as 500,000 persons transported per year, which amounts to a US$7 billion industry.

2. Kevin Bales, *Disposable People: New Slavery in the Global Economy* (Berkeley: University of California Press, 1999), 147–48.

3. Victoria Griffith, "Fighting for a Fairer Deal in America," *Financial Times*, December 4, 2000, 8.

4. Martin Dickson, "Global Inequality," *Financial Times*, September 22, 2000, 24.

5. Frances Stewart, "Income Distribution and Development," United Nations Conference on Trade and Development X: High-Level Roundtable on Trade and Development, November 23, 1999, 22, available at www.unctad.org, accessed January 17, 2001.

6. *United Nations Human Development Report*, cited in Martin Dickson, ibid. Compare Nancy Birdsall, "Life Is Unfair: Inequality in the World," *Foreign Policy* (Summer 1998), 76.

7. World Bank, *Entering the 21st Century: World Development Report, 1999/2000* (New York: Oxford University Press, 2000), table 2, 232–33.

8. Ibid., 26.

9. Samuel Brittan, "Protest Against the Protesters," *Financial Times*, September 29, 2000, 19.

10. Kevin Bales, op. cit.

11. Human Rights Watch, *The Small Hands of Slavery: Bonded Child Labor in India* (New York, 1996), 1.

12. World Bank, op. cit., table 2, 232–33.

13. Ibid., 28.

14. Joseph Stiglitz and Lyn Squire, "International Development: Is It Possible?" *Foreign Policy*, (Spring 1998), 138.

15. Martin Wolf, "Making Aid a Better Investment," *Financial Times*, March 13, 2002, 15.

16. World Bank, op. cit., 41–42.

17. "Hotting Up in the Hague," *Economist*, November 18, 2000, 81–82.

18. World Bank, op. cit., table 1, 230–31; Martin Wolf, "Kicking Down Growth's Ladder," *Financial Times*, April 12, 2000, 15.

19. World Bank, *World Bank Development News*, January 7, 2002.

20. Nikki Tait, "Divisions on World Hunger Remain as Wide as Ever," *Financial Times*, May 30, 2001, 6.

21. Nicholas Kristof and Sheryl WuDunn, "Two Cheers for Sweatshops," *New York Times Magazine*, September 24, 2000, 70–71.

22. *United Nations Development Report 1999*, quoted in Jeremy Brecher, Tim Costello, and Brendan Smith, *Globalization from Below: The Power of Solidarity* (Boston: South End Press, 2000), 6.

23. Giovanni Arrighi and Beverly Silver, "Global Inequalities and 'Actually Existing Capitalism,'" Paper prepared for the Annual Meeting of the American Political Science Association, Washington, D.C., August 31–September 3, 2000.

24. Manuel Castells, *The Rise of the Network Society* (Cambridge, Mass.: Blackwell Publishers, 1996), 92.

25. Arundhati Roy, "Shall We Leave It to the Experts?" *The Nation*, 274, no. 6 (February 18, 2002), 16.

26. Aristotle, *The Nicomachean Ethics*, I:7, translated by David Ross (Oxford: Oxford University Press, 1980), 11–12.

27. Ibid, I:9–10, 19–21.

28. Charles Taylor, *The Ethics of Authenticity* (Cambridge, Mass.: Harvard University Press, 1992), 16–17.

29. Douglas Porpora, *Landscapes of the Soul: The Loss of Moral Meaning in American Life* (New York: Oxford University Press, 2001).

30. Amartya Sen, "Capability and Well-Being," in *The Quality of Life*, edited by M. Nussbaum and A. Sen (Oxford, U.K.: Clarendon Press 1993), 31. I am deeply indebted to Amartya Sen for his seminal contributions to the understanding of the role of capabilities in human functioning. See his *Development as Freedom* (New York: Alfred A. Knopf, 1999), as well as *Inequality Reexamined* (Cambridge, Mass.: Harvard University Press, 1992).

31. World Bank, *World Development Report 2000–2002: Attacking Poverty* (New York: Oxford University Press, 2001), table 2, "Quality of Life," 276–77.

32. World Bank, ibid., 4.

33. Sen 1999, op. cit.

34. Ariel Dorfman, *How to Read Donald Duck: Imperialist Ideology in the Disney Comic* (New York: International General, 1975).

CHAPTER TWO

The Consequences of Capitalism

Capitalism and human history have been joined together for a long time. Evanescent among the commercial transactions of city-states and empires a millennium ago, capitalism slowly saddled and rode upon the backs of all manner of economies, east and west, north and south. Industrialization starting in the eighteenth century has continuously transformed life as we know it. Human labor has been harnessed to machines, and a cornucopia of goods and new ways of making them have worked in tandem to change our connections with nature and to alter our human relationships in ways that demand the great powers of art to describe.

It is our habit, perhaps, to depict this change in superhuman ways and to transform human experience into an aesthetic expression. Capitalism becomes like the mighty Colossus that bestrode the ancient world, or like the Hindu god Shiva, maker and destroyer of worlds. In American letters, writers like Theodore Dreiser and Frank Norris who witnessed the rise of industrial capitalism used such words as *titan* and *octopus* to capture the enormity of the new economic machine transforming their world.

To be sure, capitalism, like all normative institutions in human affairs, has this larger-than-life dimension. The impulse to regulate our economic activities in a capitalist way is not something we volunteer. It is as compulsory to follow its rules as it is to observe the incest taboo. Conjure it up with an inner beneficence, as did Adam Smith with his metaphor of the hidden hand, or more darkly, as did Max Weber when he suggested that the drive to labor in capitalist economies derives ultimately from the force of law and the lash of hunger. Capitalism is no less a coercive social system than systems of rank and privilege, marriage and inheritance. In our daily lives it occurs to us, when we think about it at all, as an unalterable, if not quite natural, fact. It too easily becomes a dictum for the twenty-first century as the dogma of the divine right of kings was to the Europeans in the seventeenth century.

Yet in our imaginative strivings, we tend to forget that capitalism, though an economic system that regulates human action, is nevertheless composed of billions of acts, both great and small, by billions of people. Several million minds and sets of hands make a Chevrolet. Millions more move grain from the fields to the factories and from the warehouses to the breakfast table. For each commodity we consume, for each machine with which we reproduce our societies, there are human hands that make it happen. Human labor makes the life we know possible, and most of us in both a direct and extended sense provide it.

This hardly means that in an epiphany of universal protest, we could stop capitalism simply by stopping work. That we should end the anarchy of production with the strike of simple refusal is the stuff of our dreams, perhaps possible in movies but impossible in real life. As Michael Harrington once put it, given the coercive structure of capitalism in the United States, the freedom of action we imagine exists in our nation boils down to freedom to starve. We can choose to say no and in a free fall from society lose our lives, or chomp down on the bit between our teeth and keep hauling.

Yet mass refusal, mass desire for change, and mass action to do things differently can have an impact on our economic direction. This is the value of forgoing the metaphors and thinking about capitalism concretely. It enables us to imagine specific alternatives and to act.

In this chapter, I suggest several things. First, I argue that it is reasonable to assume that the global growth of industrial capitalism has led to the greatly increased social inequality we observe worldwide, and that unchanged, global industrial capitalism is likely to lead to more social inequality in the future. Second, I suggest that capitalism is a particularly unstable, crisis-prone economic system that can cause grave and lasting damage to the cause of universal well-being. Third, I show that there is some variation in how capitalism works around the world, and that some of the variations are more conducive to universal well-being than others.

Getting the Inequality Story Straight

We have become very rich and very poor—both in huge numbers. This is the difference between life in the world before the rise of industrial capitalism and afterward. As we noted in the first chapter, 100 years ago, after a half-century industrial head start, the American family had emerged nine times richer than the average Ethiopian family. Now, after a second hundred years of the industrial revolution, an American family is seventy-two times richer than an Ethiopian family. For the first world, advantages have multiplied: wealth has measurably improved the quality of life. For the poor countries, disadvantages have multiplied. Poverty, both relative and absolute deprivation, has increased as economic integration with the Western industrial order has proceeded. Only East Asia, including China, has lifted up a significant proportion of its poor through industrialization since 1980. For the rest of the developing world, the trajectory is static or downward.

It is hard for us to assimilate these facts. Consider another set: A recent survey disclosed that despite turmoil in the world's stock markets during 2000 and 2001, the amount of wealth owned by the world's richest people rose 6 percent, to US$27 trillion. This is the equivalent of one-third of the world's wealth. The number of "high net worth individuals," as the survey calls them, consisting of people with US$1 million or more to invest, increased by 184,000 to 7.2 million individuals, a rise during the 2000 calendar year of 3 percent.[1]

Caught up as all humans are in the daily struggles of their worlds, people in the West sometimes succumb to the romantic myth that somehow a life before industrial capitalism was idyllic. The story we tell ourselves is about our own histories. Innocently, we criticize the helter-skelter quality of our lives by appealing to the folklore of our past: Somehow, grandmother and grandfather on the farm had it better, never having had to put up with cell phones, supervisors, and stock market hijinks. We ignore the facts that our grandparents had much shorter life spans, lost many more children to disease and accident, and generally led much more difficult lives marked by ignorance and periods of enormous privation.

Life in industrial capitalist societies has measurably improved. We have created a new human condition wherein one can live without hunger, raise children who will most likely live to maturity, and die at a ripe old age. We have lifted the limits of human potential for long life and the enjoyment of its fruits.

Yet, in some southern parts of the world, notably sub-Saharan Africa, life moves steadily in reverse. Life spans and living standards slip below levels of the 1980s. In parts of the world like Latin America, even where life spans have grown, the burdens of the poor remain relatively untouched by economic growth. Instead, the gaps between development's new middle and upper classes and the poor majority have grown.[2] The gap between rich and poor has grown in the rich countries as well. Since the 1980s in the United States, the distribution of income has tipped toward the wealthy, and the proportion of wealth held by the top 20 percent of the households has increased. For Western Europe (less Japan), similar trends have been noted.[3]

Some attribute this growing economic inequality to people's enduring devotion to tradition, but this is a hard argument to make. I will discuss the frailties of so-called cultural values explanations for economic success in detail in a subsequent chapter. But consider briefly some alternative explanations. Regarding cultural differences among countries, why should anyone assume that Asian societies, insofar as we can speak about them as a whole, are any less traditional than are less economically successful societies in Latin and Central America, the Middle East, and Africa? Because the United States grew at a faster pace than did Europe, are we to assume that Europe is therefore more culturally traditional than the United States? Does the economic record since 1980 signify that the United States is the least traditional nation in the world? Given Americans' devotion to "traditional" religious beliefs—95 percent believe in God and 40 percent believe they have been personally saved by Jesus Christ—how is the United States any more "modern," if by modern we mean secular, than those that fared much less well economically around the world?[4] In thinking about economic inequality within societies, does it make any sense, for instance, to argue that there are "modern" and "traditional" parts to society in the United States, and that these differences explain the growing rift between rich and poor? It doesn't seem reasonable.

Another possible global explanation, that a social variable like population growth is exaggerating economic inequality among and within nations, also doesn't seem to stand up to scrutiny. In the early twenty-first century, the overwhelming majority of nations have substantially reduced their rates of population growth, and sometimes, this has helped societies improve their overall economic health by increasing the gross domestic product per person. But neither rapidly increasing nor decreasing population growth seems to reduce inequality within or among societies.

There might be some reason to think that politics, not economics, is at the base of inequality. In classical social thought, Jean-Jacques Rousseau, for instance, believed that societies needed a new social contract establishing a state that would protect the rights of every citizen against the depredations of the rich and privileged. Karl Marx seized upon Rousseau's insight and elaborated a theory of class rule in capitalist societies that explained how the rich successfully leveraged both their economic and political power in exploiting the poor. Max Weber had much to say that was critical of the interpretive line stretching from Rousseau through Marx, believing that dominant political groups sought, often successfully, to capture economic resources through political coercion. But he also recognized how much the state guarantee of the sanctity of private property helped the capitalist class lock in their gains over the poor. Thus, we learn from Weber much as we do from Rousseau and Marx that modern capitalism in practice is composed of a mix of political as well as economic strategies that affect outcomes such as economic inequality.

In other words, both politics and economics in capitalism contribute to economic inequality, though every regime requires that something be produced—that some wealth be created by economic means. This is no less true among societies than it is within a given society, since all societies have operated within the context of a highly political world economy since at least the fifteenth century.

Can we be sure that industrial capitalism on a global scale is the cause of the dramatic rise in worldwide economic inequality we have thus far described? No, it cannot be conclusively proven, though we have suggested some ways in which other explanations for inequality are unlikely. Because of the sweep and complexity of the argument, it is also not clear what counts as sound evidence and finally a convincing proof.

But we can ascertain with greater confidence the counterfactual: Namely, that more "capitalist growth"—the only kind of growth available today—does not lead to reductions in economic inequality. In other words, economic growth is not enough to create equality. The evidence comes from the careful and exhaustive analysis of the relationship between economic growth and income equality in poor countries. Developmental economists do find that economic growth as measured by the increase in a country's gross domestic product does raise personal incomes across the board, from top to bottom, rich to poor strata. But those at the bottom do not catch up; each stratum picks up proportionately at the same rate. In other words, suppose a country's gross domestic product grows by 3 percent. Most probably, personal incomes for the bottom 20 percent and the top 20 percent would grow at 3 percent as well. The key is that while the poor can improve their standing when economies grow, and can become less poor or even escape poverty, the economic inequality between them and the rich doesn't shrink, but remains more or less the same.[5]

The worldwide economic development initiative signified in the adoption of the Millennium Declaration in 2000 by 180 countries under the auspices of the United Nations admits as much. Among its primary goals are the reductions by half of the proportions of people living on less than US$1 a day and of those suffering from hunger. Even for this modest improvement in the life chances of the world's extremely poor—*and it is important to remember that these goals in no way envision achieving greater economic equality, but are attempting instead only to reduce poverty and hunger*—the 2004 World Bank *World Development Report* minces no words: "To reach all of these goals, economic growth is essential. But it will not be enough." Accordingly, the Millennium Declaration calls for increasing the transfer of funds from rich to poor countries by US$60 billion annually until 2019. Still, the proportion of people living on less than US$1 a day will actually increase in Africa, while South Asia will fall significantly short of achieving the 50 percent reduction goal set by the Millennium Declaration.[6]

The inference is inescapable. Economic growth alone will not eliminate poverty, let alone improve economic inequality. Perhaps just as damaging, the Millennium Declaration project itself illustrates how achieving worldwide economic equality is not even being countenanced.

Thus, absent any other intervention, the best one can hope for from more or more rapid growth is that fewer people will be poor. Economic growth does reduce poverty, and this is surely a good and important thing. For instance, between 1975 and 1995, East Asian nations reduced their poverty rates by fully two-thirds, an astonishing feat if one considers that 60 percent of all East Asians began the two decades mired in absolute poverty. Economic growth both profited from and encouraged nearly universal primary school enrollments in China, Korea, Indonesia, and the Philippines, and substantially increased school participation in Malaysia. Life expectancy rose from 60 years in 1970 to 69 years in 1995. Infant mortality was halved.[7]

These are fantastic gains. But we need to recall that many of these economies were helped by land reform that provided for more agricultural productivity and resolved problems of enormous economic inequality in the countryside before industrial development began.[8] There is also evidence that nations with highly unequal distributions of income produce less economic growth than those with less unequal distributions of income.[9] And, though the evidence is by no means conclusive, there is a certain common sense to the position that if one starts with enormous chasms between rich and poor, as is characteristic of Latin America in contrast with Asia, it will be more difficult to provide as much well-being as quickly via economic growth.

Adding to increasing economic inequality are recent changes in capitalism as a global economy itself. After the world economic slowdown of the 1970s and 1980s, capitalism in the 1990s and continuing through the new millennium has found new legs in global economic integration and technological innovation. Production and finance have been reorganized on a global scale on a level not seen since the First World War.[10] The growth of large transnational corporations, foreign trade, and international investing has created a new kind of global economy. Informational technology innovations, driven by computers, telecommunications, and the Internet have bolstered further economic integration by making it possible to envision the world as one market and to supply products cheaply and efficiently to global markets.[11]

This global capitalist rebirth has quickened the pace of wealth accumulation and concentrated newfound riches in the hands of the very few located in the world's largest and most cosmopolitan urban centers. Those with capital have seen their investments flourish in this accelerated world economy. Those without capital or without the new skills demanded by the new world economy have had a difficult time capturing any of the new wealth. They amount to a vast number of people found in rich as well as poor countries.

The renewed global economy is a more efficient engine of accumulation. Though technological innovation has provided rich societies with a tremendous competitive edge, the technology itself enables corporations and their stockholders to tap markets for high-interest loans and low-cost labor in poor societies. The higher percentage paid out by a Thai entrepreneur for a loan backed by a New York City bank finds its way more easily to the city's plutocrats on the fabled Upper East Side.[12] The fewer dollars put into the hands of Mexican factory workers by U.S. firms means more money in the bank for the firms and their stockholders. Exploitation, in other words, has become more globally systematic, and its returns more concentrated in the hands of capitalholders.

Facilitating these transfers of goods, labor, and wealth are the transnational corporations (TNCs). Of the world's largest 100 economies, 51 are corporations.[13] Their sizes are truly staggering. Consider that General Motors' (GM) annual sales is larger than the gross domestic product of Thailand or Norway; Ford's, though smaller than GM's, is larger than the economies of Saudi Arabia or Poland; the Japanese Mitsui and Mitsubishi Corporations are each larger than national economies of South Africa or Greece. Wal-Mart, "the store with low prices," grosses more per year than the annual products taken singly of Malaysia, Israel, Colombia, Venezuela, or the Philippines.[14] TNCs now account for half of the world's trade in goods, and just five TNCs account for 70 percent of the world market in consumer durables, 50 percent of the market in cars, airline, electronic components, and steel, and 40 percent of world markets in personal computers, oil, and media.[15] Again, this concentration facilitates greater economic inequality, as monies are funneled to the stockholders in the form of dividends and the sales of their appreciated stocks.

Finally, there is the concentration effect of poverty itself: When poor people are massed together, their resources amount to less than if they were dispersed among otherwise wealthier people. It seems a truism to observe that the more poor people there are living in a society, the poorer that society will be, but the concentration of poverty spatially should not be underestimated in complicating the prospects for improvement. States with a poor majority are themselves impoverished and deprived of ready resources for helping the poor. Often they are captives of a predatory upper class that uses the state to pursue its own ends. Consequently, public facilities of all kinds, ranging from roads and telephones to clean water and sewers may be lacking or provided only for the rich few, and then privately. During Mobutu Sese Seko's reign over Zaire (now the Democratic Republic of Congo), for instance, some 84,000 of 90,000 miles of public roads and highways "disappeared" by virtue of disrepair, all while the president and his clique became progressively engorged with diamond wealth.[16] Or, as in the case of Pakistan, the efforts of a small circle of the super-rich to avoid taxes undercuts the state's efforts to collect taxes at all, to the detriment of the country's infrastructure.

Functioning democracies with poor majorities also find themselves severely handicapped. In Brazil fifty people die every day as a result of inadequate basic sanitation, and two-thirds of all infant admissions to hospitals are due to infections related to solid or liquid waste. Bringing fresh water and sewage treatment to Brazil's cities would require US$26 billion in capital investment over the next ten years. Though a trivial sum even by Brazil's standards, given a gross domestic product now greater than three-quarters of a trillion U.S. dollars, it is a tidy sum for a country where two-thirds of the population lives on less than US$2 a day.[17] States like Brazil either lack broad tax bases or are political prisoners of their small but rich elites.

Northern market economies once had ample welfare states that redistributed a significant portion of their countries' wealth to improve the lives of their people, but the economic crises of the 1970s and 1980s led to their downsizing. Fiscal crises of the states followed, and successive political regimes in the 1980s and 1990s began moving their societies toward markets as the answer to economic stagnation. As a consequence, starting in Britain and the United States and heading into continental Europe (save Japan), welfare state spending has leveled off.[18] Moreover, the tax burden of supporting Western welfare states has shifted dramatically from corporations to individual taxpayers, the majority of whom are working and middle class.[19] This means that their abilities to redistribute wealth and thus lower economic inequality have been diminished as well.

Whether in growth or crisis, then, capitalism is delivering more economic inequality. Here is the United Nations Development Programme summary of trends in the world distribution of income:

> World inequalities have been rising steadily for nearly two centuries. An analysis of long-term trends in world income distribution (between countries) shows that the distance between the richest and poorest country was about 3 to 1 in 1820, 11 to 1 in 1913, 35 to 1 in 1950, 44 to 1 in 1973, and 72 to 1 in 1992. More amazing is that the British in 1820 had an income about six times that of the Ethiopians in 1992![20]

Some 200 years of industrial capitalism seeded in a global economy has created a cornucopia of economic inequalities.

Global Industrial Capitalism as Crisis-Prone

As we have argued above, capitalism is industrial and global. Avoiding exaggerated characterizations, "capitalism as colossus," and so on, it is nonetheless important to stress its systemic quality. When crises occur around the world, whether in a Wall Street boardroom or a Thai trading floor, they rapidly become worldwide because global industrial capitalism is also a highly integrated set of markets for exchange of money, labor, and goods. Take, for instance, the 1997–98 financial panic in East Asia. What began as a run on Thailand's currency, the *baht*, eventually prompted emergency action by the International Monetary Fund (IMF) to save the economies of Thailand, Indonesia, South Korea, and the Philippines from imminent collapse.

Like an engine, the crisis produced more economic inequalities, and the victims were those with the least to lose. Some 13 million people lost their jobs as a result of this panic—a number equivalent to the populations of Ecuador or Angola. The poor and working classes of East Asia, according to the World Bank, suffered job and income loss, while the middle classes escaped unscathed by the financial panic that crippled their region's economy. The 1997 financial panic and 1998 recession in Thailand, for instance, cost 2 million workers with no more than a primary school education their jobs, while the earnings of those who remained employed dropped between 15 and 30 percent. Economic inequality also increased during the crisis, as earnings for workers with a university education rose 10 percent, and a bracing 30 percent for state workers during the same period.[21]

Is capitalism doomed to undergo crisis after crisis? The most charitable answer might come from Charles Kindleberger: "Markets generally work, but occasionally break down."[22] A bit forgiving, too, is the response of Joseph

Schumpeter, whose claim developed in the light of the Great Depression and the onset of World War II. Capitalism underwent a process he termed "creative destruction" that has stimulated the growth of many a hypothesis about capitalism's future direction. Echoing Marx, he argued that "there is inherent in the capitalism system a tendency toward self-destruction," as capitalism in crisis progressively sweeps away its existing institutional framework. At the same time, though, capitalism is creating a new economic context and new relations of production and consumption."[23] This occurs primarily through technological innovation; new products and industrial processes arise that render whole industries and ways of living economically obsolete. By destroying the value of capital goods as well as corporations dedicated to their use, capitalism renews itself by making space for new industries and new economic growth. Schumpeter also believed that Marx was right: Each crisis brought capitalism nearer to socialism, albeit of a democratic sort.

Others, particularly as they contemplate a newly globalized capitalism, offer less optimistic views. David Harvey believes that crisis-ridden capitalism has shifted to a global division of labor that enables business to maximize gains across national boundaries while minimizing their liabilities by employing inexpensive pools of labor around the world.[24] Giovanni Arrighi agrees, preferring to think, however, that capitalism in striking into Asia has reached its last realizable frontier for cheap labor and high profits.[25] Manuel Castells believes instead that capitalism, having undergone an organizational revolution through the development of information technologies, has warped into a global network society in which advanced productive sectors and regions will be linked economically while the rest of the world is left to marginality and decay.[26] Taking a more apocalyptic tack, John Gray argues that global capitalism, a parasite, is destroying its host, liberal civilization itself.[27]

Though its telos remains profit in the name of endless accumulation, as Immanuel Wallerstein puts it,[28] neither its long-term nor its short-term trajectory can be predicted with great accuracy. Every economic prognosticator has her favorite index for foretelling the markets' directions, ranging from the supply of money or goods to the cost of labor or money. But resting, as capitalism still does, on what Marx called "the anarchy of production," knowledge about its bearings is as fluid as quicksilver. Though some will always claim to have foreseen calamity, emerging panics, manias, and financial crises routinely appear as fortuitous events to which people react rather than act to create.

From the perspective of someone living in the United States who is too young to remember the Great Depression of the 1930s, capitalism's cycling from boom to bust and back again since the 1970s may seem but a bumpy ride to millennial prosperity. The United States's two decades of declining personal income pale in the face of the what-me-worry 1990s. What of the 1980s, Latin America's lost decade? Or the 1990s, the lost decade for Eastern Europe, Russia, the Middle East, and Africa? Whose lost decade will occur during this first decade of the new millennium?

Capitalism and Change

The process of bust and boom, crisis and recovery—and the reactions of people to the dramatically changed conditions of their lives—provide an important dynamic in shaping the trajectory of capitalism. People struggle to obtain or to recover economic well-being, either from the owners of capital or from the state that lies uneasily between them and the capitalists. As Karl Polanyi noted a generation ago, people and states in Europe, Great Britain, and the United States were in some sense forced to save society from the ravages caused by capitalism and its crises by erecting welfare programs and other forms of social insurance.[29] In a sense, they immunized societies against the pathological swings of capitalism. The need to renew this effort will concern us in a later chapter.

As an economic system of production, exchange, and labor, capitalism continues to take on an ever-broadening array of economic activities in an ever-larger number of societies. The production of goods has been joined by the production of services. Most economic flows now pass through its nets. The information revolution and improved international transportation enable businesses somewhat successfully to envision the world as one market and to buy and sell accordingly.[30]

But the expansion of capitalism from industry to industry and from region to region over the past two centuries has been a source of significant variation in its operation and functioning. First, there is capitalism's encounter with the physical and human geography of the planet. Each mountain, valley, and seashore offered unique sets of possibilities and limits on what capitalists could do; each local group, prior to being embedded in an industrial capitalist global economy, had a particular way of living, as well as modes of production and consumption that reflected their historical efforts to create a viable human ecology. Thus, specific local economies and their resource endowments have mixed with capitalism in ways to develop different organizations of labor and production, as well as different mechanisms for allocating surplus product or value.

Second, capitalism's encounter with different ways of living had a long-term impact on its organization and functioning. While we usually imagine that business firms lie at the heart of capitalist economies, societies with notable state involvement in economies might restrict their scope, size, or profitability. The firm itself can be privately, publicly, or family held, and its stock ownership traded in markets or held under various legal arrangements by banks, trusts, entrepreneurs, managers, or employees. Production of goods and/or services can occur within the firm or be contracted in part or in whole to other firms. All of these arrangements from ownership to production can be subject to collective bargaining with employees or their unions or set in state laws.

Moreover, the relations between the economic and social organization of capitalism and the social stratification of a society are highly reciprocal. Employment opportunities, skills, earnings, and the possibilities for careers and promotions affect workers' as well as owners' and managers' life chances and class standing. Their roles in firms in turn enhance or limit those very life chances for themselves and members of their households. It is important to recall the fact that, typically, a majority of people—unemployed, young, old, perhaps female—in any society do not work. Thus their status is very much determined by the possession of wealth and/or how a society distributes its resources and rewards.

All of these conditions form an institutional order for capitalism in a given society. Certain social roles and norms are implied as well. When ensconced within a particular state structure, they account for the significant social variation one encounters in the operation of capitalism worldwide.

Key to capitalism as an economic process, however, is competition. It is the crucial limiting factor on the social variations we find in the institutional and organizational structures of capitalism. As markets link competitors, making it possible for one to succeed at the expense of another, they enforce upon both parties the normative expectation that they will make a profit— or at least make back their costs of business. The recent reprise in the globalization of the world economy puts every like producer in potential competition with every other, and the rise of stockholding as a form of business ownership means that owners, the stockholders, will expect a tangible return on their investment in the form of profit. In other words, a socially different or innovative firm must make money in a revitalized global economy where profit making is also a competitive task.

That being said, there is still room for experimentation and for differing capitalist traditions.[31] For instance, stock and bond markets are central allocators of capital investment in both Great Britain and the United States; thus the norms of profitability are more stringently enforced. In contrast, Western European and Japanese firms have relied on close relationships with banks that finance company expansion in return for proprietary stockholdings in the company. The fact that banks are more patient and historically less demanding lenders than stock markets points to another important variation in capitalist business practices.[32]

State involvement in the Western economies and Japan also varies widely and creates different institutional environments for capitalism. The U.S. government took the most "hands-off" approach, relying largely on regulation to control the behavior of utilities and large firms. The Great Depression development of the federal Tennessee Valley Authority to provide electricity in impoverished regions throughout the mid-South is the single instance wherein the United States sought to replace private effort with public ownership and control of important resources. The states of Great Britain and the rest of Western Europe instead got into the business of owning and operating utilities, and in the case of the continental nations, major firms and banks. The Japanese state preferred to direct the behavior of its large firms through planning, consultation, and incentives rather than through ownership, with the exception of utilities. Again, until recently corporations found more patient masters in Europe and Japan if they were state-owned or state-guided than they did in the United States.

The relations between industries, firms, and labor varies greatly too. In the United States, business and labor have combative, historically hostile relations. In Japan, a union is often subordinate in practice to the will of the individual corporation in which it is installed as the workers' legal representative. In Europe, a corporatist tradition prevails: That is, the state, business, and labor try to hammer out agreements accommodating the interests of all in a stable, mutually beneficial relationship.[33]

Other regions in the world display a similar spread of organizational differences in the operation of their capitalist economies. Until the 1990s, Latin America combined state ownership of major utilities, banks, and some key industries with measures that protected local industry from international competition. In the past decade, privatization and freer trade have reduced the distance between Latin American practices and those of the United States and Europe, especially since Europe has been privatizing and lowering protective barriers as well. The Japanese state-guided model of industrial development was widely imitated by Pacific Rim countries, as was the Japanese policy on import restrictions.[34] Since the 1997–98 financial crisis, some barriers to trade around the Pacific Rim as well as state sponsorship of leading industries have abated.

State ownership of all industries was a hallmark of the socialist economies of the former Soviet Union and Eastern Europe. As they have moved toward more capitalist market economies, private enterprises have been tolerated, if not overwhelmingly encouraged, and state industries have been sold off. Caught in the remnants of a command economy run by cliques of politicians and bureaucrats, privatization typically led to the recapture of state assets by their former managers and/or political sponsors. Their success gives new meaning to the term "mixed economy."

In the Middle East as well as North Africa, one finds once more heavy state involvement in running major industries. An aging pan-Arab socialism and, for some, the possession of oil have combined to maintain a strong state hand in all economic matters.

The African predicament defies easy interpretation. In such cases as Tanzania and Zambia, states under enormous economic or political pressure have yielded up state-run enterprises to private ownership. In other cases particularly marked by political turmoil and anarchy, such as Congo and Nigeria, assets have sometimes been seized and operated by armed military bands. What perhaps could best be said of Africa is that its vital extractive and agro-industrial resources rest in the hands of TNCs that exploit them without creating a great deal of common good. In addition, African countries perhaps operate with less institutional autonomy than those in any other region, as their poor economic condition has involved international agencies such as the IMF and the World Bank in their salvage.

Though the cataloging of the peculiarities of capitalist economies around the globe displayed a wide range of variation, more variation still needs be considered within individual societies. Within particular societies, business organization can vary perhaps just as radically as it can between societies. The paradigm case could be China. Once socialist, a third of its economy is still state-owned and controlled, and consists of all of China's basic industries and utilities, including banks. Since the late 1970s, China has encouraged capitalist development along its southern coast; thus, another third of the national economy consists of private enterprises for profit in manufacturing and services. Most unusual, however, is the composition of the final third of the economy, which is comprised of for-profit enterprises owned, operated, or licensed by local towns and villages. Communist party cadres responsible for the economic and civic development of their local jurisdictions spearhead this collective entrepreneurship.[35]

Though certainly not every society entertains the enterprise "spread" that China does, we have observed a great deal of variation in how societies organize their capitalist economies. We have already pointed out that market pressures such as competition and the demand for increased profitability impose some real limits on what enlightened experiments are occurring worldwide or might be proposed later in this book. A second constraint consists of the long-term attempt by the United States in its role as world capitalist leader to insist that nations take up its preferred version of the way capitalism should work as the "one best way"—in short, as a local regime of production, labor, and consumption. A so-called Washington consensus composed of policy recommendations for developing countries in fiscal and monetary crisis was developed jointly in the 1980s by the U.S. Treasury Department, the IMF, and the World Bank. It held (in brief) that economic growth could be achieved through balanced government budgets, low inflation, deregulated markets, and freer trade. Government intervention and foreign aid were limited to achieving poverty reduction, not correcting large income or wealth disparities, and to the privatization of government services.[36] Jeffrey Sachs, an otherwise mainstream establishment economist, describes with scorn how the Washington consensus was enforced:

> The IMF and the World Bank have behaved with stunning arrogance in developing countries. The sequence is familiar: the IMF's negotiating positions are settled in Washington; the mission team goes to the client country to convey Washington's conclusions; the financial markets wait breathlessly to see whether the country will comply; the American government repeats the mantra 'Obey the IMF'; and journalists assess the 'seriousness' of reforms according to whether countries bite the bullet to carry out the IMF dictates, whatever they are. This process is out of hand. It has undermined political legitimacy in dozens of developing countries.[37]

Politics, no less than the economic "logic" of capitalism itself, may stand in the way of solutions providing greater equity to disadvantaged peoples around the world. Joseph Stiglitz, former chief economist of the World Bank and both a participant and an observer of IMF and U.S. actions during the 1997–98 Asian financial crisis, leaves no doubt about the role of politics in the arrangement of the world economy:

> To what extent did the IMF and the Treasury Department push policies that actually contributed to the increased global economic volatility? . . . Most importantly, did America—and the IMF—push policies because we, or they, believed the policies would help East Asia or because we believed they would benefit financial interests in the United States and the advanced industrial world? And, if we believed our policies were helping East Asia, where was the evidence? As a participant in these debates, I got to see the evidence. There was none.[38]

Economics, particularly the fight over the capitalist rules of the game, is never far below the surface of power politics. Positive changes will have to take into account the effect of both economics and politics.

As we have seen, the organizational aspects of capitalism change as a function of growth and of crisis, as well as of politics. Spatial extension of the world economy incorporates new geographical areas whose mode of local economics mixes with the features of capitalism prevailing worldwide. Hence the Chinese and Eastern European variations noted above. East Asian predilections for state direction of the development process, along with the European preferences for a welfare state to cushion capitalism's blows, are other important variations in contemporary capitalist practice. They differ from the more "hegemonic" capitalist growth agenda pursued by the United States that also often underlies the politics of economic crisis management pursued by the IMF or the World Bank.

Capitalism also expands its scope within and across societies by creating new products and incorporating new ways of living into its commercial orbit. As we have seen, technological innovation has generated new markets for products related to information. The growth of service employment in rich societies in part reflects how we turn increasingly to markets to solve basic needs in health, education, well-being, and care for children, the elderly, and the disabled. In satisfying these needs through markets, our lives become more deeply embedded in the logic and practices of our capitalist economies.

Despite capitalism's many-faceted capacity for growth and its liability to change under conditions of economic crisis, and even though we find significant variation in capitalist economies around the world, the prognosis is slim for capitalism bringing increased well-being as an economic system. Intervention to alter or amend its workings is required. The next chapter discusses how valuing equality might reorient capitalist economies in more salubrious ways.

Notes

1. John Willman, "Rich Survive Market Turmoil to Increase Wealth by 6%," *Financial Times*, May 15, 2001, 18. For corroboration, see "The New Wealth of Nations: A Survey of the New Rich," a special section of the *Economist*, June 16–22, 2001, 1.

2. United Nations Development Programme, *Human Development Report 2002: Deepening Democracy in a Fragmented World* (New York: Oxford University Press, 2002), 20.

3. Richard Freeman, *The New Inequality: Creating Solutions for Poor America* (Boston: Beacon Press, 1999), 7–9; Richard Stevenson, "Study Details Income Gap between Rich and the Poor," *New York Times*, May 31, 2001, C4.

4. Douglas Porpora, *Landscapes of the Soul: The Loss of Meaning in American Life* (New York: Oxford University Press, 2001).

5. Recent evidence suggests that a hypothesis offered by Simon Kuznets that economic inequality increased temporarily with economic development is probably incorrect. At the same time, development doesn't even up the distribution of income appreciably. See Michael Bruno, Martin Ravallion, and Lyn Squire, "Equity and Growth in Development Countries: Old and New Perspectives on the Policy Issues," In *Distributive Justice and Economic Development: The Case of Chile and Developing Countries*, edited by A. Solimano, E. Aninat, and N. Birdsall (Ann Arbor: University of Michigan Press, 2000), 37; and also, in the same volume, Andres Solimano, "Beyond Unequal Development: An Overview," 27; and Frances Stewart, "Income Distribution and Development" in United Nations Conference on Trade and Development, *UNCTAD X: High-Level Roundtable on Trade and Development Directions for the 21st Century*, Bangkok, February 12, 2000, available at www.unctad.org, accessed January 17, 2001. Anthony Giddens, *The Third Way and Its Critics* (Cambridge, U.K.: Polity Press, 2000), 131, reports the same ratio of improvement for development assistance.

6. World Bank, *World Development Report 2004: Making Services Work for Poor People* (New York: Oxford University Press, 2003), 1–3.

7. World Bank, *Poverty and East Asia*, available at www.worldbank.org/eapsocial/sector/poverty/povcwp2.htm, accessed December 13, 1999.

8. World Bank, *World Development Report 2003, Sustainable Development in a Dynamic World: Transforming Institutions, Growth, and Quality of Life* (New York: Oxford University Press, 2002), 87–90.

9. See also Andres Solimano, op. cit., 24.

10. Michael Bordo and Korneilia Krajnyak, "Globalization in Historical Perspective," in International Monetary Fund, *World Economic Outlook* (May 1997), 112–15.

11. Manuel Castells, *The Rise of the Network Society* (New York: Blackwell, 1996).

12. Saskia Sassen, *Cities in a World Economy* (Thousand Oaks, Calif.: Pine Forge Press, 1994), 61–76, shows how assets are being reconcentrated in major metropolitan areas as one consequence of the revitalized global capitalist economy.

13. John Gershman and Alec Irwin, "Getting a Grip on the Global Economy." In *Dying for Growth: Global Inequality and the Health of the Poor*, edited by J. Y. Kim, J. Millen, A. Irwin, and J. Gershman (New York: Common Courage Press, 2000), 36.

14. United Nations Development Programme, *Human Development Report 1999* (New York: Oxford University Press, 1999), 32.

15. Raymond Vernon, *In the Hurricane's Eye: The Troubled Prospects of Multinational Enterprises*, (Cambridge, Mass.: Harvard University Press, 1997), 10; Anthony Giddens, op. cit., 143.

16. *New York Times*, November 11, 1979, cited in Peter Evans, *Embedded Autonomy: States and Industrial Transformation*, (Princeton, N.J.: Princeton University Press, 1995), 43.

17. Raymond Colitt, "Open Sewers Give Brazil's Cities a Waste Water Stomach Ache," *Financial Times*, July 27, 2000, 5; World Bank, *Entering the 21st Century: World Development Report 1999/2000* (New York: Oxford University Press, 2000), tables 1 and 4, 230–37.

18. Martin Wolf, "The Golden Age of Government," *Financial Times*, July 12, 2000, 15, cites recent studies that show that Western state spending (as represented by countries of the Organisation for Economic Co-operation and Development [OECD]) in toto, after a bracing upward run for the Great Depression, leveled off at 46 percent of gross domestic product by 1996.

19. Vernon, op. cit., 172.

20. United Nations Development Programme, op. cit., 38.

21. World Bank, *Thai Workers and the Crisis*. A summary reported in *World Bank Development News*, July 20, 2000, 4. For regional unemployment figures, see United Nations Development Programme, *Human Development Report 1999* (New York: Oxford University Press, 1999), 4. The country population comparisons are made with the aid of the World Bank, *World Development Report, 2000–2001: Attacking Poverty* (New York: Oxford University Press, 2001), table 1, 274–75.

22. Charles Kindleberger, *Manias, Panics, and Crashes: A History of Financial Crises*. 3d ed. (New York: John Wiley, 1996), 4.

23. Joseph Schumpeter, *Capitalism, Socialism, and Democracy*, 3d ed. (New York: Harper and Row, 1950), 162.

24. David Harvey, *On the Condition of Postmodernity* (New York: Blackwell, 1989).

25. Giovanni Arrighi, *The Long Twentieth Century* (New York: Verso, 1994).

26. Manuel Castells, op. cit., 92–97.

27. John Gray, *False Dawn: The Delusions of Global Capitalism*, (New York: The New Press, 1998).

28. Immanuel Wallerstein, "The West, Capitalism, and the Modern World-System," *Review* 15 (Fall 1992), 561–619.

29. Karl Polanyi, *The Great Transformation* (Boston: Beacon Press, 1945).

30. Manuel Castells, op. cit.

31. For a discussion of differences among OECD countries, see Herbert Kitschelt, Peter Lange, Gary Marks, and John Stephens, *Continuity and Change in Contemporary Capitalism* (Cambridge, U.K.: Cambridge University Press, 1999).

32. Joseph Stiglitz, *Whither Socialism?* (Cambridge, Mass.: MIT Press, 1994), 254.

33. For a discussion of the European corporatist tradition, see Colin Crouch, *Social Change in Western Europe* (Cambridge, Mass.: Blackwell, 2000).

34. Robert Wade, *Governing the Market: Economic Theory and the Role of Government in East Asian Industrialization* (Princeton, N.J.: Princeton University Press, 1990).

35. Michael Blim, "Can NOT-Capitalism Lie at the End of History?" *Critique of Anthropology* 17, no. 4 (December 1997), 351–64.

36. Andres Solimano, op. cit., 28–29.

37. *Economist*, September 12, 1998, 24–25.

38. "What I Learned at the World Economic Crisis," *New Republic*, April 17, 2000, available at www.tnr.com/041700/stiglitz041700.html.

CHAPTER THREE

Values and Action

The world we live in is a scene of often appalling contrasts, as if the world were Bombay or New York City, where plutocrats of inestimable worth live a stone's throw from people struggling for subsistence in the midst of unrelieved, crushing poverty. Or conjure up another image—that of landless day laborers working on the great sugar estates of the Caribbean or of Africa who, while making little for themselves, line the pockets of that tiny fraction of the world who are its corporate shareholders. If these scenes are metaphors for the human condition, how shall we orient ourselves? What shall be our stance? How shall we act?

Much depends upon our values. People have values, notions of what is good or worthy and what is bad and unworthy of human life, regarding the most fundamental questions of existence. Our choices, our actions in the world, are guided by them. They are the ultimate ends against which we measure our actions.

Values point toward appropriate actions. For instance, suppose we value human beings leading long, disease-free lives. Of course the concepts "long" and "disease-free" would need further definition in a given society through discussion among peers. Assuming that we could satisfy the demand to be more precise, we would proceed to evaluate goals and courses of action in light of the degree to which they advance that which we hold dear. Some goals would be appropriate, and some would not. In this case, perhaps the goal to be rich, for instance, may be less relevant to our value of long, disease-free life than the goal of universal health care.

Let us take another case. Suppose we value living without experiencing physical violence. Again, assuming we can adequately define "physical violence," we can then proceed to evaluate our goals. Is retaining the use of force as a foreign policy option consonant with our values? Is the action of keeping a standing army compatible? Is state administration of the death penalty appropriate? Is corporal punishment in schools fitting? On the other hand, if we think about goals that would enhance our abilities to live in a violence-free world, we might look at courses of action that lessened the frequency and impact of violence in our lives. We might consider it advisable to teach children peaceful approaches to conflict resolution. Or we might want to argue that lowering the degree of poverty and economic inequality among us would lower rates of crimes that include physical force and violence.

The relationships between values, goals, and actions are reciprocal. Considerations of a goal or action invoke our values, and vice versa. All three are part of the materiality of our existence and change as the conditions of our lives change. Thus, values are not some fixed essence, like the North Star, by which we guide ourselves. They are more like road maps we use to cross the rough and changing terrain of everyday life.

But are values commensurable? That is, can they be understood from person to person, society to society? To be compared, they must be understood in some meaningful sense. A second and equally challenging question: Can they be shared from person to person, society to society? If they can be, then the project here—to provide a new common value base for changing how we operate economies that advance human flourishing—can proceed. If not, then we face the dismaying prospect that no common project is possible. Humanity by default would have to rely upon each person or each society, depending on how incommensurable people's values are, none of which might be connected with the project envisioned here—or any other collective project for the improvement of the human condition, for that matter.

In other words, a great deal hinges upon how we answer these questions. We also need to be mindful that understanding and sharing are not the same things. Understanding only implies an agreement on what a concept means, while sharing implies that we jointly espouse the belief that we have agreed the concept has. We shall tackle the first—the problem of understanding—immediately below. The problem of sharing will preoccupy us later in the chapter when we discuss the necessary role of power and politics in improving the prospects for human flourishing.

The Human Rights Revolution and
Creating Mutual Understanding

More than two centuries ago, Jean-Jacques Rousseau launched his famous discourse *The Social Contract* with the provocative observation that humans, while born free, were everywhere in chains. Society had absconded with liberty, reducing humans to the status of social chattel. The revolutionists of the eighteenth century, the United States's founders among them, responded to Rousseau's cries of human bondage with the fervent belief that every person had the right to life, liberty, and the pursuit of happiness. For them, there was no doubt that there existed a plateau of universal human values whose fulfillment was reachable by all over the course of their existence. The common task was to assure that societies provided the context wherein their expression and results were manifestly available to all.

In so doing, as Claude Lévi-Strauss has noted, Rousseau laid down for the world "the only possible basis" for ethics and the foundation for the human sciences.[1] The human capacity to recognize something of us in others, our ability to identify with others, was the foundation for the Enlightenment. Today, we recognize Rousseau's first principle, that we humans are empathic creatures in our more empirical appreciation of the human capacity for language. Through language we come to know the thoughts and desires of others. Mutual intelligibility between speaker and listener is the fundamental basis for human communication. In this sense, we have improved upon the speculative philosophical anthropology of Rousseau by lodging his emphasis on empathy as a defining human sentiment in the modern scientific understanding of the potentialities of human language for opening up worlds of possible mutual understanding.

Our human linguistic skills are a highly useful place to start figuring out how human beings can share common values that have positive consequences for life on the planet. One of the discoveries of modern anthropology through its exhaustive exploration of every nook and cranny of human habitation of the twentieth century is that every spoken human language can be learned and used by a nonnative speaker. Thus, empirically, there appears to be a potential bilingual speaker whose competence includes making sense and translating meaning for every one of the thousands of human languages spoken on Earth.

To residents of the United States, a nation predicated on cultural contact, immigration, and migration, this realization must seem as if it were no more than a bit of obvious common sense. At a bus stop, in an emergency room, at the post office—in short, amidst the banalities of everyday existence—we experience the profound challenges, as well as satisfactions, of multilingual living. The everyday experiences of asking or giving directions, telling a doctor where it hurts, asking a clerk how much a first-class stamp costs occupy a certain amount of our time for understanding even when we speak the same language. We expend even more energy establishing what we mean when these exchanges take place between speakers of different languages.

In the multilingual contexts in which many U.S. citizens find themselves, another, larger lesson can be learned. It is that our exercise in nation-making, if only ideally a result of multiethnic, multicultural negotiation, closely resembles in theory the process of achieving common understanding that we suggest here is increasingly a universal fact of human endeavors. We resolve differences in meaning from one concept to the next in the line-by-line translation of living among peoples whose concepts of living in all their detail are different. When we are participating in the activities of social institutions, whether they be of learning, curing, business, or jurisprudence, to name a few focused settings, agreements in meaning form the basis for most social interaction.[2]

Agreeing to what something means is not the same as saying that one understands completely what the other is saying. More often than not, translations between one language and another are imperfect. More often than not, translations *in the same language* from speaker to speaker involve a great deal of ambiguity. Each of us imparts some fraction of meaning that is particular to us based upon the unique coloring of our experiences. For instance, my concept of justice may include a meaning that we can agree to, such as equal treatment before the law. But my concept of justice also bears reflections of my personal history, such as how the law may have treated me or how I may have observed others being treated by the law. All of our experience imparts meaning to concepts.

Moreover, language cannot always express completely our moods, feelings, and dispositions. Perhaps we notice this most in more intimate conversations, when we might even use the conventional phrase "Words cannot express how I feel." It is an admission that we sometimes struggle very hard to put our thoughts and experience into concepts and concepts into words. There is often some remainder, some aspect of our thought and feeling, that eludes successful communication.

Values are particularly tricky and easily misunderstood concepts. In contrast, when we use language to refer to things, we have many options and more security that mutual understanding can be achieved. Suppose two persons bilingual in English and Italian were looking at what an English speaker would call a barn and trying to decide what color to call it. They could compare the red color terms of both languages to see which term best represented what they were seeing. They would soon find that in addition to English's "red" and Italian's "*rosso*" they had such red color terms as "*magenta*," "*violetta*," "*cremisino*," and "*scarlatto*" in common, both languages having derived some terms from the same Latin or Greek linguistic roots. Perhaps both speakers thought that "magenta" in both languages adequately described what they were seeing—a decision that obviated most translation problems. (Of course, a magenta barn would certainly cause comment in either country!) On the other hand, they could just as easily choose to modify a term in one language with one from the other. One can imagine an English speaker inventing terms like "Italian red" or "rosso red," for example; similarly, one can readily imagine the Italian speaker's "*rosso americano*." In the language of things, there are many options for obtaining mutual understanding, not the least of which is that two parties can point to an object and agree to a term for use.

Instead, values as concepts present more problems because they connote many meanings to both speakers of the same and different languages. You cannot point to a value in the same way as you point to a barn. What does "life, liberty, and the pursuit of happiness" mean, exactly? What does it mean to citizens of the United States, for whom the phrase refers to the ambitious opening of the Declaration of Independence? What does it mean to citizens of other countries, for whom life, liberty, and happiness have different histories and significances? And what would the "right to" life, liberty, and the pursuit of happiness mean?

The first United Nations (UN) conference in 1948 to define universal human rights struggled mightily over the precise significance of saying that persons had the "right to" something. In the atmosphere of an oncoming Cold War, East and West prescribed entirely different domains of meaning to the concept of "right to." The capitalist West, following the nineteenth-century liberal tradition, defined "right to" negatively: A person could pursue life, liberty, and happiness free of intrusion by another person or state. The socialist East, acting within an evolving twentieth-century revolutionary tradition, defined "right to" positively: It wanted any human rights covenant to spell out affirmatively those goods owed to each member of humanity. For example, the "right to" included full-time employment for adults, health care, and a minimum of material prosperity guaranteed for all. The resulting Universal Declaration of Human Rights included rights of both kinds, negative and positive, in its ringing endorsement of a wide range of human freedoms.[3]

It is precisely the movement for human rights ignited by the UN declaration more than a half-century ago that improves our prospects for mutual understanding. We are currently undergoing a human rights revolution in which the world is fast becoming one highly contentious, but communicative, reference group. This means that through constant and significant interaction we are creating common sense and reference about certain essentials of human life. And, perhaps more than mutual understanding, we may also be creating through the same process a set of shared values.

It seems an overly ambitious claim. It also raises the problem of politics and power that we will discuss later in the chapter. Yet there is some sense in which it can be verified within the context of the past decade. Persons accused of war crimes and crimes against humanity, ranging from the former Chilean dictator Augusto Pinochet and many former Yugoslavian politicians to civilians accused of abetting the ethnic massacres in Rwanda, have either been brought to justice or attempts have been made to bring them before national or international tribunals. Powerful banks and international corporations have been compelled to provide compensation for their complicity in the murder of European Jews during the Holocaust.

Even the United States, its current economic and military supremacy notwithstanding, receives sharp criticism for what is perceived by large portions of the international community to be substantial human rights violations. That the United States resorts to the death penalty for offenses such as murder and kidnapping, for instance, routinely draws disapprobation from religious leaders, citizens' groups, and states around the world. Our rates of incarceration as well as the character of offenses that trigger life sentences in the United States are also held up to a critical glass by respected human rights groups like Amnesty International, the exemplar of agencies that many praise for uncovering cruel and unusual punishment in other lands.[4]

The resort to war in Afghanistan under the rubric of frontier justice, and the claim of the right wing to "hot pursuit" of terrorists wherever in the world they may be as a result of the events of September 11, 2001, is a disturbing setback to the prospects for advancing a common code and procedure for international justice, if international justice is conceived as a collective global institution like the United Nations. The refusal of the United States to ratify treaties establishing international courts of justice, both criminal and political, also contributes to the inescapable inference that the United States is substituting imperial might in the place of a more legitimate and humane solution of universal human rights with international procedural guarantees. So, too, the Anglo-American war on Iraq was prosecuted without the explicit endorsement of the United Nations and without the support of more than half the nations of the world.

Fortunately, we do live in a world where the actions in or of one society are increasingly subject to the scrutiny of others. The values of a person, of a group or section within a given society, or of the society as a whole pass an inevitable world review, as people around the world compare particular value commitments with their own. To be sure, there is no advantage in imagining that people will come to subscribe to common values only to ignore that people disagree in their practices. Some normatively acceptable range of practices given certain values is bound to emerge, thus casting a deviant aspersion on some activities while positively acknowledging others.

For instance, let us take up a controversial issue in the United States's public domain and put it into a world context. U.S. reliance on capital punishment draws significant worldwide rebuke because its practices are "deviant" with respect to those of the majority of other developed nations. This suggests that there is a real sense in which we are forming a new global reference group in which rewards as well as sanctions on the part of other peoples become a relevant consideration in the value commitments we make over the course of our lives. Reluctant though it may be, there is no doubt either that even the United States finds itself compared with others, and thus compares itself with others, according to an evolving set of human rights and humane practices.

In the words of the Vienna Declaration of the World Conference on Human Rights in 1993, to which 172 countries, including the United States, assented: "The universal nature of these rights and freedoms is beyond question. . . . Human rights and fundamental freedoms are the birthright of all human beings; their protection and promotion is the first responsibility of Governments."[5]

Anthropology and Human Values

Despite the fact that anthropology has been the historical interpreter and translator of human values from culture to culture, the discipline has a long and complicated history with human rights and the study of values. In the retelling of the story, we find important lessons for how complicated and difficult the subject of values can be.

Anthropology's first stance on human rights might best be seen as an expression of the classical liberal endorsement of "negative" liberty. The American Anthropological Association's 1947 opposition to the UN Universal Declaration of Human Rights rested on the rejection of any set of "universal" norms and values that might infringe on those of any particular culture. "The Rights of Man in the Twentieth Century," the association's statement of the same year read, "cannot be circumscribed by the standards of any single culture, or be dictated to by the aspirations of any single people."[6] The formula was that no group or nation could prescribe to another, that such an action would constitute "imperialism," as anthropologist Julian Steward put it at the time.[7] This view placed anthropology in the highly ambiguous position of seeking to protect the rights of some—at that time largely indigenous peoples—in lieu of advocating rights of the many. As Terence Turner points out, the post–World War II anthropological position "fail[ed] to deal with the common humanity or species-being of all people, as members of all cultures."[8]

The position was also inconsistent with some of the beliefs of the founding figures, whose positions are worth considering in some detail, for we may be able to get an answer this time that is more congenial with the view expressed here, that universal values are important. Franz Boas and his students were attached to two important assumptions underlying their work. First, though anthropology was to explore the ways of life of peoples around the world, it was also supposed to use the knowledge gained abroad to critically reflect on Western ways of life. Second, as anthropology was committed to exposing the particular rhyme and reason of every society, it was further compelled to protect each society's cultural integrity. This actually meant that the social practices that differed from those of Western societies were justified as deriving from the logic of people's local lives. This last assumption became described as a belief in "cultural relativism": that is, the view that peoples had the right to live their lives as they saw fit, without suffering the disparagement and prohibitions of more powerful outsiders. The 1947 American Anthropological Association statement on human rights puts the principle well: "Standards and values are relative to the culture from which they derive so that any attempt to formulate postulates that grow out of the beliefs or moral codes of one culture must to that extent detract from the applicability of any Declaration of Human Rights to mankind as a whole."[9]

Let us take up the first assumption, that anthropology should engage in cultural critique of Western ways. For Franz Boas, disabusing oneself of the essential "rightness" of one's own cultural practices was necessary if anthropology as a human science were to prosper. Like the impulse to estrange oneself from one's native land through ethnographic fieldwork, so too it was important to alienate oneself from one's native beliefs and practices to understand the beliefs and practices of others different from one, and thus make room for the practice of science. According to Boas, the anthropologist "reaches a standpoint that enables him to view our own civilization critically, and to enter into a comparative study of values with a mind relatively uninfluenced by the emotions elicited by the automatically regulated behavior in which he participates as a member of our society." This end can be reached, he continues, "only by patient inquiry in which our own emotional valuations and attitudes are conscientiously held in the background."[10]

While Boas imagined that the exercise creates a dispassionate faculty of critical intelligence, his student Ruth Benedict saw anthropology as a form of moral corrective to be practiced on our civilization. Benedict argued:

> There is, however, one difficult exercise to which we may accustom ourselves as we become increasingly culture-conscious. We may train ourselves to pass judgment upon the dominant traits of our own civilization . . . which deserve special scrutiny. We need to realize that they are compulsive, not in proportion as they are basic and essential in human behavior, but rather in the degree to which they are local and overgrown in our own culture.[11]

In the hands of Margaret Mead, the story of Samoan female adolescence becomes an object lesson in how to liberate the generations of adolescents coming of age in the twentieth-century United States from the neurosis-inducing strictures that bore down so heavily upon them.[12]

Yet, as much as Benedict and Mead explored anthropology as a redemptive project for Western societies, the possibility of a comparative study of values, also raised by Boas, finds its way into the work of another Boas student, Alfred Kroeber. "How is it possible," Kroeber wrote, "without the most sterile stultification, to make intellectual study of social man who is cultural man, and yet permanently leave out of consideration his product, culture, and that essence of culture, its forms and values?" Values, Kroeber continued, "can obviously be described; their differential qualities as well as common characteristics can be compared; their development phases, sequential relations, and connections can be investigated."[13]

For Kroeber, then, the values of another are accessible knowledge, and something that is done in "every study of the history of an art, in every attempt to present a religion, in all ethnographic accounts that rise above mechanical itemization."[14] If one can understand the values of others through the commonplace of anthropological study, what are the prospects for understanding the values of others in everyday social interaction? Does one need to observe Boas's priestly injunctions before one can understand? And if one can understand in ordinary discourse, what are the prospects for sorting out differences, or even greater, for agreement?

It depends on how tightly we hold onto the principle of cultural relativism, the founders' second assumption. If we believe, as Boas argues at one point in *Anthropology and Modern Life*, that the social ideals of various peoples are "so different from our own that the valuations given by them to human behavior are not comparable," then limited understanding is possible. "What is considered good by one is considered bad by another," he continues,[15] and we might add "and never the twain shall meet."

This would be the strong view of cultural relativism. It means that values from one society to the next are incommensurable: No understanding and thus no basis for agreement is possible. But Boas himself leaves the door open for something more flexible, and something more philosophically real. No society is an isolate, a thing unto itself:

> It might be thought that primitive societies were isolated and that the laws governing their inner development may be learned directly from comparative studies of their cultures. This is not the case. Even the simplest groups with which we are familiar have developed by contact with their neighbors.[16]

Here is the link, the bridge over which the conversation on values and the possibilities for mutual exchange between groups are possible: the inevitability and significance of intersocietal contact. As every society grows in contact with others, so, too, do its values. Thus, there is no society whose values cannot be discussed by another, as they share a mutual origin in contact with another. The problem of the "truth" of cultural relativism is that it describes no living situations. You might say that all societies are talking about universal human values—only at times from their particular points of view. The values themselves, however, are based in and change with dialogue between societies as well as dialogue that occurs within every society.

Anthropology as a human science bears important witness and brings important agency to this process. Anthropologists are like lenses placed over the world's eyes to improve human perceptions of others and ourselves. Anthropologists are part of the ongoing project of enlightenment, articulating a vision of human life and values that constitutes the beginnings of a world culture. Though patchy, and fought over, the cultural conversation—and conflict—grows.[17]

Defending a native group's right to be different—their right not to have their rights of self-determination taken away by modern states—still reflects the discipline's outlook. The American Anthropology Association's Commission for Human Rights in 1993 reaffirmed the rights of groups to their cultural, social, linguistic, and biological differences, while expanding its purview to include individuals as well.[18] Terence Turner, a member of the commission, argues that it sought to combine a universal principle of difference, by which it intends to underscore the human activity of individual and collective distinction, with "a cultural relativist recognition of the fundamental importance of cultural, social, and individual difference."[19] This position, Turner believes, makes universal principles and local differences compatible.[20]

Perhaps a small, but significant, amendment to Turner's conception of rights is in order, and it has to do with the distinction he draws between "universals" and "local differences." As we argued above, values are not some sort of fixed essences, standing above and apart from the experience of everyday life. Quite the opposite: They only make sense when we use them to guide our actions in very specific contexts. Like any conceptual abstraction, they can only take on meaning with reference to some concrete situation or act, and do not "reside" in any other human space other than lived experience. Thus, they also change through use or application, and part of the task of scientists, intellectuals, and other interested parties is to keep track of their historical use and application so that we keep in constant contact with our experience, both present and past.

One way of accomplishing this task is to consider values from the philosopher John Dewey's point of view: Values don't exist apart from practice, and the consequences of their use; in fact, they change with use. A moral law, he argues (and here we might interpolate a value-based prescription):

> is not something to swear by and stick to at all hazards, it is a formula of the way to respond when specified conditions present themselves. Its soundness and pertinence are tested by what happens when it is acted upon. . . . The test of consequences . . . secures constant development, for when new acts are tried new results are experienced, while the lauded immutability of eternal ideals and norms is in itself a denial of the possibility of development and improvement.[21]

Consequently, the distinction drawn between "universal values," on the one hand, and "local values," on the other, dissolves. This is because if we stipulate that the context of use is the world, then "local" practices are expressions of the current state of values for the world as a whole. It also means that a practice anywhere in the world can be scrutinized with appeal to a value or values with which we are all familiar, being "hard at work" through our practice in applying them. Value "disagreement" is inevitable, but the very disagreement itself points to the value or values we currently hold and use.

In this less-than-"ideal" world, universal values are not simply possible, but actual. The struggle is to make them what we want them to be.

Proposing Values

So let us propose some values to guide our economic actions. In so doing, let us recall the basic premise of the book, that the overall goal of living is that we might flourish under a condition of universal well-being. We argue that human life worth living is invested with dignity and equipped with some prospect of satisfaction. The implication of this stance is that life is something fuller and richer than mere survival. Instead, living in good spirits and with enthusiasm is envisioned as the atmosphere and outcome of human striving.

This premise requires two important extensions. The first, recalling Amartya Sen's injunction from an earlier chapter, is that the virtues of living are not enjoyed "on average." This means that not only are persons' capabilities for satisfaction highly differentiated, but that one cannot take a measure of average improvement in the human condition and consider the job of enhancing human flourishing as done. Individual differences and capacities must be taken into account when enhancing human prospects.

The position is a matter of fundamental importance because we propose that one cannot choose who shall flourish and who shall not, and thus whose interests should count and whose should be ignored. The only defensible claim is that all human beings as human beings are worthy of living rich, fulfilling lives. Any other position has the burden of proof of showing why any individual(s) or group(s) should be advantaged over others—something, I would venture, that is actually much harder to prove than its opposite. Our case can rest upon the fundamental identity of the human species, without which the assumption of a common human consciousness and cognition would be an impossible claim.

There is a second extension, stemming from the recognition of individual differences just above, that also becomes necessary. It follows from our assessment of the different needs of each person that each person constitutes a distinctive self, and that selfhood is integral to human dignity. Citing the philosopher Charles Taylor earlier,[22] we argued that selfhood in the modern world means that each person believes or is entitled to believe that she has a personal destiny. Fulfillment of that destiny thus becomes an essential characteristic of our concept of well-being. We might defend this choice by arguing that the quest for self-fulfillment has a long history, and trace its lineage back to the Socratic imperative to know thyself. We might the trace the growth of self-fulfillment in civilizations and cultures around the world. Or we could settle for Taylor's assertion that self-fulfillment is an attribute of the self in the modern world. Any and all of these arguments support the belief that self-fulfillment is an integral part of modern human experience.

In any case, making our conception of universal well-being more robust by including specific attention to individual differences and to the distinctive needs of a person's quest for self-fulfillment sets the bar for the pursuit of values that can satisfy this broad requirement a bit higher than before. It implies in terms of negative liberty that no person should be deprived of her destiny because she is physically handicapped or disabled. It also means that neither should she suffer economic or social impairment based upon her race, gender, class, or social status. It also implies liberty in the positive sense that a person should be supported affirmatively in her personal quest for self-fulfillment, which in turn is central to what was earlier called "the human vocation."[23]

But what values, if put into practice, might reconcile well with this robust view of human development? One could consider many possible contenders. Following from our discussion of the way global capitalism has accelerated economic integration since World War II, the value of autonomy arises almost immediately. People experience a diminished capacity to regulate their economic destinies, whether as individuals, as members of groups, or as citizens of regions and states. The terrors of capital flight, currency crashes, bank panics, and other economic calamities that are contagious in this interconnected world economy have tamed outsiders and insiders alike to respect the imperatives of profit-driven, but accident-prone, world capitalism.

Individuals, if we entertain for a moment the conservative prescriptions of economist Milton Friedman, must be "free to choose." Persons, Friedman believes, create an economy by expressing their personal needs and desires and seeking to satisfy them. For an economy to function, persons must be free to act on their preferences so that the economy can be mobilized to satisfy them. So, too, communities, regions, and states as entities composed of individuals engaged in social cooperation for the fulfillment of their needs arguably need the freedom to choose among alternative courses of action so that the economic interests of their constituent individuals can be satisfied.[24]

The world is so interconnected, as has been argued repeatedly here, that the value of autonomy for individuals and societies is inevitably relative, and probably should be so. Modern autarchic societies, such as Albania after World War II, Perónist Argentina, and present-day North Korea, suggest that societies that are immune to the influence and even the criticism of others are not necessarily good in advancing human flourishing. Moreover, all actions taken by individuals and societies have impacts on others who are uninvolved in or external to the decision-making process. For example, as a smoker in a closed room endangers the health of everyone in the room, so every society that pollutes the atmosphere in ways that foster global warming injures every other society on the planet. Every decision has consequences that in a fair world would weigh in and affect the decision-making process itself. Thus, autonomy is a useful, if limited, value that we might identify to guide our actions in making a better world.

Similarly, following the useful advice of the World Bank, we might also nominate opportunity, empowerment, and security as the values by which we measure our progress. People can overcome poverty and degradation by acting on opportunities that arise because a society values creating opportunities for its citizens. Economic growth, according to the World Bank, is the source of opportunity. The more growth, the more general opportunities, and the more likely that they will reach the poor and disadvantaged.[25]

Empowerment, that people have a voice in their destinies and that institutions are responsive to people's needs and desires, is surely also among the cardinal virtues. And powerlessness is one of the most common of human experiences, as a Gallup poll surveying 50,000 persons in 60 countries found out. Only one-third of the respondents worldwide felt that their country was governed by the will of the people. Only 10 percent felt that their government was responsive to citizens' needs and desires.[26] According to the World Bank, responsive institutions not only help the poor and disadvantaged but also contribute to economic growth.[27]

Security, too, is a good candidate for a paramount value. The vagaries of human existence necessarily impose upon us the condition of uncertainty. Disadvantage often deepens our state of objective insecurity deriving from want whose fulfillment is denied. Subjectively, we also often carry a palpable sense that our lives are in some jeopardy, and that a sudden lurch will transport us into the unknown or into a hell of material and/or spiritual deprivation.

Rich societies in the twentieth century have sought to hold their citizens harmless from the effects of ill health, unemployment, and old age. Their responses, welfare states of varying degrees of effectiveness, have been their answers to pervasive economic and social insecurity. Generally speaking, they have put a floor of economic and social protection underneath our feet, seeking to establish a minimum level under which human existence cannot fall. As the World Bank sees it, security and the social and economic risk management that it implies should be at the center of our efforts. Success in reducing risk also encourages investment in human capital and higher-gain economic activities.[28]

The values we have thus far discussed—autonomy, opportunity, empowerment, and security—form only a partial list of the many we might put forward. Each has its merits; none seems superfluous to our aim of enhancing human flourishing. Quite the contrary: each seems to complement the other in a search for better human lives.

However, more fundamental than these values—and I would argue instrumental in their accomplishment—is the value of equality. It is the keystone in the arch of well-being, without which the other virtues are unattainable or only fleeting opportunities. There are two rather different reasons why I believe this to be true.

First, if we approach this issue from a moral stance, then it seems inescapable to me that we must argue for equality. Human beings, it is important to say, compose a species, and all of us share a basic nature that produces basic capabilities as well as needs. Our individual capabilities may vary, but fundamental characteristics such as needing and desiring well-being and happiness are identical. Sometimes prejudice and ignorance blind us to the fact that every human life departs from these same premises. As an exasperated Shylock in Shakespeare's *The Merchant of Venice* cried out to his tormentors: "Hath not a Jew eyes? If you prick us, do we not bleed?" A regard for every human life is a moral corollary to our concern for our own lives. An insistence on well-being for ourselves imposes upon us to demand it for others. Equality becomes a moral minimum, a kind of default position, I believe, because it is much more compatible with acceptance of our common human nature. Following the conventions of normal reasoning, and applying Occam's razor to determine which argument has more basic sense, it becomes clear that the argument for equality is much more economical and straightforward than one for inequality.

Try a mental exercise. Starting from the facts presented in the first two chapters, seek to justify the enormous economic inequalities among us, acknowledging the suffering and indignity they visit on billions of our fellow human beings. One dubious premise follows another, and the justification of wealth and privilege begins to seem just a form of special pleading, an artifact of advantage. My suspicion is you may find yourself reverting to the position set forth more than 200 years ago by Jean-Jacques Rousseau, as I noted at the beginning of the chapter, that economic and social inequalities derive not from human nature but from the concrete historical struggles among people. Inequality in this kind of scenario thus becomes the booty of victors, an unenviable outcome incapable of being defended in a principled manner.

There is a second and empirical reason for making equality the keystone in the arc of human well-being. An exhaustive reading of the social science research, I believe, would support the conclusion that *unless persons achieve important forms of economic, social, and political equality, it is very difficult to defend any gains they achieve in well-being.* Equality, as I show in the next chapter, is *being* equal. Thus, every person needs the capabilities of acting and experiencing life as every other, for itself as a human virtue to be enjoyed and as an instrument with which to gain access to resources necessary for the possibilities of well-being.

Though I could appeal to our intuitive sense of what equality means, that will not suffice for our purposes ultimately. We will need to explore what we mean by "equality" as a term of use and as a value. I will show that if we delineate carefully several important dimensions of equality as the value is applied to social life, then we have some prospect of being able to speak with insight and probity of what would make a better world.

Notes

1. Claude Lévi-Strauss, *Structural Anthropology, Volume II* (New York: Basic Books, 1976), 43.

2. See Harold Garfinkel, "Some Rules of Correct Decision Making That Jurors Respect," in *Studies in Ethnomethodology* (Englewood Cliffs, N.J.: Prentice-Hall, 1967), 104–15, for a paradigmatic discussion of how deriving an agreement on meaning drives most focused social encounters.

3. I am only using part of Isaiah Berlin's distinction between negative and positive liberty. While his notion of negative liberty is meant to mark the individual's maximum freedom from the interference of others or of the state, a distinction I adopt, he describes positive liberty in a less charitable light, suggesting that it stands for the process of the usurpation of individual freedom, typically by state despotism. See Berlin, *Four Essays on Liberty* (New York: Oxford University Press, 1970), xliv–xlvi, 121–22, 131–34. I prefer to use Alain Touraine's notion of positive liberty in the sense my text suggests—that is, the affirmative actions that persons, groups, and states can take to increase human potential to exercise liberty. See Touraine, *What Is Democracy?*, translated by David Macey (Boulder, Colo.: Westview Press, 1997), 131, 185. For a comprehensive examination of the various political and social forces that produced the Universal Declaration of Human Rights, see Ellen Messer, "Pluralist Approaches to Human Rights," *Journal of Anthropological Research* 53, no. 3 (Fall 1997), 293–317. See also Ellen Messer, "Anthropology and Human Rights," *Annual Review of Anthropology* 22 (1993), 222–23.

4. See Amnesty International's *Annual Report 2000* (Washington, D.C.: Amnesty International, 2000) for a statement of alleged current human rights abuses in the United States, ranging from the death penalty (which it calls "judicial killing") to inhumane prison treatment and police brutality, as well as state violence practiced upon illegal immigrants.

5. Quoted in Michael Perry, "Are Human Rights Universal? The Relativist Challenge and Related Matters," *Human Rights Quarterly* 19 (1997), 481.

6. Quoted in Ann-Belinda Preis, "Human Rights as Cultural Practice: An Anthropological Critique," *Human Rights Quarterly* 18 (1996), 286–87.

7. Ibid. See also Elvin Hatch, "The Good Side of Relativism," *Journal of Anthropological Research* 53 (1997), 371–81.

8. "Human Rights, Human Difference: Anthropology's Contribution to an Emancipatory Cultural Politics," *Journal of Anthropological Research* 53 (1997), 278.

9. "Statement on Human Rights," *American Anthropologist* 49, no. 4 (October–December 1947), 542.

10. Franz Boas, *Anthropology and Modern Life* (New York: W. W. Norton, 1928), p. 207.

11. Ruth Benedict, *Patterns of Culture* (Boston: Houghton Mifflin, 1961 [1934]), 249–50.

12. Margaret Mead, *Coming of Age in Samoa: A Psychological Study of Primitive Youth for Western Civilization* (New York: William Morrow, 1961 [1928]).

13. Alfred Kroeber, "The Concept of Culture in Science." In *High Points in Anthropology*. 2d ed. Edited by P. Bohannon and M. Glazer (New York: Alfred A. Knopf, 1988), 116.

14. Ibid.

15. Franz Boas, op. cit., 204.

16. Ibid., 211–12.

17. Preis, op. cit., 290, makes this point nicely, arguing that our new concepts of culture, which affirm contestedness rather than static holism, allow us to describe human rights as human culture, in this more robust sense.

18. Terence Turner, op. cit., 286.

19. Ibid., 287.

20. Ibid., 278.

21. *The Quest for Certainty: A Study of the Relation of Knowledge and Action* (New York: Minton, Balch and Company, 1929), 278.

22. See chapter 1.

23. Douglas Porpora, *Landscapes of the Soul: The Loss of Meaning in American Life* (New York: Oxford University Press, 2001).

24. Milton Friedman and Rose Friedman, *Free to Choose* (New York: Harcourt Brace Jovanovich, 1980).

25. World Bank, *World Development Report 2000–2001: Attacking Poverty* (New York: Oxford University Press, 2001), 6–7.

26. United Nations Development Programme, *Human Development Report 2002: Deepening Democracy in a Fragmented World* (New York: Oxford University Press, 2002), 63.

27. World Bank, op. cit., 7.

28. World Bank, ibid.

Valuing Equality

This chapter puts forth the case for valuing equality. After a discussion designed to clarify what equality can mean, we go on to discuss its value as a guide to social action. We specify how focus on three of its dimensions—economic, social, and political equality—can help us clarify how we might use the concept to advance the cause of human betterment.

"Equality" in ordinary language is an ambiguous term. It can refer to persons having the same, meaning *identical*, things or qualities. For example, persons may have identical civil rights before the law, the same degree or academic certificate, or mathematically the same chances in a given lottery, to name a range of possible conditions we would describe as equal. Included is a sense of same access and treatment. But equality can also signify persons having *equivalent* things or qualities. This means that by some criterion applied to two things, nonidentical or unlike things are taken to be the same for some purpose. In exchange settings, for instance, we trade equivalents such as a determinate amount of money for a good or a service. Sometimes, though things might be different in the sense of how things were done or achieved, we accept them as functional equivalents, as in the case of a high school diploma and a high school equivalency degree, where both degrees satisfy requirements for employment, college admission, and other matters.

When we address human needs, the distinction between identity and equivalence becomes trickier, and the less satisfied we become with relying on the simple principle of identity instead of the more complicated, but more experientially real, notion of equivalence. For illustrative purposes, given our interest in advancing human well-being, people's health becomes one of several primary concerns. To be "in good health" connotes an ability to function in physically, cognitively, and emotionally adequate ways in the course of everyday life. It is our shared belief and expectation, that is, a norm that we agree upon, as to what being "in good health" is.

Persons have different requirements for being "in good health." For one person, it is enough to get plenty of sleep and eat a hearty breakfast to start the day. For another, a surgical intervention, say an open-heart operation, may have been necessary so that she can function adequately in everyday life. Still another may need the conditions of everyday life modified so that she can function adequately in such settings as home, a job, commuting between the two, and so forth. Barrier-free environments, prostheses, physical aids, flexible hours—a wide range of conditions may need modification so that she can function adequately.

In these three instances, people do not share identical health. They share a functional equivalent that we call "good health." In other words, we define in societies common understandings of what things like "good health" are. Highly valuing equality would mean in this instance that we would undertake to assure that every person is functioning "in good health."

The question of equality is complicated, though, because we lack the experience of what we might call "absolute" equality, which might be what we mean by referring to equality in the first sense as meaning "identical." We experience ourselves as distinct, thus as different, and become cognizant as time passes that we do not share the identical bodily integrity, access to or enjoyment of social goods and resources, or just plain luck that others do. Since the 1960s, a time of struggle for civil rights and of actions to end poverty, the United States as a society has thought hard and long about how to actualize the value of equality. This experience suggests that there are two important questions to ask. First, to what should equality apply? Second, how should equality be applied?

The Dimensions of Equality

Let us take up the first: To what should equality apply? Amartya Sen believes that we must make a determination of what kind(s) of equality we want to propose. First there is the matter of what "spaces," as he puts it, we want to work for equality in.[1] I believe there is a warrant for focusing our energies on three spaces or dimensions of equality: economic, social, and political. In everyday life, these different dimensions of inequality often figure jointly in creating situations of profound disadvantage. For instance, women often find themselves poorer, stigmatized by virtue of their gender, and more powerless politically than men. Each dimension of inequality contributes to their disadvantage. Action in one domain can help diminish the effects of disadvantage in another. Thus, though concepts such as "social," "economic," and "political" seem clear at the abstract level, actions in a practical sense tend to blur the distinctions a bit—not enough, I would argue, to entertain restricting our analysis to a generic concept of equality and leaving it at that.

In the preceding chapters, I have shown that economic inequality, deprivation absolute and relative, stands in the way of a project of universal well-being. It is here—in changing people's material circumstances for the better—that I will place most of my emphasis. Though the book pays serious attention to the social and political causes and consequences of inequality, the bottom line, to use perhaps the most unmistakable phrase I can find to describe this effort, will be the economic benefits one can derive by acting on behalf of equality in all of its dimensions.

This said, the social dimension of inequality does need our specific attention. Many an economic remedy has had little or no lasting effect because people suffer under the yoke of socially structured inequalities. And what might appear as an individual disadvantage fast becomes one that is socially shared by a group of like-identified persons. The philosopher Ronald Dworkin provides a highly instructive illustration of how social barriers can prevent persons and groups from tackling head-on the problems of economic inequality. Taking up a hypothetical case from India in which two persons find themselves in different castes, one inferior to the other, Dworkin argues that it is conceivable that both persons, even the person from the lower caste, would consider greater equality inadvisable as an effect of their life experiences in a caste-ridden social structure.[2] Thus, the social dimension of inequality presents itself as a reality demanding direct, not indirect, attention, for it cannot be assumed that an economic remedy addressing the totality of inequality will touch in meaningful ways the lives of socially disadvantaged persons.

Gender is another outstanding example. Despite being a majority of the world's population, women comprise two-thirds of the world's illiterate. Lower skills and restrictions on work and workplace account in part for the fact that women earn less than men in all societies, notwithstanding the economic differences between poor societies like Belize or Algeria and Sweden or the United States.[3] Women have objectively diminished capabilities in learning, work experience, and access to resources that limit their economic choices. Fostering self-fulfillment among women requires building up the resources that men in these respects do not need.

Or take the equally insidious case of race in the United States. Persons of color are historically disadvantaged. Native Americans were killed or driven from their ancestral homes and placed in settings of permanent disadvantage on reservations throughout North America. Some 250 years of slavery, coupled with 150 years of continued institutional discrimination, created a legacy of disadvantage that afflicts African Americans even now. Then, too, it is important not to forget that both Asian Americans and several groups of Latino/Latina Americans, especially those from Mexico and Puerto Rico, endured several generations of stoop and indentured labor, doing jobs on America's railroads and in its farm fields that no "American" would do, a situation still true for many Latinos and Latinas throughout the southern and western parts of the United States. Each group leaves the mark of its oppression in its discrete performances in U.S. labor markets in the phenomenon we call ethnic segmentation, whereby job opportunities are restricted to certain, and often less remunerative, occupations. Their consequently divergent patterns of savings, income, and wealth can be tracked over time.[4]

Elsewhere in the world, discrimination against minority groups has the same endemic quality. For instance, a recent study in Vietnam showed that basic services are geographically much less accessible to ethnic minorities. A minority member of Vietnamese society has to travel at least twice as far to market, the post office, schools, hospitals, and administrative centers than do majority group members.[5] Given that use is related to access, it suggests how even the location of services typically puts minority groups at economic disadvantage.

Similar arguments for diminished capabilities due to disadvantage could be made for the physically handicapped and otherwise socially stigmatized. The reality that many persons share diminished capabilities based upon memberships in disadvantaged groups qualifies the question of equality greatly. It means that we must evaluate remedies for their impact on the equality of social chances made available to persons marked in some way by group disadvantage. The social dimension of equality, in other words, needs special attention, as we propose and examine economic remedies.

Further, political equality is fundamental to the achievement of both economic and social equality. In state societies, if a person does not possess equality before the law, how shall she press her claims for redress of her economic and/or social inequality? We are human beings and members of societies but, finally, it is as citizens of states that we present ourselves in the search for equality. Thus, political equality, while something good in itself, is instrumental in gaining the other two.

Valuing political equality is not the same as valuing democracy. Rather, the degree of political equality is what one values about a democracy when it is functioning optimally. Political equality becomes a measuring stick whereby we evaluate the quality and effectiveness of governments in action. I begin by assuming that democracies are clearly better than other alternatives for the organization of state societies. But we are holding democracies, which we have taken as an acknowledged good, to a higher standard. Can every person exercise the same civil and political rights as every other? How routinely does she, and in what contexts? These become the questions we must ask when the political dimension of equality is at stake.

In contrast, there are very strong tendencies at large to judge democracies in purely formal terms. Democracy is often regarded as a thing that exists fully formed, in a given society, or it doesn't. For instance, though aware that much more is at stake, the United Nations Development Programme (UNDP) in a recent study of democracy still takes something of a laundry-list approach to the evaluation of democracies. Does society X have multi-party elections? Does it have an elected head of state? Are all adults eligible to vote? And so on.[6] These kinds of checklist variables are necessary but not sufficient conditions for democracy. It is not enough to scan the political institutions of given societies and score them as democratic or nondemocratic. In each case, and with knowledge of political practices around the world, we should measure the effectiveness of any given democratic process.

That said, let us begin by transforming democracy from a form of politics and government into a process of political equality. Italian political theorist Norberto Bobbio, for instance, describes democracy as a set of procedural rules for arriving at collective decisions in a way that facilitates "the fullest possible participation of the interested parties,"[7] a simple, but clarifying way to judge democracy's efficacy. By borrowing from the Greek meaning of the root "demos," which refers to common people, we could expand Bobbio's characterization by specifying that political equality also implies that a democracy is a context in which every person makes her position count in any collective deliberation.

The "opportunity" to practice democracy is not enough. If, following Bobbio, it is the "fullest possible participation" we look for, then theoretical rights as mere opportunities do not measure up. The key is action, participation. Take the case of declining voter participation in Western Europe and the United States. Though Europe can still boast that a majority, though shrinking, of its citizens elects its parliaments and presidents, in the United States, less than half of the voting age population actually votes in federal elections. In the case of the close presidential election in 2000 that resulted in George W. Bush's taking office, this means that no more than a quarter of the nation's voting age population actually voted to elect him president. Participation, not the opportunity to participate, should be our test of the effectiveness of a democracy.

Then, too, we need to recognize that many nations are merely pro forma democracies, and that their actual quotient of political equality is in many cases alarmingly low. The UNDP's exhaustive 2002 study argued that of the 140 out of 200 nations that hold multiparty elections, only eighty are "real democracies." In the other sixty, either their election processes are flawed or an overweening state apparatus or ruling group throttles the democratic exercise of government. The study also finds that civil rights are abridged in more than 100 nations, some of which it counts as formally democratic in governance.[8]

Let us push even harder here by asking another tough question. Are societies rife with economic and social inequality even able in theory to satisfy the minimum requirements of political equality based upon the fullest participation of all? Can they be really be considered effective? For the philosopher Ronald Dworkin, the answer is unreservedly and emphatically no:

> No government is legitimate that does not show equal concern for the fate of all those citizens over whom it claims dominion and from whom it claims allegiance. Equal concern is the sovereign virtue of political community—without it government is only tyranny—and when a nation's wealth is very unequally distributed, as the wealth of even very prosperous nations now is, then its equal concern is suspect.[9]

It is important to measure political equality as it affects the human condition. If a society were governed under conditions of political equality, then one would expect a different result: Inequalities of the sort we have described would be dramatically curtailed or one could at least observe a clear pattern of government action to remedy the effects of disadvantage.

People's interests are reflected in their politics. Here one can include a variety of possible interests, from strict self-interest to interest in the well-being of others, or some mix of the two. In the first instance, it is hard to know how all persons' self-interests would be served in a society where the lives of these same persons are marked by significant disadvantage of some sort. In the second instance, it is hard to know how the interests of those concerned about the welfare of others would be served in such a society either, for the presence of disadvantage would mean that either the self-interests of some are not being met, or that even the designs of the holders of more altruistic interests were not being satisfied, and Dworkin's rather straightforward requirement of "equal concern" on the part of a legitimate government is going unmet. The point is that democracies governed by political equality are necessary to human well-being, insofar as they make efforts to improve economic and social equality. They do not contribute to human well-being by simply assenting to some people's oppression.

As we finish here with the introduction of the specific economic, political, and social contexts in which we should like to see equality made salient, I think it is useful to be flexible about the issue of the scale of the context. In other words, "the fullest possible participation" as called for by Bobbio might suggest a smaller scale of operation than the nation-state. In fact, given that political equality involves face-to-face discussion, representation by parties and interest groups in governing institutions, as well as community and institutional conflict—it is not just a series of plebiscites—a smaller arena might in many cases make sense. There is nothing argued here that would prevent regions and communities from being important loci of political equality-making. Quite the opposite: Movements for greater decentralization and local control might be quite instrumental in achieving "the fullest possible participation" now lacking in so many parts of the world, including our own.[10]

Applying Equality

How shall equality in its three dimensions be applied? Across the board, we need to answer the question: "Equality of what?"

In our discussion of political equality just above, I alluded to something of the answer. The "opportunity" to practice democracy was not enough. Practice and result were our watchwords. That is, we expected to see societies with Bobbio's "fullest possible participation" *and* societies that were not rife with economic and social inequality. We relented a bit by positively evaluating societies that were at work eliminating social and economic disadvantage, to which in a general sense we would add working to achieve political equality as well.

Let us apply the lessons of political equality to social and economic equality. Is it enough to offer "equality of opportunity"? That is, is it enough to provide each person with something like a passport to opportunity that admits him or her to the common struggle for happiness and well-being? Think of our earlier distinction between negative and positive freedom. Negative freedom was a guarantee that a person would not encounter barriers to well-being—that she had the "freedom" to become a full-fledged person in her society. Positive freedom, on the other hand, was an explicit attempt to aid or provide support for people's growth in well-being. Perhaps the goal we should be seeking is a certain "equality of outcome" as regards certain aspects of people's attempt to improve their well-being. We shall have to explore what "equality of outcome" or some formula like it means, and how it might be usefully applied.

The difference, as a reader with experience in U.S. battles over affirmative action can tell, is significant. "Equality of opportunity" refers to providing people with the capabilities to engage in the economy and social life successfully. "Equality of outcome" implies actions that assure that people receive certain goods or opportunities in due course. While mindful of the distinction, it will become clear as we examine how to introduce more equality into our economies that some measure of each—opportunity and outcome—is necessary to tackle the problem of the yawning inequalities we have described from the outset.

To clarify what we might mean by pressing on with the notions of certain guaranteed outcomes in reducing social and economic inequality, it is useful to turn to some of the hypothetical situations that philosophers themselves have used to obtain more clarity. Let us consider scenarios created by John Rawls, Ronald Dworkin, and Amartya Sen. Each tries to figure out what mix of opportunity and outcomes is most appropriately their respective concern for the prospects of human betterment.

Rawls's *A Theory of Justice*[11] is the touchstone for contemporary discussions of equality. He assumes that humans are equipped with two moral powers—a sense of justice that he takes to be fairness and a conception of the good—as well as the capacity for reason.[12] Rawls argues that if persons were to construct a society from scratch, finding themselves in an hypothetical space he calls "the original position," they would choose equality in the assignment of all rights and duties, and would hold that social and economic inequalities were just only if they resulted in compensating everyone, most especially the least advantaged members of society. They would be egalitarian regarding rights and concerned with the disadvantaged because "a veil of ignorance" would prevent them from knowing whether they were or would be disadvantaged. Thus their self-interest would prudently push them to assure that disadvantaged persons would be compensated or aided in the task of living, since they could find themselves disadvantaged once the veil of ignorance were removed and their fate known.[13]

Each person in society, according to Rawls, would receive *social primary goods* that consist of "rights and liberties, powers and opportunities, income and wealth," as well as less tangible items that society can confer on individuals, such as self-respect. The list of social primary goods is not exhaustible, because they are basically means that persons agree would aid them in their pursuit of rational ends. But the outcome of the "original position" is that "everyone has similar rights and duties, and income and wealth are evenly shared." *Natural primary goods,* such as "health and vigor, intelligence and imagination," are beyond the capacities of society to bestow upon its members, and can be sources for inequalities among persons.[14] However, inequalities of wealth and power that arise are acceptable if their existence improves the lot of everyone else. So, for instance, the extra income and power granted to the professions or to captains of industry is justified if the exercise of their privileges or the rewards they receive result in increased aggregate wealth and well-being for all of society's members.

"The general conception of justice," Rawls writes, "imposes no restrictions on what sort of inequalities are permissible; it only requires that everyone's position be improved."[15] Thus, for instance, society is not required to "try to even out handicaps as if all were expected to compete on a fair basis in the same race," but could be expected to "allocate resources in education . . . so as to improve the long-term expectation of the least favored."[16]

For Rawls, "undeserved" inequalities of birth and natural endowment do call for redress. Genuine "equality of opportunity," Rawls says, requires that "society must give more attention to those with fewer native assets and to those born into less favorable social positions." These inequalities are to be "compensated for," by spending greater resources, for instance, "on the education of the less rather than the more intelligent." The object is:

> to regard the distribution of natural talents as a common asset and to share in the benefits of this distribution whatever it turns out to be. Those who have been favored by nature, whoever they are, may gain from their good fortune only on terms that improve the situation of those who have lost out. The naturally advantaged are not to gain merely because they are more gifted, but only to cover the costs of training and education and for using their endowments in ways that help the less fortunate as well. No one deserves his greater natural capacity nor merits a more favorable starting place in society.[17]

We live under a social contract,[18] Rawls believes, that enjoins us to act with concern toward others. We do not need absolute economic and social equality, but we do need to assure that disadvantaged persons have access to equality of opportunity in obtaining that which is valuable in society. So, socially valuable positions in society, for instance, are "to be not only open in a formal sense, but that all should have a fair chance to attain them."[19] Thus, following Rawls, one assures justice through fairness, and fairness is achieved by equality of opportunity, not equality per se.

Though artful in its design and execution, Rawls's position is not completely satisfactory. Could we guarantee more equality per se? If we could, wouldn't it be better than simply assuring equality of opportunity?

Ronald Dworkin's position as elaborated in *Sovereign Virtue*[20] might offer some prospects for improvement. Once again, we have a hypothetical instance: In this case, a group of immigrants settle an unpopulated desert island. By using an auction, the settlers create a market in which the total resources of the island are divided equally. The results become final when every claim that is raised about the advantage of someone's resource bundle over that of another is satisfied, by swaps, trades, and other adjustments. In this way, the auction and its results pass what Dworkin terms "the envy test." An initial "equality of resources" is attained.[21]

Equality, by dint of people's different choices, efforts, and luck, cannot be sustained indefinitely. Inequalities inevitably arise. In contrast to positions that guarantee equality only at the initial distribution of resources, a stance Dworkin calls "the starting-gate theory of fairness," he argues that a society must undertake activities that periodically redistribute resources. People need protection from the effects of bad luck. Something like catastrophic insurance could be established for conditions such as disease, disability, and handicap, as well as other conceivable misfortunes such as job or income loss that people as a society agreed to insure. The premiums would be redistributed as resources to the insured victims. The income tax would be based in part on the hypothetical premiums people would pay for insurance against the various misfortunes, and thus resources would be redistributed on a continuing basis.[22] He emphasizes, though, that it is important that tax rates not undercut some market allocations to individuals that are rewards based upon their superior effort and/or ability.[23]

Dworkin believes that his concept of "equality of resources" is superior to Rawls's framework because it is more flexible and more attuned to individual needs. In contrast to Rawls's social primary goods, which are enumerated and agreed to in the hypothetical space of "the original position," Dworkin imagines a continuing process whereby people through the insurance process decide what needs should be valued and how much they should be valued. Insurance premiums are decided in a market where the value of compensations for a handicap, injury, or financial loss, and other needs that people value are being set in comparison with all other needs. Thus, people under Dworkin's scheme decide what Rawls's "social primary goods" should be. Dworkin also believes that his approach allows people to be treated as individuals who address their particular needs through the insurance mechanism. He argues that Rawls, in contrast, deals with individual needs only insofar as people are members of disadvantaged groups. Thus, according to Dworkin, Rawls provides only "flat equality" because primary goods are provided "without regard to differences in ambition, taste, occupation, or consumption, let alone differences in physical condition or handicap"—all of which Dworkin believes his scheme provides for.[24]

Dworkin's proposal advances our interests here in important ways. First, he delivers resources continuously based upon people's needs and, importantly, a society's collective estimation of these needs and their remedies. While both Dworkin and Rawls offer resources as compensation for accidents of nature or birth, Dworkin's method is more direct. It offers affected individuals money with which to construct or reconstruct their lives; in contrast, Rawls offers public goods like education in recompense for disadvantages that persons as a group experience. More education, as we have seen above, is an answer Rawls provides to disadvantages such as poverty and racial discrimination.

The indirectness of Rawls' method places him a bit more on the "equality of opportunity" side of the equation. Dworkin's directness places him more on the "equality of outcomes" side of things. People under Dworkin's scheme, I would argue, would have a better chance of receiving equal resources than they would with Rawls's program. Moreover, Dworkin with his insurance plan provides the space whereby people through markets collectively decide what should be indemnified and how much indemnities should be. Thus, markets perform something they do well—namely, set prices—while the state through the tax system seeks to spread the risks and assure compensation in the widest possible manner.

By now, the proposals of Amartya Sen should be familiar, as we have already discussed them in part. For Sen, the goal is to strengthen people's capabilities to function in ways that satisfy their goals for a good life. Sen's central insight is that people are differently capable of converting resources into satisfying lives, and thus the provision of equal resources will miss the mark for advancing equality. For one thing, there are the simple differences of situation: A pregnant woman, Sen argues, may have to overcome disadvantages that a man of same age and income need not face. More resources may be necessary for her to achieve adequate functioning. A handicapped person may be greatly disadvantaged in converting her income into achievements she desires and, once more, additional resources may be necessary for her to achieve optimal functioning.[25] Sen directly contrasts his approach with that of Rawls and Dworkin:

> a poor person's freedom from undernourishment would depend not only on
> her resources and primary goods (e.g., through the influence of income on the

ability to buy food), but also on her metabolic rates, gender, pregnancy, climatic environment, exposure to parasitic diseases, and so on. Of two persons with identical incomes and other primary goods and resources (as characterized in the Rawlsian or Dworkinian frameworks), one may be entirely free to avoid undernourishment and the other not at all free to achieve this.[26]

People can be differently capable. Their "handicaps," or characteristics that promote relative disadvantage, can include their gender, geography, and degree of bodily integrity. They can also include the disadvantages of class, race, and caste membership.[27] Each of these must be assessed in any given context, and remedies found that will improve people's capabilities.

But, as the quotation above with its three references to freedom within the space of two sentences tells us, we need to address the importance to Sen of the concept. Why freedom? What does it mean to be "free from undernourishment"? Isn't it enough to be nourished? By pressing the notion of freedom, Sen is reflecting a desire he shares with Rawls and Dworkin that people remain able to choose how they wish to live. All of them are defending, and Sen in an explicit fashion, the freedom of a person to reject the suggested direction of others. Sen does not want to insist that people be compelled to live a certain way; he wants a person to have the capabilities to function in a manner she sees fit:

> A person's "capability" refers to the alternative combinations of functionings that are feasible for her to achieve. Capability is thus a kind of freedom: the substantive freedom to achieve alternative functioning combinations (or, less formally put, the freedom to achieve various lifestyles). For example, an affluent person who fasts may have the same functioning achievement in terms of eating or nourishment as a destitute person who is forced to starve, but the first person does have a different "capability set" than the second (the first *can* choose to eat well and be well nourished in a way the second cannot).[28]

Freedom for Sen is both a means and an end: Its exercise enables people to be free to be something, and the experience of freedom is virtuous in and for itself.[29] Rawls places freedom first, by ranking personal liberty ahead of the needs for equality.[30]

While Dworkin also prizes liberty, he believes that equality has priority. If there were equality of resources, something like true justice, as it were, then liberty would be an attribute of equality. It would share the property of a society that had divided itself justly, and was thus a "community of equal concern" in which both liberty and equality might flourish.[31] But both he and Rawls harbor a second motive for prizing liberty: Both fear a society in which there is in effect a disincentive to excel, to work hard, to do for oneself, and so forth. As we have seen above in the case of taxation, Dworkin is explicit about safeguarding the incentives as well as the rewards of work for those who do. Rawls as a general matter worries that the general efficiency of society will decline the degree to which persons with superior capabilities are discouraged from doing their utmost.[32] As we have seen above, Rawls wishes to socialize the result of people's talents as "common assets," the benefits of which can profit everyone. Sen, in contrast, believes that egalitarian policies that attempt to undo disadvantages based upon human differences have relatively few incentive problems, as compared with those that concern effort. The fear of "free riding" on the part of the disadvantaged, or the slacking of the advantaged, for that matter, is greatly reduced when fundamental gaps in equality are addressed.[33]

Synthesizing Equality

Our examination of the complexities of equality that began with a consideration of some of its facets and ended with analysis of its enlightened treatment by three prominent philosophers of equality leads us to draw several conclusions.

First, a robust notion of equality, that is, achieving full economic, social, and political equality, is better. Rawls's reticence in this regard should not deter us. The fundamental question is, What other standard can we apply that would assure optimal functioning for all humans? Following Sen here, we want to provide equality of capabilities so that every person can achieve her human potential. Equality of opportunity as distinguished from equality of resources in this context is not a strong enough remedy to offset the inequality created by birth and nature.

Second, achieving equality requires distributing and redistributing resources. Remedies for social and political equalities require resources no less than do remedies for economic inequalities. With sufficient resources, people can plot their ways to more satisfying lives. Regarding our opposition of equality of opportunity to equality of outcomes, we shade toward outcomes, provided that we amend our notion to take into account both Dworkin's and Sen's accounts. Something of a melding of Dworkin's call for equality of resources with Sen's insistence on measuring those resources in terms of their capability of enhancing people's freedom to achieve a good life seems warranted.

Third, political equality is a dimension of equality no less important than either economic or social equality. From Rawls's notions of the binding social contract and society "as a cooperative venture for mutual advantage,"[34] to Dworkin's insistence on "equal concern" as the bedrock of any state,[35] and finally to Sen's belief that individual freedom is just as much an end for itself as it is a means,[36] we can see how deeply entangled the realities of economic and political equality are. Mutual advantage, equal concern, and freedom to become a fully functional person all require a fundamental equality among all participating in the running of society.

An Answer to "Yes, but . . ."

Kurt Vonnegut, in the short story "Harrison Bergeron," describes a future world, the year 2081 to be exact, in which all talented people must be handicapped so that those who are handicapped can be made equal. Ballerinas toting around bags of birdshot and hiding their beauty behind masks, highly intelligent persons with implanted radio transmitters that block novel and creative thoughts, mellifluous speakers made to stutter— these were among the persons whose lives were circumscribed on orders of a "Handicapper General," whose job consisted in making everyone perforce equal by handicapping the talented. The environment they live in is totalitarian. The protagonist, Harrison, is shot dead after refusing to submit to his handicapping. His parents, watching his execution live on television, cannot cry because they cannot remember what they saw. Their short-term memories had been handicapped, leaving them incapable of sadness.

A fine mess! Is this what happens when one takes equality seriously? As one friend put it to me, it isn't a good idea to allow the mediocre easy access to the reins of power throughout the institutions of society. Merit should be rewarded with money, power, and prestige, and thus, given the uneven distribution of talents, inequality is inevitable. Another friend objected: If inequality makes the world better for everyone, then who cares if there is inequality?

These are terrific objections, and you might agree with one or the other points. But there are counters. Taking the first, that merit should be rewarded, finds support in the work of Rawls and Sen that we have discussed above. Meritorious people help improve society as a whole, Rawls argued, and should not be discouraged from doing so by limiting their freedom. Sen also believed that people should be free to choose whether and how they use their capabilities. Fair enough. While the life paths that people choose, those personal vocations we spoke of above, should never suffer abridgement, the compensations owed the meritorious need not be limitless. If, to achieve equality, some of the surplus they generate is redistributed via taxes, for instance, this is a relative rather than an absolute deprivation of their freedoms. Unlike Harrison Bergeron's fate, no one's fundamental freedom to become the person she strives to be is extinguished. It is meretricious, it seems to me, not to recognize the plain difference between redistributing a portion of a reward and abridging a fundamental freedom.

The second objection—who cares about inequality if everyone can be made better off—poses what I think to be a long-term impossibility. It seems highly unlikely to me that everyone can be made better off, and that they can stay better off, without equality. Persons whose resources make them equal or who by the social redistribution of resources become equal can defend equality as a value that in their own self-interest is worth keeping. Without equality, what are the prospects for defense of the transfer anew of resources from the better off to the disadvantaged? Granted, societies make decisions to remedy the problems of disadvantage, and this provides us with reasons for supposing they will do so again. But unless the objective is equality, and unless significant equality is achieved, those gains are not only not assured, but can be fleeting. People need the capacities that equality can provide to defend themselves and their own life choices. Unfortunately, societies not dedicated to achieving equality easily countenance inequality and become complacent to its consequences.

This rejoinder to a "yes, but . . ." argument may not yet have eased your qualms about valuing equality. You are invited in the next chapter to compare equality with other value frameworks that can orient our economic choices, and see if it is not the better option. Then observe whether the consequences of the proposals based upon equality set out in the remainder of the book are better alternatives than the ones we make now.

Notes

1. Amartya Sen, *Inequality Reexamined* (Cambridge, Mass.: Harvard University Press, 1992), 130–39.

2. Ronald Dworkin, *Sovereign Virtue: The Theory and Practice of Equality* (Cambridge, Mass.: Harvard University Press, 2000).

3. Martha Nussbaum, *Sex and Social Justice* (New York: Oxford University Press, 1999), 31–34.

4. For income disparities by race and ethnicity, see Leslie McCall, *Complex Inequality: Gender, Class and Race in the New Economy* (New York: Routledge, 2001); for racial and ethnic discrepancies in savings and assets, see essays collected in

Thomas Shapiro and Edward Wolff, editors, *Assets for the Poor: The Benefits of Spreading Asset Ownership* (New York: Russell Sage Foundation, 2001).

5. United Nations Development Programme, *Human Development Report 2000* (New York: Oxford University Press, 2000), 32.

6. United Nations Development Programme, *Human Development Report 2002: Deepening Democracy in a Fragmented World* (New York: Oxford University Press, 2002), 1–2.

7. Norberto Bobbio, *The Future of Democracy* (Minneapolis: University of Minnesota Press, 1987), 19.

8. United Nations Development Programme, op. cit.

9. Ronald Dworkin, op. cit., 1.

10. Jeremy Brecher, Tim Costello, and Brendan Smith in *Globalization from Below: The Power of Solidarity* (Boston: South End Press, 2000), speak of the necessity of placing democratic participation and decision-making closer to or at the grassroots.

11. John Rawls, *A Theory of Justice* (Cambridge, Mass.: Harvard University Press, 1971).

12. Ibid, 505. See also John Rawls, *Political Liberalism* (New York: Columbia University Press, 1993), 18–19.

13. Ibid., 14–15.

14. Ibid., 62–63.

15. Ibid., 62–63, 93.

16. Ibid., 101–2.

17. Ibid.

18. Ibid., 11.

19. Ibid., 73.

20. Ronald Dworkin, op. cit.

21. Ibid., 65–68.

22. Ibid., 98–109.

23. Ibid., 86–89.

24. Ibid., 116.

25. Amartya Sen, op. cit., 27–28.

26. Ibid., 33.

27. Ibid., 117–28.

28. Amartya Sen, *Development as Freedom* (New York: Alfred A. Knopf, 1999), 75.

29. Ibid., 36–37; Amartya Sen, op. cit., 50–51.

30. John Rawls, ibid., 60–61.

31. Ronald Dworkin, op. cit., 120–23.

32. John Rawls, op. cit., 78–80.

33. Amartya Sen, op. cit., 143.

34. John Rawls, op. cit., 4, 11.

35. Ronald Dworkin, op. cit., 1–3.

36. Amartya Sen, op. cit., 56–72.

CHAPTER FIVE

◦━━◆━━◦

Comparing Values

If we suppose that our values orient our actions, then it is important that we place them under greater and more demanding scrutiny. Much depends upon how we interpret them and how we connect them to the empirical world. This is because values differ less in their formal meaning than in their specification through use. It is how we use them, in other words, that finally matters.

The value of equality advocated here is certainly not an especially novel choice, as it has been one of the well-known products of liberal thinking since the European Enlightenment. Yet it acquires its particular edge, its particular stimulus to thought and action, when we consider what we would do differently in the world in light of believing in it.

This chapter is an attempt to compare equality in its three dimensions with other value frameworks that are currently available as guides to our actions. We take a look at the value commitments of three diverse, yet sympathetic accounts. The first is offered by Thomas Friedman in *The Lexus and the Olive Tree: Understanding Globalization*,[1] a U.S. best seller that offers a clear picture of what globalization is coming to mean in our lives and suggests the values that are associated with its rise. The other two frameworks to be examined consist of extended policy statements by the World Bank and the United Nations Development Programme (UNDP) in which their value commitments are made readily available for analysis. We will compare each of them to the value of equality in two ways. First, we look at the assumptions underlying the value commitments themselves and compare them with those we make here. Second, we directly compare the values to determine what they imply for action.

The Technological Revolution and New Global Values

Friedman's *The Lexus and the Olive Tree* provides a compelling portrait of how the globalized economy is dramatically altering everyday life. The technological revolution in information processing has accelerated the growth since World War II of a unified, virtually instantaneous world market fueled by trillions of dollars in capital seeking the highest possible returns. It is a destroyer of traditional worlds as well as a conveyor of a new culture that emanates directly from economic processes now flowing freely through international circuits of technology, finance, and data. These tumultuous flows of money, information, and goods, in Friedman's words, "democratize" the societies they touch, by which he means that people from all walks of life in highly stratified, unequal societies gain access for the first time to the technological levers of their liberation. As people become empowered with goods, information, and contact with worlds outside their own, Friedman believes that their societies face the choice of adapting to a U.S. style of life or of being left behind world economic development.

Successful societies find ways to adopt the values that spring directly from the processes and prosperity of the new economy without obliterating local customs that provide peoples with familiar local identities. Peoples, according to Friedman, absorb influences that fit, reject those that don't, and compartmentalize those that can be enjoyed without having to change. The democratization of business, however, leads to political liberalization and eventually to democracy per se. The leader of political reforms will not be a James Madison, as was the case for the United States, or an Andrei Sakharov, in the case of the former Soviet Union. The engine of change, as Friedman puts it, will be Merrill Lynch.[2]

Describing himself as a social democrat, however, Friedman believes that every society should provide its citizens with a social safety net designed to cushion the blows of rapid social and economic change. Globalization, as Friedman notes, kicks up plenty of resistance among those who are poor or who are losing out in the struggle for their piece of the new economy. These "used-to-bes" include the middle and lower-middle classes of capitalist market societies who have lost their safety nets or who find themselves unprotected in the new era of open economies and stepped-up international competition. According to Friedman, they need to adapt to the cyclonic nature and pace of economic change by becoming more engaged with the new technological revolution.

The value commitments Friedman makes derive from his belief that globalization, accelerated by technological revolution, brings with it its own values. They include what he sees as the values of free markets, such as openness, greater efficiency, and greater rationality. For instance, in describing the causes of the 1997–98 Asian economic crisis, he argues that Asian countries lacked "a basic feel and understanding of how real free markets, and a free-market based society, work—that they are not run by the arbitrary judgments of individuals, but by the anonymous working out of every value judgment in the marketplace."[3] The market itself is a primary virtue.

So, too, is democracy. The spread of the global economy newly invigorated by the "three democratizations" of technology, finance, and information brings about changes in society that add up to greater democracy in all its institutions, but most especially those of firms and governments. Globalization and democracy form a virtuous dyad, one spurring the development of the other.

If we step back a bit and examine Friedman's claims, we can notice several things. First, a sort of technocratic bias is at work. Friedman believes that the market is a kind of technical arbiter of human progress: What works in it must be a necessary harbinger of human social evolution. Thus, the progressive development of the market is synonymous with greater human progress.

The market, in the case of this current surge of globalization, is propelled by a microelectronic technology that radically increases the spread of information, and which, when coupled with communication via media such as the Internet, cannot help but increase democratic access and participation. For example, Friedman predicts that China will have a free press because "China's leaders simply can't control and monitor their bursting free markets . . . without the other institutions that must go with free markets—from an effective Securities and Exchange Commission to a free and responsible press backed by the rule of law."[4]

Second, the values and institutions propagated by globalization turn out to be those endemic to the experience of the United States. Friedman is not shy about it: The United States stands at the pinnacle of world progress. Balancing the radical innovations of markets with everyday life is:

> what America, at its best, is all about. America at its best takes the needs of markets, individuals and communities all utterly seriously. And that's why America, at its best, is not just a country. It's a spiritual value and role model.[5]

There is no sense in which Friedman imagines variations on the American formula for nations becoming rapidly globalized; as noted above, straightforward replication is his watchword.

Third, his conception of democracy is less than full. As we have seen, he imagines democracy as consisting of a voice in the marketplace, at the office, and in the voting booth. Though, to his credit, he argues that democracy means more than simply political elections, he nonetheless, once again, treats the United States as the paragon of democratic values. To a critic, this poses the question of how effective one considers democracy in the United States. As he points out, globalization brings on a "winner take all" system of material rewards that creates ever greater social inequalities in the United States. He notes, as we have in an earlier chapter, how the rich are getting richer and the poor poorer, citing with concern how the United States had 170 billionaires in 1998, even as income for the poorest one-fifth of the population dropped 21 percent between 1979 and 1995, adjusted for inflation.[6] If democracy in the United States were really effective, would social inequalities of this sort, involving significant portions of the country's population, be tolerable?

Let us turn now to confronting Friedman's value commitments with those advocated here. When speaking in the previous chapter about political equality, we stressed how it need be effective rather than merely formal. That Friedman can lionize the United States while countenancing the alarming social and economic inequalities he himself notes suggests that he possesses a different notion of democracy than one that might follow our concept of political equality. If our democracy rested upon the effective representation of all concerned, then the kinds of significant economic and social disadvantages Friedman accepts as normal wouldn't be. Or, put another way, our notion of political equality would entail finding a democracy that is striving to eliminate the disadvantages of birth and nature.

Something of the same could be said with respect to our valuing economic equality. Friedman accepts as an inevitable consequence of globalization that intensive social differentiation will increase, both within and between countries, "as some choose prosperity, get wired, become shapers and adopt the habits of effective countries, and others do not."[7] Once more, Friedman believes that the market should be maximally freed up from government supervision so it can provide opportunity. Where there are "market failures" in reaching the poor, states should provide disadvantaged groups and communities with access to capital for investment in new businesses. Workers in transition from one job to another or from one field of employment to another should be given job-training grants. And finally, traditional social safety nets, which in the United States include social security, Medicare, Medicaid, food stamps, and welfare, are needed "to catch those who simply will never be fast enough or educated enough to deal with the Fast World, but who you don't want just falling onto the pavement."[8]

Friedman, in other words, offers a palliative, opportunity and protection, for those who fall on the wrong side of the inequality divide, instead of strategies that prize achieving equality.

Moreover, there is something particularly disempowering about Friedman's scenario for the world's future. People in their states, regions, and localities are given a choice of adapt or decline. The swirling, engulfing pools of capital flow toward those providing rewards to investors whom he calls "the Electronic Herd," and on terms investors understand and prefer. Ignoring investors' wishes and their rules is to call down a capital strike on oneself, a futile gesture when survival in a globalized economy depends on trade, commerce and, most important, the capital of others. His advice is direct, and nothing if not candid: "[E]ither run with the Electronic Herd and live by its rules or run alone and live by your own rules but accept the fact that you are going to have less access to capital, less access to technology and ultimately a lower standard of living for your people."[9]

The task of states, regions, and localities is not greater political equality but rather to provide a suitable macroeconomic climate in which capital can flourish. This means that they perform public services efficiently and do so without running up the public bill and thereby burdening private capital. In fact, they should learn how to do those regulatory tasks that facilitate capital accumulation by enforcing the law against economic malefactors and assuring transparency and the rule of law in all commercial transactions. In other words, states, regions, and localities are being asked to conform to a universal international standard that is being set outside of them by the forces of global capital.

The difficulty with this position is that the "universal standard" envisioned by Friedman is in fact a particular set of norms that reflect the interests of only one group of persons in societies composed of many, many more groups. What are the interests of the others? How are they to be actualized in this accommodation to big capital? Friedman's only reply can be that the effects of investment will indirectly serve the interests of the others in the form of increased economic activity and, presumably, employment opportunities—the "trickle down" effect once more. Confronted with the demands of equality, it is an insufficient, even inappropriate, response.

In sum, Friedman's account, as he acknowledges, lies close to the intersection between neoliberalism and social democracy that has been occupied over the past decade by forces such as the Clinton administration and Tony Blair's Labor Party in the United Kingdom. As such, it bears many of the same virtues and faults. It is virtuous because it offers a realistic analysis of what globalization as a new international discipline means for all involved.

It identifies the forces of global capital as the antagonists of local democracy and of efforts to achieve equality because it costs something. It is flawed because it makes the capitalist market the highest value and assumes, albeit with minor repairs by a safety-net-providing state, that its operations will bring on prosperity for all.

Planning to End Poverty

"Our dream is a world free of poverty." This slogan found on the outside cover of every World Bank Development Report perhaps best describes the mission of one of the most important development agencies in the world. Since the end of World War II, the World Bank has been the principal international agency dispensing multilateral development loans and assistance from the rich countries to the poor. Its annual World Development Report is among the most important documents written on economic development today. It describes in great detail the economic and social state of the world in a manner that is helpful to the expert and layperson alike. Policy prescriptions are offered that should give every thoughtful reader pause. Over the past decade, the World Bank has expressed the neoliberal view of how the world can overcome the chronic problems of capitalism through greater involvement of peoples in markets. Since the head of the World Bank is by custom nominated by the United States, it is of no surprise that its line during the 1990s was in concert with that of the Clinton administration. The World Bank's answers, whether they be private corporations building sewers in poor countries or polluting rich countries buying rights to pollute permits from poor countries, are more market-driven capitalism.

At the World Bank, process is policy. It advocates a "comprehensive development framework" that serves as "both a planning and a management tool for coordinating . . . a holistic approach to development" for each nation.[10] The framework envisions a process whereby consultations between a state, the private sector, nongovernmental organizations, and other actors in civil society result in the articulation of a common vision of national needs and solutions that all can support. The plan, identified "as a compass, not a blueprint," is intended to balance social with macroeconomic concerns and to focus on four areas of development—structural, human, physical, and sectoral. Structural elements include goals such as honest government, as well as strong personal and property rights. The human development area highlights the importance of universal primary education and access to secondary education and health services. Physical development centers on the provision of efficient infrastructure, from sewers to mass transit systems. Finally, the World Bank advocates adoption of rural and urban sector development strategies that facilitate private investment.[11]

The plan is unavoidably bureaucratic. The World Bank is in the business of disbursing loans and advice to poor countries, and thus has its own criteria for how to analyze a problem or design a solution. As such, the plan reflects values that are important to bureaucrats, such as the reduction of unique aspects of a phenomenon to certain universal descriptions and the use of a prescribed methodology for the documentation of a particular situation. Because the plan itself forms part of the "contract" between bank and lender, it takes on importance equal to—and, in some cases, greater—than the planning process itself.[12]

Moreover, one cannot forget that the World Bank itself is an instrument of foreign policy for the rich nations. Prevailing economic nostrums at any given time—take the case of the so-called Washington consensus view of how poor countries could put their economies aright that prevailed among Reagan administration–influenced elites during the 1980s at the World Bank, the International Monetary Fund, and the U.S. Department of the Treasury, discussed earlier in this book—become planning imperatives for World Bank officials who set the agendas for loan negotiations. The priority of human development factors such as education and health care in the World Bank's framework during the 1990s reflected the Clinton-era consensus that investments in the "human capital" of poor countries would accelerate economic growth. The George W. Bush administration (2000–2004) has renewed emphasis on "hard-targeted" grants and loans designed to increase the productivity of labor in poor countries, rather than devoting resources to the "softer" human capital projects of education and health care.

These concerns of any of the decades or of the changing Washington elite, voiced by the powerful in negotiations with the needy, have certain impact on the plans of poor communities, regions, and states. Pet policy prescriptions become so-called conditions, or riders on loan agreements that obligate local officials to undertake specific kinds of actions.[13] Proposals are solicited for policy ideas that have caught the fancy of the elites rather than having emerged from the planning activities of local people. A whole nomenclature is invented and adopted by persons at all levels of interest to describe local problems. Indeed, local problems only "count," or are found worthy of close attention, if they can be redescribed successfully in the changing international argot.

So, we are learning an important lesson as we compare the value of equality advocated here with those discussed immediately below, advocated by the

World Bank. "Who" has particular values is as important as "what" the values are. Inescapably for the World Bank as a bureaucratic institution and as a foreign policy instrument of rich countries, the production and execution of a "plan" becomes a value in itself. I would argue it is a more fundamentally important value than others that the World Bank identifies as important for its mission, because it underlies any particular value set that the World Bank identifies from year to year and decade to decade. How much the World Bank's newfound "values" approach to eliminating poverty is vitiated by its nature and its obligations is a highly relevant question that we must keep in mind below.

For the World Bank believes in values too. In fact, in *Attacking Poverty: World Development Report, 2000–2001*, the World Bank identifies three values fundamental to its war on poverty: opportunity, empowerment, and security.[14] In addition to eliminating poverty, the World Bank believes that opportunity, empowerment, and security have intrinsic value for poor people. That is, the well-being of poor people improves when they are the mainsprings of action.[15]

Opportunity depends upon accelerating economic growth that is generated in turn by expanding markets. Liberalizing trade, shrinking the size of the state, and deregulating markets, among other reforms, are recommended. Also important is the redistribution of resources for education and health care so that they reach poor people. This formula amounts to combining two decades of development thinking, "market-friendly" macroeconomic reforms envisioned in the Washington consensus of the 1980s with the Clinton-era concerns for enhancing human capital through education and health reforms.

Can opportunity, expressed in these terms, bring greater economic equality, thus satisfying one dimension of our value requirements? In the case of the macroeconomic reforms, evidence gathered by the World Bank itself suggests the answer is no. The poor benefit as much as anyone else from these reforms—but not more. The gap between rich and poor remains the same in societies that have successfully implemented the elements of the Washington consensus. As the World Bank notes:

> Cross-country evidence suggests that macroeconomic reforms on average have had little effect on income distribution. For example, recent studies have examined the impact of market-friendly policies—such as openness to international trade, low inflation, a moderate-size government, and strong rule of law—on the incomes of poor people in a large cross-country sample. The findings: these policies on average benefit poor people as much as anyone else.[16]

So just getting the economic "big picture" right by balancing budgets, privatizing basic industries and services, and lowering tariffs and other barriers to trade—all part of the Washington consensus advocated by the United States and other rich countries as the cost of further developmental aid support—will affect the poor no more positively than the rich. These measures do not reduce economic inequality. The poor can become less poor, but not less unequal.[17]

Moreover, the World Bank's faith in the underlying process of economic growth, by its own analysis, would seem misplaced. As the World Bank notes: "Many studies show that on average there is no systematic relationship across countries between growth and summary statistics of income inequality such as the Gini coefficient."[18] In other words, greater equality cannot be achieved solely by revving the engines of economic growth.

Perhaps resorting to the emphasis on expanding access to education and health care for the poor would put the World Bank back on the road to greater equality. If poor people received an adequate education and good health care, their life chances would be substantially improved. Better-educated people have healthier, better-fed children and higher crop yields, for instance.[19] In the United States, the more education one receives beyond a high school degree, the more likely one finds oneself with a "middle-class" income.

The trouble is that education and health opportunities are not equally distributed in most societies, precisely as a consequence of inequalities between rich and poor in the first place. "Public spending on education and health is not progressive but is frequently regressive," the World Bank notes.[20] In fact, the World Bank's 2000–01 report shows that in eighteen of twenty-one poor countries for which there are data, the lowest one-fifth of the population receives less than 20 percent of their states' educational expenditures. The same is true of health expenditures: comparable data show that in eight of twelve countries reported, the poor received less than 20 percent of public health spending. The accounts of individual countries show the depths to which these inequalities can sink. In Nepal, for instance, the richest 20 percent of the population receives four times as much public education spending as the poorest 20 percent. In Ghana, the richest one-fifth of the population receives nearly three times the public health monies received by the poorest one-fifth.[21]

The culprit is the relationship between the rich and the state, as the World Bank rather obliquely acknowledges: "States generally mirror the unequal political structure they are founded on, and government action often reflects this."[22] It might have added "unequal social structure" as well, because economic and social inequalities usually form the base for political inequalities.

The existence of significant inequalities between rich and poor regarding education and health expenditures in poor countries means that any reform program is in reality a remedial program to redress inequities rather than provide additional opportunities. And it suggests symptomatically what is true for the value of opportunity with respect to the poor majorities in poor countries—and no few rich ones as well: Namely, strategies based upon valuing opportunity are insufficiently powerful to address the vast existing inequalities one finds. Valuing equality instead identifies the value that is the master key to finding solutions.

With empowerment, the World Bank seeks to provide poor people with the abilities to change their fates. It seeks to assure "the choice and implementation of public actions that are responsive to the needs of poor people."[23] The World Bank advocates a state structure that is honest, ideally decentralized to the maximum extent possible, with legal systems that are accessible to poor people and provide equal protection under the law for all.[24] Beyond access and participation, empowerment for the World Bank means democracy:

> Democracy—both representative and participatory—is a good in itself. . . . Democratic process must permeate all major levels of decision-making. . . . Citizens must be given systematic access to information so that they can hold their civil servants and politicians accountable. . . . Strong civil society organizations can promote the political empowerment of poor people.[25]

Democratic decisions, accountability, and a resilient civil society are crucial to the World Bank's recipe.

The World Bank also argues for decentralization of some of the powers of government to local decision-makers. The rationale is that moving a program closer to its users helps assure accountability and can lower the costs of delivering a service. It also helps build the social infrastructure necessary for a vibrant civil society.[26]

However, even in reasonably democratic milieus, the World Bank fears that poor people may find themselves voiceless. Social barriers such as discrimination on the basis of gender, ethnicity, race, religion, or social status often exclude poor people from the market and lock them into "poverty traps."[27] Gender discrimination, the World Bank finds, is particularly insidious as it occurs in the very building block of social life: the household. Affirmative action consisting of programs and policies of special assistance to women and other historically disadvantaged groups, the World Bank believes, is often necessary to combat discrimination.[28]

There is much to admire in the value the World Bank places on empowerment. The extension of its meaning to include universal democratic process is consistent with our own valuation. The acknowledgment of structural inequalities that prevent people from becoming empowered and the call for targeted affirmative action are also highly compatible with the emphasis here. There is also a refreshing sense of realism when the World Bank candidly admits that more privileged groups in a society often hijack the democratic process and put it to their own ends, and once more concedes that a nation's legal system is typically constructed in ways that favor the rich and powerful.[29]

Nonetheless, there are points of important divergence, if one advocates, as we do, effective political equality. First, there is a persistent tendency toward proceduralism on the part of the World Bank's treatment of democracy, rather than an evaluation of democracy on the basis in part of its results. Can a democratic process be said to be effective if the structure, large or small, acts against the interests of the majority? Having a voice is not a strong enough criterion. Materially affecting the life circumstances of a majority of persons in a positive way redresses the problem of how one knows whether a really effective democracy exists or not.

Second, the World Bank's call for decentralization, while once again laudable, prompts a question about the extent to which it countenances the devolution of political power. For instance, health and education service funding, job creation programs, community-run schools, as well as community planning of the sort carried out in Porto Alegre, Brazil, all receive favorable mention. Economic efficiency in terms of lower costs of service delivery, better data retrieval for estimating program effectiveness—bureaucratic criteria, in short— weigh heavily in the World Bank's endorsement of decentralization. Suppose it were to discover that local control and delivery of a service, say a maternal education program, was found to be more expensive handled locally. Would it still favor decentralization? Suppose more radical proposals to effectively sever regions from states were put forward. What would be the World Bank's response to a break in the chain of responsibility that leads from the local through the national, and to the consultant role of the World Bank itself?

The reason for placing these hypothetical questions into discussion here is to raise the issue of whether one can highly value democracy simply as empowerment. Can people have an effective democratic process without the freedom to match their needs with their desires in a manner whereby their choices have direct impact on their world? If one values political equality in the robust sense as described above, then one would find the World Bank's formulation wanting.

The World Bank's high valuation of security seems eminently sensible at the outset. In convincing fashion, the World Bank argues: "Reducing vulnerability—to economic shocks, natural disasters, ill health, disability, and personal violence—is an intrinsic part of enhancing well-being and encourages investment in human capital and in higher-risk, higher-return activities."[30] It is important to note that the World Bank gives two reasons for reducing vulnerability—one to enhance well-being, and another to improve the operation of markets. It argues that safety nets should be constructed for poor people in poor countries, not unlike those that exist in rich countries. "The tools" of securing security "include health insurance, old age assistance and pensions, unemployment insurance, workfare programs, social funds, microfinance programs, and cash transfers."[31] In short, security means welfare states for poor countries, and the World Bank is persuasive that the need for them is dire. It notes how only 16 percent of the world labor force—less than 10 percent in South Asia and sub-Saharan Africa—has old age pension coverage of any sort.[32] It points out how the absence of income or its equivalent in health insurance is directly correlated with vulnerability to medical epidemics like AIDS and tuberculosis. The World Bank also argues that harvest failures are human catastrophes for poor people, while farmers in rich countries rely on technologies such as irrigation, pesticides, and disease-resistant varieties of seeds, as well as direct government support, for survival in lean times.[33]

The World Bank's focus on security reflects its adoption of Amartya Sen's conception of poverty as a deprivation in well-being. Quoting directly from Sen's *Development and Freedom*, the World Bank acknowledges its reliance on Sen's view of poverty as severely restricting what he calls "the capabilities that a person has, that is, the substantive freedoms he or she enjoys to lead the kind of life he or she values."[34] As noted in earlier chapters, the account offered here is also deeply influenced by Sen. Consequently, the degree to which our view and that of the World Bank's are congruent in this respect is not surprising.

Instead of adding security to our value of equality, however, I would argue that we treat security as one of those capabilities that arise in the course of people pursuing economic, social, and political equality. Achieving greater security for those without it would seem to be one of the principal tasks of the pursuit of equality, and one of those areas of concern we address when exploring economic alternatives. The reason for subordinating security to equality is that equality is a larger, more inclusive concept that implies a more thorough or maximal redistribution of resources. In contrast, security has more to do with the provision of minima such as a durable safety net of welfare to which all should have equal access. Our job, however, would not be complete if we settled for welfare minima.

Consider the following scenario. Suppose it were possible to establish an old age pension in all poor countries, equal in proportion regardless of sex. This would surely meet the burden of valuing security, but would it meet the demands of equality? The latter, I think, demands more. For instance, old age pensions might have to be structured so as to compensate women in those societies where their access to resources prior to retirement was restricted when compared with that of men. Equality, in other words, requires additional effort to secure justice than does security. In our usage here, it presupposes not simply equality of opportunity, but an effort after equality of outcome.

Lessening Globalization's Impact

The United Nations Development Programme wants a globalization that works for people. It argues that:

> The challenge of globalization in the new century is not to stop the expansion of global markets. The challenge is to find the rules and institutions for stronger governance—local, national, regional, and global—to preserve the advantages of global markets and competition, but also to provide enough space for human, community and environmental resources to ensure that globalization works for people—not just profits.[35]

This remedy—a globalization that works for people and not simply profits—is a kind of populist version of the World Bank's neoliberal stance. Put simply, while the World Bank embraces the advance of the market, the UNDP is more wary of its potential to wreak havoc on persons and communities. It is populist because the underlying belief of its program is that "we, the people"—that is, all of us—have the same interest in making globalization more humane. Yet, when its rhetoric contraposes a globalization for people and not just profits, it is acknowledging that some, notably those who benefit from the workings of capitalism, might choose profit over the needs and interests of people who don't.

Its wariness of the market is observable in its statements of the new threats posed by globalization. Rising human insecurity due to financial volatility and economic turmoil endangers jobs and incomes. Also part of the rising insecurity for the UNDP are the dangers posed by AIDS, a monocultural as opposed to a multicultural world, environmental degradation, and the decline in personal safety due to crime and the political instability of states. The

UNDP fears that the information technologies driving globalization will marginalize the poor and increase their number; greater inequality between and within nations is anticipated. It is also apprehensive that the caring labors of persons that support fundamental social structures such as households will be squeezed out by the actions of competitive labor markets and the neoliberal withdrawal of state support for families.[36]

As the quotation above indicates, the UNDP is very concerned about governance. Global governance, by focusing almost exclusively on economic growth and financial stability, suffers from too narrow a scope. Moreover, such economic coordination and burden sharing that occurs takes place among the rich industrialized countries at the cost of further marginalizing poor countries. It calls for a reinvention of global governance that commits itself to global ethics and human rights; human well-being as an end with open markets and economic growth as the means; respect for national diversity; and accountability of all the governing actors. A more coherent and more democratic global governance system is needed for the twenty-first century.[37]

The UNDP sets forth six values that should orient our actions in the ongoing rush of globalization. They include ethics, equity, inclusion, human security, sustainability, and development. They are stated in such a way that having fewer violations of each is a desirable outcome. Thus, having fewer violations of human rights is equivalent to having more ethics in the world. Likewise, less income disparity within and between nations means more equity, and so on.[38]

Having more or less of something creates the possibilities for measurement. The metric used by the UNDP called the Human Development Index was invented by Amartya Sen as a means of measuring the overall capabilities of people in every society to live a fulfilling life. It assigns numbers or scores that reflect national levels of adult literacy, life expectancy, school enrollments, as well as per capita income expressed in terms of purchasing power parity with the U.S. dollar. The numbers, combined and rationalized proportionally, yield an index that includes human accomplishments as well as income levels.[39]

Though Sen himself is critical of utilitarian views of human betterment, as represented in the expression "the most good for the most people,"[40] the index of which he is author, when expressed in the more-or-less terms of the UNDP, takes on a utilitarian character. Thus, the index shares in part the problem of missing important dimensions in human differences by seeking average or aggregate measures of success in strengthening capabilities.

However, regarding the specific values proposed in the UNDP report, we find some sympathetic choices. To substitute the positive for the UNDP's negative characterization of its values, we find much in common with the organization's call for more human rights, more equity within and between societies, more inclusion of marginalized peoples, more human security, a more sustainable environment, and development that reduces poverty and deprivation.

But there is a significant difference in meaning between "more equity," to put the UNDP position affirmatively, and the value of equality. More equity is more elastic than is equality; that is, many more conditions would satisfy the state of more equity than would approximate equality. Equality, in this sense, is a more restrictive concept and envisions the substantial removal of inequalities of the sort we have discussed above. One knows when that job is finished. How does one know when one is finished with more equity?

Let us take up the others. Inclusion is a worthwhile value, but it can be subsumed under equality. One is not equal if one is not included in the mix of societies, as well as in their rewards and resources. Hence, working on equality should wear down barriers of exclusion. The same would be true of more human rights. One cannot have equality without a political equality of rights. Also valuing democracy, as argued above, entails the exercise of equal rights and access, as well as the elimination of poverty and deprivation.

Still remaining for consideration is the value of sustainability. In the UNDP's view, it stands for less environmental destruction, or put positively here, for more environmentally sustainable living. This is a highly appropriate stance, but, I would argue, one that should not be expressed as a value, but as a limiting condition on the solutions we propose in eliminating all forms of inequality. I will have more to say about sustainability in the pages below.

Values Compared

After a careful comparison of the value of equality proposed here with those proposed by Thomas Friedman, the World Bank, and the UNDP, we have tried to show how a single-minded pursuit of equality can yield the same and often better results that the other formulas discussed here. But, now we must face the question: Can economies be run well enough with equality as their guide, or are the values that brought us all of this inequality the only ones that can support viable economies? The short answer is that equality will do quite well, but we will need to show how it can do as well as the existing orientations to which we cling.

Notes

1. Thomas Friedman, *The Lexus and the Olive Tree: Understanding Globalization* (New York: Anchor Books, 2000).

2. Ibid., 166.

3. Ibid., 161.

4. Ibid., 183–84.

5. Ibid, 474.

6. Ibid., 309. New estimates by the *Economist*, June 16, 2001, show that the United States had 274 billionaires by the end of the year 2000. For data, see supplement entitled "The New Rich," 1.

7. Ibid., 212.

8. Ibid., 449.

9. Ibid., 168.

10. World Bank, *Entering the 21st Century: World Development Report, 1999–2000* (New York: Oxford University Press, 2000), 21. See James Ferguson, *The Anti-Politics Machine: "Development," Depoliticization, and Bureaucratic Power in Lesotho* (Minneapolis: University of Minnesota Press, 1994 [1990]), for a trenchant, as well as telling, analysis of a World Bank national development plan for Lesotho.

11. World Bank, ibid.

12. James Ferguson, op. cit.

13. The June 16, 2001, issue of the *Economist* discusses how the IMF places conditions on its loans, a practice with which the World Bank routinely joins in aiding with the bailouts of the failing economies of poor countries. See 70.

14. World Bank, *Attacking Poverty: World Development Report, 2000–2001* (New York: Oxford University Press, 2001), 7.

15. Ibid., 33.

16. Ibid., 66.

17. Ibid., 52.

18. Ibid., 52.

19. Ibid., 119.

20. Ibid., 80.

21. Ibid., 80–82.

22. Ibid., 80.

23. Ibid., 7.

24. Ibid., 99–106.

25. Ibid., 113–14.

26. Ibid., 106–8.

27. Ibid., 115, 117.

28. Ibid., 125–26, 131.

29. Ibid., 103, 106, 107.

30. Ibid., 7.

31. Ibid., 40.

32. Ibid., 153.

33. Ibid., 137–39.

34. Ibid., 15.

35. *Human Development Report 1999* (New York: Oxford University Press, 1999), 2.

36. Ibid., 3–7.

37. Ibid., 8–13.

38. Ibid., 3, 44.

39. Ibid., 23, 127.

40. Amartya Sen, *Development as Freedom* (New York: Alfred A. Knopf, 1999), 62–63.

CHAPTER SIX

Putting Values into Economies

Thus far, I have tried to show that valuing equality can enhance human flourishing, and that it is a superior choice to other value frameworks against which it can be compared. I have implied that the value of equality should modify how we do things economically or change the economic outcomes so that human well-being is enhanced. This means that either we must change the way capitalism works, or successfully blunt its impact in ways that dramatically improve people's lives.

One important argument stands in the way. It is the belief that if capitalist economies are to succeed, they need one tried-and-true set of values with which to orient the economic activities of people. The implication is that if societies don't have or replicate a particular set of values, their economies are destined to fail. In contrast, we will show that there are already a number of different sets of value orientations operating in contemporary capitalist economies that are achieving at least average or modest success in the world.

There Is No "One Best" Value Orientation

There is no "one best" value battery that is needed to produce a satisfactory economy. A variety of values motivate and shape reasonably functioning economies in this capitalist world of ours. The arguments for the "right values" have become popular once again in our discussions of how to make economies grow. During the 1960s and 1970s, they were grouped under the general rubric of modernization theory. In brief, proponents believed that there were certain cultural preconditions or sentiments that people in the West and Japan had and that newly industrializing countries needed for successful economic development. Walt Rostow, one of the theory's most important proponents, imaginatively summarizes from the historical record of the West how these new ideas about life and progress enabled whole societies to economically "take off":

> The idea spreads not merely that economic progress is possible, but that economic progress is a necessary condition for some other purpose, judged to be good: be it national dignity, private profit, the general welfare, or a better life for the children. . . . New types of enterprising men come forward . . . willing to mobilize savings and to take risks in pursuit of profit or modernization.[1]

These visions, transformed into ambitions, finally become values. The modernization paradigm, perhaps best expressed when formalized by Talcott Parsons into what he called "pattern variables," was essentially a list of the values a modernizing society must have in order to succeed economically. They included prizing achievement over ascription, universalism over particularism, and specificity over diffuseness, to name a few. Achievement over ascription was well fixed by Rostow: "Men must come to be valued in the society not for their connection with clan or class, or even, their guild," Rostow wrote, "but for their individual ability to perform certain specific, increasingly specialized functions."[2] A preference for universalism, for instance, enables people to appreciate things beyond their narrow personal interests, while specificity refers to the ability to separate and act on a particular problem without getting tangled up in what we might call the "big picture" of reality.[3] These new values, then, became emblems as well as measures of the social progress of postcolonial nations in the 1960s and 1970s on the road to modernization.

This "right values" argument has never really died out. Rather, we find it reemerging in reinvigorated form over the past decade. Once more, a particular value or value set is essential for long-term advantage. Leaders of Asian states, such as Singapore's former president Lee Kuan Yew, have argued that Asian values based upon the teachings of Confucius have been responsible for Asian economic ascendancy during the 1980s and 1990s. Values such as respect for authority, hierarchy, and the group—not "Western" values such as individualism, democracy, and personal freedom—have enabled Asian societies to achieve economic success.[4]

In contrast, Francis Fukuyama identified "trust" as the essential ingredient in the economic success of the United States, Germany, and Japan. The social structures of these societies resisted the confinements of the kin group and found ways to channel bonds of trust into the complex organizational achievement we know as the modern corporation, itself the master rationalizer and renewer of capitalist economies. Armed with this hypothesis, Fukuyama neatly divides Asian societies into two groups: the ultimately unsuccessful developers, who cannot move beyond the kin group, which includes China and the Chinese diaspora, and the successful developers, like the Japanese, who can expand their notion of kin to include the corporation.[5] Given the economic news since the beginning of the 1990s, there has been a reversal of fortunes that Fukuyama, among others, did not expect, as China has soared ahead and Japan has stagnated.

Others have put forward more ambitious value agendas. Lawrence Harrison, for instance, in his contribution to a book he coedited with Samuel Huntington called *Culture Matters: How Values Shape Human Progress*,[6] lists ten values that progressive cultures have, and that they need, in order to successfully develop economically:

1. Time orientation (to the future)
2. Work (diligence and achievement for self-respect)
3. Frugality
4. Education (for progress orientation)
5. Merit (as basis for advancement and rewards)
6. Community (trust bonds beyond family)
7. Honesty (business and personal ethics)
8. Justice and fair play
9. Authority (dispersed, horizontal)
10. Secularism

Though Harrison notes that few countries would be graded a "ten" on all the factors, he asserts that "virtually all of the advanced democracies—as well as high-achieving ethnic/religious groups like the Mormons, Jews, Basques, and East Asian immigrants in the United States and elsewhere—would receive substantially higher scores than virtually all of the Third World countries."[7]

Harrison's enthusiasm reveals, albeit in extreme form, the tendency of this view to identify the moral ideals of economically successful societies and to attribute success to the practice of these ideals, regardless of whether he can demonstrate that these ideals are actually in practice. "The power of culture is demonstrable," he writes, adding the activities of ethnic Chinese diaspora businesspeople throughout Southeast Asia to his list of favorites.[8] Though Fukuyama, as we have seen, would disagree with Harrison about the ethnic Chinese, whose ultimate economic success, he argues, is limited precisely by their devotion to family—as opposed to corporate—ties,[9] we can nonetheless see in the work of both the tendency to award particular cultural values a causal role.

They are not alone. "Max Weber was right," writes the economic historian David Landes: "If we learn anything from the history of economic development, it is that culture makes almost all the difference."[10] With the invocation of Weber, Landes makes the lineage claims for the culture argument. And, in fact, our value inquiries still hearken back to the example of Max Weber's classic study of the role of Protestantism in generating the original motivations for the investments, efficiencies, and savings that modern capitalism assumes as its orders of the day. His radical notion that the ascetic Protestant sects of northern Europe ignited the growth of modern capitalism because their religious values and those of capitalism's exactly coincided in their habits and life practices is a fascinating study in the powers of a social personality in human conduct. It also set a standard for investigations over the course of the twentieth century.[11]

Yet, even in Weber's lifetime, there were disagreements about the "value causes" of capitalism, and here begins our argument against the "one best" or "right values" argument. Weber's colleague Werner Sombart put the desire for riches at the center of capitalist motivations,[12] while the U.S. economist and Weber contemporary Thorstein Veblen emphasized "pecuniary emulation" of the rich and conspicuous consumption as the keystones of modern capitalism.[13] Faced with their mutual contradiction, sociologist Daniel Bell does the sensible thing to conserve both readings: He historicizes them. Max Weber may have been right once upon a time, Bell writes, but Sombart's stress on "greed and gold" best captures the spirit of today's capitalism. For Bell, the value of acquisitiveness underlies capitalism's historic switch from extolling the virtues of production and savings to embracing the rewards of consumption.[14]

Moreover, Weber himself, having propounded the famous thesis of the Protestant ethic, nonetheless associated different types of value orientations with a variety of forms of capitalism. In other words, while he argued that the historical origins of modern, Western capitalism lay in the existential anxieties and compulsive habits of certain northern Protestant sects, he acknowledged that other kinds of capitalism derived from the diverse value orientations of other historical societies. Thus, for instance, he recognized that a more "financial" capitalism based strictly upon business speculation in currencies, rather than the production and trade in goods, was present in scores of societies before and after the Protestant invention of Western capitalism. He also notes that what might be termed a kind of "predatory," or politically oriented, capitalism, that is, a form of enterprise in which persons or organizations made money via their connections to a political leader, class, or state, was practiced in the West from the time of the Roman Empire. Though Weber awarded pride of place to modern capitalism with its origins in the historical development of Protestantism because it was more rational than either the financial or political variants in the use of labor and capital, he nonetheless took cognizance of the other modes as occasionally present whenever events like financial crazes or wars were visited upon modern economies.[15]

In this, then, we find Weber something of a compromise figure for our argument. On the one hand, he finds for a plurality of value systems producing a plurality of capitalisms—a position very much in line with ours. On the other hand, he picks his favorite, the modern Western variety, because the values he traces to the religious conflicts of certain groups of Protestants best fit his preference for a model with an instrumental rationality, that is, one in which a person is constantly calculating the most efficient means for accomplishing her ends. Does he find the others deficient? In this virtue, yes. But in other respects, were we to ask Weber whether one could make a "satisfactory" economy on the basis of financial or political capitalistic values and practices, one can imagine—and only imagine, unfortunately—that he would answer equivocally, but yes, the possibility exists.

Yet we need not rest our argument solely on a theoretical footing. We can support it with empirical evidence. Our fundamental point is that contemporary capitalist economies vary greatly in their natures and in the values that motivate them. The first way in which they differ is how they make money—that is, how they are structured to make money. For instance, the economies of rich countries tend toward postindustrialism: a major part of their economies makes money by producing services rather than goods. They also devote a significant portion of their moneymaking activities toward the financial sector, in effect making money with money.[16] A second batch of countries, ranging from those in East and Southeast Asia to Latin America and Eastern Europe, heavily depend upon industrial production for their livelihoods. Another batch of middle-income countries bases their economies on the extraction of oil and vital minerals and metals. The poor countries of Africa and other regions find market activities in the formal economic sense other than trade in basic commodities internationally hard to sustain. Their economies are largely informal, meaning that activities revolve around subsistence, rather than profit, and households and kin rather than firms operate them.

Moreover, they differ in the way that economic institutions are interconnected. One key is how banks fit into the economic equation. In poor countries, the great majority of the population and the informal economic activities upon which their subsistence is based have no access to banking services and no means of saving money. The absence of commercial banking activity puts these countries in the hands of international lenders such as the regional development banks and the World Bank or, when their economies are growing, those of the large private banks of the rich countries.

Though the differences between their plight and that of rich countries is apparent, it is also important to note how the economies of rich countries use banks very differently among themselves. Banks in East and Southeast Asia, as well as those in Western Europe, for instance, maintain proprietary relations by owning stock in their clients' firms; thus, loans from banks are sorts of equity contributions made effectively by co-owners. In contrast, though banks are powerful and important sources of loans for companies in the United States and Great Britain, they are not typically co-owners of firms, nor do they supply the lion's share of investment capital. For a major share of their investment capital, firms resort to stock and bond markets.[17]

These differences have important consequences. In Great Britain and the United States, banks, because they are guarantors of their subscribers' money, play a regulatory role in the economy at large, lending to the creditworthy and denying the uncreditworthy loans.[18] In contrast, banks in Western Europe and in East and Southeast Asia, as co-owners of large corporations, play a supportive rather than a regulative role. During economic crises, such as the 1997–98 Asian crisis and the decade-long Japanese slump, banks were much more exposed to direct harm from the economic difficulties of firms in which they were heavily invested as well as being prime lenders. For these regions, when international agencies like the International Monetary Fund (IMF) and the World Bank, as well as the U.S. Treasury Department, insisted that Asian banks reform themselves by shedding bad loans and selling their depreciated stock in a nation's industrial companies, this had very serious implications. The portion of the nation's wealth locked up in banks, and that which provides the liquidity keeping economies going, was reduced not once, but two times: first by the bad debt, and second, by the depreciated stock they held and were urged to sell. This lowered the value of the assets in their resale and rapidly depleted a nation's wealth.[19]

Another vital relationship, in addition to the one between banks and businesses, is the one between states and businesses. Once again, there are enormous differences between rich countries, as well as between rich, middle-income, and poor countries. The issues are to what degree and when do states lead or direct businesses and their investments. In two decades of industrial competition and strife between the United States and Japan, the differences between the two were stereotyped and exaggerated. It was said that in "Japan, Inc.," the Japanese government fixed the trajectory of economic growth, picked industries for development, subsidized innovations, and rewarded winning businesses with market share and political protection.[20] The United States, in contrast, was said to be a laissez-faire operator, leaving businesses to rise or fall by their own lights without any governmental interference, save antitrust regulation.

Though there may have been some truth to the original comparison, the differences between the two nation's state roles in their economic development became much more similar than usually supposed. Reacting to "the Japanese threat," the U.S. government involved itself directly in promoting the development of advanced technologies like microchip production and the Internet; in addition, during the 1980s, it financed research and development of innovations in optics, lasers, and industrial materials through defense efforts such as the Strategic Defense Initiative (popularly known as "Star Wars").[21] And through trade sanctions and acrimonious bilateral negotiations, the United States intervened directly to support its international businesses against their Japanese competitors, even seeking to interfere with Japanese state regulation of its national economy. Since the beginning of Japanese economic troubles in 1990, the United States has missed no opportunity to tell the Japanese precisely how they should restructure their economy in ways compatible with the direction of the international economy, as the United States saw it.[22]

That said, and in appreciation of the fact that these kinds of political stances affect the direction of national economies and change over time, the addition of a hard-charging, state-directed Chinese economy has strengthened the hand of those throughout Asia who prefer national industrial policies administered by interventionist state bureaucracies. There is an expectation in such countries as Malaysia and Singapore, and no less in South Korea and Indonesia, that the state will act to set direction for the future and facilitate economic growth of the sort that the elites in both government and business prefer.[23] Though the economic crisis in 1997–98 shook some of the confidence in this arrangement, quick economic recovery quieted some of the more strident demands made by the United States and the IMF for greater separation between businesses and state, as well as banks and businesses.

The Western European case, and to a lesser extent the larger Latin American economies, provide another alternative to U.S. and British claims to laissez-faire economic practices: corporatism. Again the state plays a starring role, except that it shares the economic planning stage with its two costars, business and labor. All three in concert seek to set economic policy, the conditions for production, the rate of innovation, and its impact on the workforce, as well as wages and compensation. The state acts as a guarantor of good faith between the parties, the font of extra monies needed to satisfy the other two parties' demands, and something of a spokesperson for the public interest. This last role is perhaps the most fragile, as the state elite in the interests of its own survival often finds common cause with the business and labor elites at the sacrifice of its public fiduciary role.[24]

Before pausing to consider the value implications of each of these kinds of institutional adaptations, we need to assay the differing relations that obtain between businesses throughout the global economy. National economies differ in the way that businesses conduct their everyday transactions: The choice that every business faces is whether to perform every phase of its production itself or whether to buy that product or service from another firm.[25] Historically, for instance, Japanese and United States firms handled this problem very differently. The United States developed large corporations that subsequently became transnational corporations that largely provided for all their production and service needs by developing a branch of the corporation that could serve all the other branches. Perhaps the most famous example of this tendency was Henry Ford's manufacturing plant at River Rouge, Michigan. In its day, two generations ago, the plant began its production with such raw materials as coal, iron ore, coke, and energy, and at the other end of the plant, out rolled a finished Ford motorcar.[26] This model of self-sufficient production for U.S. firms lasted until the 1980s when the Japanese industrial revival, relying on outsourcing as much of the product as possible to separate, though cooperating firms, showed some prospect of overtaking American carmakers even in their home market. The U.S. response, a radical restructuring of all of its major manufacturing and service industries to mirror the Japanese model, has since remade the face of American industry to more closely resemble our Japanese counterparts.[27] This is the basis for the so-called flexible mode of production.

Other societies resolve the problems of how to organize businesses differently. While the United States recently has found it possible, as we have just described above, to have big corporations and quasi-Japanese patterns of outsourcing at the same time, Italy has handled the same organizational imperative by networking small firms into virtual, not actual, long production lines. This "small is beautiful" strategy has been successful since the early 1970s among industries composed of microenterprises of no more than ten people that, when working in a production chain, compete successfully in international markets.[28]

What we learn from these examples is that the organization and functioning of businesses are historically fluid. Businesses must make a profit, and, typically, make a bigger profit than their competitors, or suffer eventual elimination. International competition, especially since the world economic slowdown in the 1970s, has driven most national economies to try any number of new means, new institutional lineups, different labor policies, and the like to obtain a marketplace advantage.[29] This increases variety in one moment and fosters imitation in another.

We live in a period of U.S. economic, political, and military dominance, in which the primary objective of U.S. foreign policy is to encourage harmonization of economic policies worldwide around an agenda of free markets and free trade. Directly or through intermediaries such as the IMF or the World Bank, the United States seeks to encourage like-minded economic practice the world over, as our discussion of the so-called Washington consensus in earlier chapters illustrates. Despite these efforts, many observers believe that continued economic "divergence"—that is, differences in the structure and functioning of national economies—is a much more likely outcome than "convergence," a situation in which national differences gradually disappear.[30]

The second major point we need to examine is that what differentiates economies is whom they serve; that is, not only is it important is how money is made, but it is equally relevant who gets the money. Economies pay off individuals and groups directly. The state also redistributes the surplus it claims through taxation. Both, then, are factors in who benefits from a particular economic configuration.

Once again, there are differences—even among closely grouped economies such as those in Western Europe and Japan when compared with the United States and Great Britain. Put simply, Japan and Western Europe are "stakeholder" economies, while the United States, and to a lesser extent, Great Britain, are "shareholder" economies.[31] The key is the economic surplus produced by corporations. In stakeholder economies, corporate profits go to long-serving employees; in shareholder economies, the profits are paid out to the corporations' owners, those who own the companies' shares. This means that stakeholder economies reward the steadfast corporal of the corporation over the capitalist risk-taking investor, the implication being that organizational loyalty is more important to society than individual accumulation of capital.[32]

In addition to these qualitative distinctions, aggregate data concerning the distribution of income in societies also become highly relevant in showing us who receives the rewards of a particular economic system. A measure like the Gini index, which indicates the degree to which incomes are equally distributed in a given society, can be very helpful. It tells us the total results of distribution, either through direct compensation to employees on the part of corporations or through the redistribution of corporate surplus through state expenditures. We can ask the question: When all is said and done, which economies produce more equal distributions of income and which do not? We find some very interesting clusters of countries. First, incomes are more equal in Western Europe and Japan than they are in the United States and Great Britain. This finding would be consistent with the stakeholder/ shareholder distinction: Corporations in Western Europe and Japan would be distributing more of their surplus to their employees, a larger number, than to their shareholders. In contrast, corporations in the United States and Great Britain would be paying out larger sums to the smaller proportion of their citizens who are shareholders.

Other patterns suggest themselves. The Scandinavian countries have the most equal distributions of income, followed, with the exception of Russia, by Eastern Europe. The United States finds itself in the same league as Australia and New Zealand but, most significantly, is as unequal in income distribution as the majority of poor countries and less-poor countries in Africa, Asia, and Latin America. In what must be one of the great ironies of contemporary history, the United States and China find themselves tied with Ethiopia, Tunisia, and the Kyrgyz Republic among the higher-inequality countries, with identical Gini indexes of forty.[33]

Aside from the stakeholder distinction, what accounts for these differences? The presence of active welfare states in Scandinavia and Western Europe would figure in any explanation for why inequality is lower in these countries than others equally as wealthy by other measures. Could the absence of a robust welfare state explain why the United States finds itself in such anomalous company? In part, yes, because the overall taxation rate of the United States, the crucial component of any welfare system consisting of the amount of money the state claims for redistribution, is significantly lower than that of its rich country counterparts. Less money, in other words, is taken by taxation from the rich and given to the poor, or poorer.[34]

Poor countries find themselves in the same position as the United States, and partly for the same reasons. Once again, they typically tax less than other more income distribution–equal countries, and thus, like the United States, have less to redistribute. In addition, like the United States, they have powerful ruling classes that use political influence to insulate them from paying proportionately higher taxes. Thus, they have penurious welfare states—if they have one at all—that returns little to their poor.

In sum, we have looked at how economies make money and to whom they spread the rewards and noticed significant differences. They are not only evidence of continued divergence, but forces for continued divergence.

Different Economies, Different Values

Perhaps another reason why complete convergence is unlikely concerns the relationship between economies and values: Different economies generate and are generated by different values. To be sure, economies and values utterly incompatible with the world economy as it stands over the past 200 years presumably no longer exist in their differences. Capitalism and the rule of profit are powerful enough to discipline extreme outliers over the long haul. That said, economic differences breed value differences, and vice versa.

The economic differences we have discovered suggest significant differences in value orientations. Taking up the stakeholder/shareholder comparison once more, there are several implications. First, employees' institutional loyalties among stakeholders are rewarded at the expense of individual royalties of the shareholder. The relationship between persons and institutions, consequently, is valued as a deeper social attachment than merely one of economic opportunity. While the job of the firm may be to make money, it is supposed to distribute the surplus in a way that takes care of the economic needs of its loyal members, not simply provide a wage at the market rate. This valuation of deep loyalty finds its fullest expression perhaps in the postwar Japanese corporate practice of lifetime employment, a commitment honored in the breach over the past few years of economic crisis, but fundamental to how Japanese business views its obligations to some of its members.

Second, there is an implicit valuation of group ties over individual abilities. In the same way that stakeholder economies hold the individual shareholder less highly, so too they tend to reward employees for their role and tenure in the organization rather than for their individual accomplishments. Compensations, bonuses, and benefits accrue with time and responsibility within the firm; the competitive bidding process that occurs to hire or retain an individual's services in U.S. corporations is rare. Again, the historical example of the Japanese "salaryman," the manager brought in, paid, and promoted as a member of a cohort of fellow managers over a lifetime career, is almost a paradigm case.[35] Further evidence can be found by noting the controversy over the high rates of executive compensation among U.S. corporations: Europeans find it scandalous and inappropriate, and while many Americans may agree, it is nonetheless the norm that executives bargain for their market price as compensation for their work in a U.S. corporation. The proof, however, is in the pay: The average chief executive officer (CEO) in the United States is paid three times as much as a comparable CEO in Britain and four times as much as comparable CEOs in France and Germany.[36]

Next, let us take up again the issue of corporatism—the effort, primarily in Western Europe and some Latin American countries, to establish an ongoing negotiating process between labor, management, and the state with respect to vital industrial and labor policies. If we compare this sort of regime with practices in the United States, for example, value differences become plain. In corporatist societies, value is placed on cooperation among parties who are urged to see themselves in a sort of common effort for keeping society going and growing. There is value placed upon competition, but it is usually displaced from the realms of interfirm and labor-management relations to external, preferably foreign, actors. A German company, for instance, typically has employee union members on its board of directors, and it meets regularly with its unions to plan the operation of the firm and resolve differences between sides in an industrial work council. Even cooperation among industrial competitors is muted, as both employers and employees are encouraged to think for the good of the industry and for the nation. The state reinforces the value of cooperation by acting as a guarantor of benefits for both sides.

In the United States, by contrast, the historic antagonisms between labor and management have seldom yielded to the corporatist persuasion of the occasional presidential administration that has sought smoother industrial relations or restraints on prices or wages.[37] Instead, the state has intervened to aid one side or the other at different points in time, depending upon the administration's political coloration. The Reagan administration, it will be remembered, abandoned the state-as-mediator tack more typical of the Nixon-Ford-Carter years when it acted as management, fired U.S. air traffic controllers, and led a national effort to reduce the influence of unions in the country's economic affairs.[38] The Clinton years were marked by an uneasy return to both limited union advocacy in the halls of Congress and pleas for labor-management cooperation in industrial councils. We have tried to show that these kinds of value orientations vary over time. It is still important to observe that when compared with European orientations toward cooperation at home and competition abroad, the United States in the spirit of "may the strongest prevail" still implicitly values competition among economic parties, including between labor and management. So, too, it places a much more limited value on cooperation, which occurs typically in the limited cases where labor and management find their interests coinciding in a particular trade matter.

Regarding the significant differences in economic equality among societies, the findings seem neither mysterious nor new—except perhaps for the discovery that the United States shares its record of economic inequality with many of the poor countries in the world. It thus seems an obvious implication that some societies value equality more than others do. But this judgment needs refinement, as people's beliefs about the value of equality are complicated. For instance, economic inequality in the United States is treated as the outcome of the economic competition between individuals for economic rewards. So long as persons have equality of opportunity, Americans generally believe and the country's laws uphold, America's obligations to equality are satisfied. Such inequalities as exist are rationalized by the fact that economic competition has occurred, and the distribution is consequently a just result. If the reader finds this argument familiar, it is because the country has been discussing the issue via disputes over the policy of affirmative action since the early 1970s. For all of the tugging of those favoring affirmative action, the policy has been limited to equality of opportunity instead of being extended to take into account equality of outcomes.[39]

Other societies value equality differently. Some seek equality of outcomes as well. For example, India since its independence has sought to guarantee preferences by reserving employment and university slots for historically disadvantaged social groups such as the *dalits* or outcasts, and indigenous tribes. In Malaysia, the state has sought to guarantee greater ethnic Malay economic success vis-à-vis ethnic Chinese citizens by requiring Malay economic participation in most of the country's major industries and businesses. It has also buttressed Malay representation in government bureaucracies through preferential hiring. Both the Indian and Malaysian cases are relatively modest attempts to achieve equality of outcome as well as that of opportunity, but they are different from the approach to equality taken by the United States. One can say that they share, therefore, different values with respect to economic equality.

The regional differences in national distributions of income also suggest value differences. The combination of taxation and welfare policies in Scandinavia attempts to equalize the usual inequalities that arise in industrial societies in the workplace and in the accumulation of capital over time. The Scandinavians capture the surpluses produced through taxes and redistribute them both through taxes and services with an eye toward significantly reducing economic inequality. To a lesser extent, Western Europe and the former socialist countries of Eastern Europe attempt the same, though their redistributive reach does not equal that of the Scandinavians. One would be hard put to describe any of them as attempting to provide equality of outcomes, though a finer-grain analysis of the history of taxation and welfare policies in particular states might yield cases that more approximate the ideal. Their differences in value orientations at this level of generalization, then, might be described in terms of degrees rather than of type.

Do the Differences Make a Difference in People's Lives?

We have discussed how economies are differently organized and how they are motivated by different values. The questions that arise now have a deeper relevance. They have to do with whether one can choose the values and the kind of economy that arises from those value choices and still produce an economy that adequately provides for human flourishing. Some showing of general equivalent effectiveness on the part of differently oriented economies would not only lessen the imperative to chase after the "one best way"—the one best economy that all societies must achieve or imitate. It would also afford us more latitude in envisioning economies that offer greater prospects of human satisfaction.

Suppose we ask the simplest and most obvious question: What economies are most successful by the conventional criterion of wealth generated? An uncontroversial measure of wealth generated is gross national product (GNP) per capita. Using figures for 2000, we can generate the following list:[40]

Table 6.1. Top Ten Economies By Gross National Product Per Capita, 2000 (in Purchasing Power Parity with US$)

1. Luxembourg	$50,061
2. United States	$34,142
3. Norway	$29,918
4. Ireland	$29,886
5. Switzerland	$28,769
6. Iceland	$29,581
7. Canada	$27,840
8. Denmark	$27,627
9. Belgium	$26,765
10. Austria	$26,765

It is an interesting mix of nations. With the exception of the United States and Canada, it is composed of Scandinavian and Western European nations with fairly robust welfare states. Once more with the same exceptions, it features Western European and Scandinavian societies that organize the interests of labor, capital, and the state along corporatist lines.[41] The inference we can draw is that a variety of economies, albeit confined to the parameters we have discussed in this chapter at least, can produce reasonably satisfying outcomes by strictly economic measures.

Suppose we raise the bar a few notches and ask the more demanding question: Can a variety of economies achieve a broader set of goals more closely related to the concept of human well-being? We can resort to the use of the United Nations Development Programme's Human Development Index (HDI), developed for the program by Amartya Sen. The index is based on three components, Sen explains: ". . . indicators of longevity, education and income per head—it is not exclusively focused on economic opulence (as GNP is)."[42] As in table 6.1, a measure of the gross national product, the gross domestic product per capita, is calculated with respect to how much in goods and services a nation's income would buy if an amount equivalent to it in U.S. dollars were spent in the United States. This measure, "purchasing power parity," is an attempt to estimate a nation's standard of living when compared with that of the United States, which is used by the World Bank as an international benchmark.[43] Regarding longevity, the index uses average life expectancy at birth. The education quotient of the index is calculated by combining the adult literacy rate with the proportion of population's six through eight year-olds enrolled in primary school. This generates a "top ten" list somewhat different from our earlier rendition:[44]

Table 6.2. Top Ten Societies, UNDP Human Development Index, 2000

1. Norway
2. Sweden
3. Canada
4. Belgium
5. Australia
6. United States
7. Iceland
8. Netherlands
9. Japan
10. Finland

What is interesting about the nations in the Human Development Index "Top Ten" (table 6.2) is that even though their scores on the HDI were virtually identical (they are separated by 0.012 of a point), and the inference warranted that they are providing roughly the same quality of life, their incomes vary widely. Among the new top ten, incomes range from the $34,142 per person in the United States to $24,277 per person in Sweden, a difference of $9,865 in wealth per capita available for consumption. Put another way, Sweden produces the equivalent high quality of life with only 70 percent of what the United States spends. Thus some societies produce more well-being for substantially less than others do.

What explains the ability of some societies to produce equivalent well-being for less? The answer is highly redistributive welfare states. Societies such as Austria, Belgium, and Denmark collect more of the gross domestic product in taxes and redistribute it to their citizens in the form of income and services than does, for example, the United States. Called "high-income, high-equity societies," they succeed in keeping their overall economic inequality very low—about 40 percent lower than does the United States.[45]

Suppose we tailor an index even further, so that it reflects the degree of relative equality between the sexes, in addition to the other measures already used in the Human Development Index. The UNDP has constructed an index that incorporates gender differences in life expectancy, literacy, school enrollment, and income. The more equal the outcomes between men and women, the higher a society's ranking is. Here is the result:[46]

Table 6.3. Top Ten Societies, UNDP Gender-Related Development Index, 2000

1. Australia
2. Belgium
3. Norway
4. Sweden
5. Canada
6. United States
7. Iceland
8. Finland
9. Netherlands
10. United Kingdom

As inspection reveals, the two human development indexes, one accounting for gender equality and the other not, are virtually identical. The exceptions are that Japan, though ranked ninth on the Human Development Index, when ranked for gender equality falls below the top ten on the Gender-Related Development Index (table 6.3). In its place, we find the United Kingdom ranked in the top ten with regard to gender development, but absent from the other two indexes. But the overall continuity between the two development indexes suggests that human development and gender equality, at least as measured by the UNDP, go hand in hand.

Thus, between the three indexes, the differences in countries nominated are slight. By eliminating duplication, we find that in all, only sixteen societies are represented on the lists. This is a narrow range of countries—the "top" by measures of income, well-being, and gender equality. This should caution us against making sweeping claims that wealth generation is a secondary matter or that a very wide band of values can produce successful economies. Neither statement is warranted. The range of variation among the 173 countries surveyed is vast, and no doubt we could learn lessons from studying them all.

Still, among the societies measured, there are important differences. We can argue two things. First, wealth can be generated by economies that differ from each other in some important respects. Two, well-being, here using the HDI and the gender-related development index as proxies, can be achieved in societies whose economies differ by the degrees or qualities we have tried to describe above. Perhaps these points are strong and buoyant enough to allow us to countenance satisfactory economies that can be based upon the value of equality advocated here.

This is our next task.

Notes

1. W. W. Rostow, *The Stages of Economic Growth*. 2d ed. (Cambridge, U.K.: Cambridge University Press, 1971 [1960]), 6–7.

2. Ibid., 19.

3. Talcott Parsons, *The Social System* (Glencoe, Ill.: Free Press, 1951), 58–67.

4. Fareed Zakaria, "Culture Is Destiny: A Conversation with Lee Kuan Yew," *Foreign Affairs* 73 (March–April 1994). For an argument claiming that there is a great diversity of "Asian values," no one set of which is responsible for economic development in Asia, see Amartya Sen, *Development as Freedom* (New York: Alfred A. Knopf, 1999), 231–48.

5. Francis Fukuyama, *Trust: The Social Virtues and the Creation of Prosperity* (New York: Simon and Schuster, 1995).

6. Lawrence Harrison and Samuel Huntington, *Culture Matters: How Values Shape Human Progress* (New York: Basic Books, 2000).

7. Ibid., 299–300.

8. Ibid.

9. Francis Fukuyama, op. cit.

10. Lawrence Harrison and Samuel Huntington, op. cit., 2.

11. Max Weber, *The Protestant Ethic and the Spirit of Capitalism* (New York: Charles Scribner's Sons, 1958).

12. Werner Sombart, *Luxury and Capitalism*, translated by W. Dittmar (Ann Arbor: University of Michigan Press, 1967).

13. Thorstein Veblen, *The Theory of the Leisure Class* (New York: Viking Penguin, 1994 [1899]).

14. Daniel Bell, *The Cultural Contradictions of Capitalism* (New York: Basic Books, 1996 [1976]), 295.

15. Max Weber, *Economy and Society*, edited by G. Roth and C. Wittich (Berkeley: University of California Press, 1978), 164–66.

16. Fred Block, *Postindustrial Possibilities: A Critique of Economic Discourse* (Berkeley: University of California Press, 1990), 1–20.

17. Joseph Stiglitz, *Whither Socialism?* (Cambridge, Mass.: MIT Press, 1994), 254.

18. Fred Block, *The Vampire State and Other Myths about the U.S. Economy* (New York: The New Press, 1996), 150–55.

19. Robert Wade, "The Asian Crisis: The High Debt Model versus the Wall Street-Treasury-IMF Complex," *New Left Review* 228 (March–April 1998), 3–24.

20. Chalmers Johnson, "Political Institutions and Economic Performance: The Government-Business Relationship in Japan, South Korea, and Taiwan," in *The Political Economy of the New Asian Industrialism*, edited by Frederic Deyo (Ithaca, N.Y.: Cornell University Press, 1987), 136–64. See also Chalmers Johnson, *MITI and the Japanese Miracle* (Stanford, Calif.: Stanford University Press, 1982).

21. Robert Kuttner, *Everything for Sale: The Virtues and Limits of Markets* (New York: Alfred A. Knopf, 1997), 221–24.

22. Some of the flavor of the ongoing economic conflicts between Japan and the United States is captured in Lester Thurow, *The Future of Capitalism: How Today's Economic Forces Shape Tomorrow's World* (New York: William Morrow, 1996), 194–208.

23. See articles collected in Frederic Deyo, editor, *The Political Economy of the New Asian Industrialism*, op. cit.

24. For a cogent rendering of the strengths and frailties of corporatism in Western Europe, see Colin Crouch, *Social Change in Western Europe* (Cambridge, U.K.: Cambridge University Press, 1999).

25. Oliver Williamson, "The Economics of Organization: The Transaction Cost Approach," *American Journal of Sociology* 86, no. 3 (1981), 548–77. See also Oliver Williamson, *The Economic Institutions of Capitalism: Firms, Markets, and Relational Contracting* (New York: Free Press, 1985).

26. Robert Lacey, *Ford: The Men and the Machine* (New York: Ballantine Books, 1986).

27. Bennett Harrison, *Lean and Mean: The Changing Landscape of Corporate Power in the Age of Flexibility* (New York: Basic Books, 1994), describes the Japanese production system and the attempts of U.S. corporations to imitate Japanese success.

28. For background, see Michael Blim, *Made in Italy: Small-scale Industrialization and Its Consequences* (New York: Praeger, 1990). As an update on how these Italian industrial districts are doing, see Josh Whitford, "The Decline of a Model? Challenge and Response in the Italian Industrial Districts," *Economy and Society* 30, no. 1 (February 2001), 38–65.

29. Robert Brenner, "Turbulence in the World Economy," *New Left Review* 228 (1998), 1–273. This phenomenon has been explained at length historically by Giovanni Arrighi, *The Long Twentieth Century* (New York: Verso, 1994).

30. Testimony arrives from very different camps. For samples, see Herbert Kitschelt, Peter Lange, Gary Marks, and John Stephens, "Convergence and Divergence in Advanced Capitalist Democracies," in *Continuity and Change in Contemporary Capitalism*, edited by H. Kitshelt, P. Lange, G. Marks, and J. Stephens (Cambridge, U.K.: Cambridge University Press, 1999), 427–61; and Stiglitz, op. cit., 254–75.

31. Anthony Giddens, *The Third Way and Its Critics* (Cambridge, U.K.: Polity Press, 2000).

32. Giddens may be a bit optimistic about the degree to which Britain is a "shareholding" economy. Kevin Brown, "Poll Shows Britons Are Ceasing to See Capitalism as Profits of Doom," *Financial Times*, August 16, 2001, 7, reports that only 29 percent of the British public supports a firm's right to big profits, as against 43 percent who do not. A polling company executive analyzing these findings argues that Britons "want companies to make a profit, but not at the expense of their staff or the wider community."

33. The source for these Gini index comparisons is the World Bank, *World Development Report 2000/2001: Attacking Poverty* (New York: Oxford University Press, 2001), table 5, Distribution of Income or Consumption, 282–83.

34. See Organization for Economic Cooperation and Development (OECD), "Revenue Statistics, 1965–1996," available at www.oecd.org, accessed January 23, 2003.

35. Ezra Vogel, *Japan's New Middle Class* (Berkeley: University of California Press, 1967), 32–39.

36. Alan Krueger, "When It Comes to Income Inequality, More Than Just Market Forces Are at Work," *New York Times*, April 4, 2002, C2.

37. For a history of the particularly violent and contentious industrial and labor history of the United States, see James Green, *The World of the Worker: Labor in Twentieth-Century America* (New York: Hill and Wang, 1980).

38. Robert Kuttner, op. cit., 99.

39. For a detailed look at what affirmative action could have been, see Gertrude Ezorsky, *Racism and Justice: The Case for Affirmative Action* (Ithaca, N.Y.: Cornell University Press, 1991).

40. United Nations Development Programme, *Human Development Report, 2002: Deepening Democracy in a Fragmented World* (New York: Oxford University Press, 2002), table 12, Economic Performance, 190–92.

41. See Colin Crouch, op. cit., 349–52.

42. United Nations Development Programme, *Human Development Report 1999* (New York: Oxford University Press, 1999), 23.

43. The United Nations Development Programme uses the World Bank data for this part of its Human Development Index. For its explanation, see United Nations Development Programme, *Human Development Report 2002*, op. cit., 193 note.

44. Ibid., table 12, Economic Performance, 190–92.

45. David Dollar and Paul Collier, *Globalization, Growth, and Poverty* (Washington, D.C.: World Bank, 2002), 122, available at http://econ.worldbank.org/prr/subpage.php?sp=2477, accessed June 27, 2002.

46. United Nations Development Programme, op. cit., table 22, Gender-Related Development Index, 222–23.

CHAPTER SEVEN

The Necessity to Choose

We are all connected. What you do, and what you believe, has a significant impact on the world.

Try this exercise. Take out your wallet and examine its contents. Look at what you find. The dollar bills link you to a nation-state—and to a common way of economic life. A driver's license and voter's registration card signify your citizenship: You count somewhere in a democratic world. Bank and credit cards tie you into a system of worldwide finance. Health care and Social Security cards entitle you to medical care, and eventually income support assistance. A union card and a membership to an advocacy or charitable group bind you to particular people and ideas. From a Red Cross donor's card to the one that gets you into a gym, all the cards are tokens of connection and responsibility in your life.

You may consider your influence slight, but your connections are vast. The bills you put in the church collection basket, the United Way pledge you honor, the yearly donation to Amnesty International or Doctors without Borders—these are ways, aside from your work, that you link yourself to the world. Moreover, they reflect some of the moral choices you make.

Not all our moral choices are so obvious. For instance, the clothes you wear are commodities, their origins, save the nametags, obscure. Yet any reader of a daily newspaper knows that the means of their manufacture can be discovered, the identities, hourly wage, and employment conditions of their makers known. By implication, then, your choice of clothing has moral significance. Your purchase, this knowledge now available to you, becomes a moral choice.

Thus, many of the choices we make have a moral dimension. Their number grows as our knowledge increases. Each of us develops a moral horizon, a kind of conceptual field where we can assess the direct consequences as well as the implications of our actions. We begin to see that even the banal contents of our wallets reveal an immense set of circumstances in which we are involved or to which we are connected. More knowledge and reflection further expand our moral horizon, and we find ourselves deeply co-involved in the far-flung affairs of the world.

This poses a problem as well as an opportunity for our analysis here. Against what sets of circumstances should we counterpose our valuing equality? What situations should concern us?

We are related to the problems of economies in several important ways. First, we are producers and consumers in both international and domestic economies. We are thus stakeholders in economic operations great and small; in countless transactions, our interests and our values are in play. Second, we are citizens, and this ascription involves us in the affairs of state. It becomes incumbent upon us to sort out according to our values what the appropriate role of our nation should be in international economic matters with respect to other nations and peoples, and toward international organizations such as the United Nations, the International Monetary Fund (IMF), and the World Bank. Just as important to us as citizens is the part our state plays in our national economy, for it not only sets the conditions for economic activity, but redistributes a significant percentage of the national income through taxation and transfer payments. It behooves us, then, to evaluate both how the state regulates the economy and how it distributes its welfare.

The third area of our engagement is the wide swath of commitments we make through membership in voluntary organizations. Each person makes up something of a social biography through her membership or participation in organizations that stand apart from her efforts at work or at home. A common thread tying these activities together is that the organizations to which we belong are becoming more international in character. Some solicit our aid directly for activities overseas; others like unions and the Red Cross, among others, are reaching out to embrace organizations of their sort all over the world. Thus, local commitments implicate us in the fates of peoples whom we can only know directly through association with a group or indirectly through the media.

Still other forms of association demand attention. Many of us partake in activities as parts of social movements that know no organizational charters and formal memberships. A block club, a civic initiative, a political rally—

their very informality does not diminish their social and cultural importance. Quite the contrary: They deeply engage our commitment and energies.

Thus, we are deeply involved in the affairs of the world as persons with some critical awareness of the planet's problems and possessed of a set of values that we think should guide human actions. As our connections to the plight of others become clearer, so too the imperative grows to act.

The Costs of Doing Nothing

But suppose we did nothing. Or suppose that nothing was done that we might advocate to correct the problems we have discussed thus far. Imagine, instead, that the world undertook a phase in its development that we might call "muddling through." Let us suppose that no new initiatives were undertaken worldwide to enhance universal well-being and, specifically, nothing was done to diminish inequality.

Would we find we had a dystopia, a kind of concrete reflection of the failure of human society on our hands? We would probably find a world very much like our own. Of course, given our discussion in the preceding chapters, this would mean that our societies would be grossly economically unequal both inside and outside national boundaries. We could expect that the consequences would include widespread poverty, lower life spans for those caught up in lives of desperation and degradation, and lives marked by suffering of various types, whether it be physical, psychological, and/or social. More often than not, we would be entitled to imagine that many people, perhaps the vast majority, possessed a gnawing feeling of dispossession, of the inability to live lives they were capable of imagining and desiring.

Surely ordinary human experiences could become worse than they are today. Doing nothing more to combat the spread of AIDS could lead to an absolute decline in life expectancy in fifty-one countries by 2025. Of these, eleven countries could have average life expectancies close to age thirty, a level not seen since the nineteenth century.[1] Doing nothing to redirect the flow of medical research would mean that 99 percent of our efforts internationally would continue to go into finding new treatments for diseases found in rich countries, rather than in poor countries. Little would be done to stop such killers as malaria, lymphatic filariasis, tuberculosis, and dengue fever that literally plague poor countries.[2]

Some new demographic directions now underway in poor countries might improve the situation of many people. For instance, birthrates are declining measurably in many poor countries, increasing the proportion of able-bodied adults in the population. More adult labor increases the potential economic output of societies.[3] These possible gains are particularly threatened, however, by the AIDS pandemic, which afflicts precisely those "able-bodied" persons, young and middle-aged adults in their prime, upon whom improved economies depend.

Then, too, demographic changes of the sort we look upon as hopeful—fewer children, more adults—has its downside: namely, if adults begin to live longer, there can be too many adults in need of elder care, and too few children, absent state intervention, to provide it or to pay for it. The story is familiar to rich countries: Birthrates dropped, longevity increased, and the number of people retired from active work increased as well. Even Western societies with well-established pension systems have found it increasingly difficult to financially support their elderly populations. They have redefined who is "old" by raising the age for pension eligibility, and have offered stingier pension payments to their elderly than before.

Longevity is coming to poor countries. By the year 2050, 21 percent of the world's population will be sixty years of age or older; today only 10 percent of the world's population is older than 60, and many of the elderly live in richer countries. This doubling of the world's elderly will come primarily from poor countries, many of whom, according to the United Nations, will see their older populations quadruple over the next fifty years.[4] Complicating the picture is the fact that most workers in poor countries, and increasingly in rich countries, do not receive pension benefits as part of their employment contracts. The International Labor Organization calculates that 4 billion people—90 percent of the world's workers—have no old-age pension, private or public, upon which they can rely. Add to this fact that workers in both rich and poor countries are increasingly finding new jobs in the so-called informal sector, that is, in parts of economies where state rules and regulations governing labor like pension rights do not apply, and you redouble the likelihood that old people around the world will find themselves poor people.[5]

But perhaps most striking of all, doing nothing would mean consigning 2 billion people to increasing poverty, according to one World Bank estimate. This is because while our attentions have been taken up with the Asian economic miracle (albeit with its crises as well, if one remembers the panic of 1997–98), the economies of other countries, home to the 2 billion people in jeopardy, actually shrank during the 1990s.[6] To be sure, the number of poor people declined in fast-growing Asian countries. Economic growth in China, home to three-quarters of a billion poor rural people, has pulled many out of poverty, and because of its size reduced the numbers of poor people worldwide significantly. The introduction of peasant proprietorships in a rural society in which agriculture was collectivized following the Chinese Revolution dramatically increased crop yields and higher incomes for farm people, lifting many families out of abject poverty.[7] With newfound efficiency derived from more highly motivated labor, households found they could afford to let one or more of their number migrate to the seacoast cities, thus furnishing a vast supply of cheap labor—an estimated 200 million persons—to fuel China's industrial boom.

A virtuous circle in which efficiency in the countryside led to industrial success in the cities? A victory for self-reliance and an autonomous "Chinese" road to economic development? Not completely. Though tremendous sacrifices were made by Chinese workers and peasants to move China forward, it is important to recall that foreign capital—more foreign investment than has flowed into all the other poor countries combined—as well as large injections of industrial know-how helped China make such startling economic progress. In fact, the lesson of Chinese economic development, aside for a wish that one might find oneself in a big as opposed to a small country, may be that poor countries need the capital and industrial know-how of rich countries in order to escape poverty.

Moreover, suppose the poorest nations, with or without increased development assistance, were able to reverse their negative economic growth and begin expanding their economies at something like the rate of Chinese economic growth of the 1990s. The United Nations Conference on Trade and Development (UNCTAD) estimates that if poor countries could boost their annual growth rates to 7 percent, they could reduce extreme poverty, that is, the number of people living on less than US$1 a day, by one-half by the year 2015. This would mean that if the thirty-three countries in their sample, taken from the poorest countries for which there are reliable data, were able to sustain a 7 percent growth rate between now and 2015 instead of the average 3.5 percent growth rate they sustained for the 1990s, they would have a little less than 200 million of the extremely poor than a projected approximately 400 million without accelerated economic growth.[8]

This would be welcome, indeed astonishing progress, were it to come to pass. But is it sufficient progress? If we were to do nothing, and these thirty-three poor countries were to do in a sense *everything* for themselves, we could be consoled by the fact that they would *not* have 400 million abjectly poor, but would still have the disagreeable result that 200 million persons would be living by 2015 in extreme poverty. How do we rationalize these facts with goodwill or something like Ronald Dworkin's "equal concern"? On the part of the poor who pull themselves up at sometimes unspeakable sacrifice, it seems warranted. But for our part, having done "nothing," we cannot congratulate ourselves on the results of our charity. In fact, we run something of a moral risk. It is now foreseeable that by fair estimate one of the consequences of doing nothing is that there will remain 200 million abjectly poor. The moral risk is: How can we hold beliefs about equality and countenance this quite predictable, in fact wildly optimistic, outcome? We run the moral risk of having worthless, devalued beliefs, for if one sees the consequences of action as going against one's valued beliefs, and one does nothing, can one be said to hold those values?

I would argue that doing nothing is not an option if one values equality on moral grounds. As we have seen above, there is further no reason to suppose that the world economy would somehow correct itself and deliver well-being to the poor and extremely poor. Thus a person valuing equality has no reason to expect that doing nothing will still result in an acceptable improvement in human well-being. Quite the opposite. So-called normal growth rates in poor countries, that is, those true of the 1990s, will result in more abject poverty, not less. AIDS unhindered will damage and possibly destroy populations and their economies. Other epidemic killer diseases will at least ensure that no greater economic progress is possible. In terms of equality, however, the result is worse: Rich countries will get "better," thanks to a pharmaceutical industry dedicated to our ills, while poor countries ignored by same will slip further behind in key indices such as life expectancy and economic productivity. Better fed, better educated, and disease-managing peoples will produce more per capita in rich countries, pulling further away from their brethren in poor countries. In all, doing nothing entails accepting more inequality in the long run.

What Is to Be Done?

Let us agree, then, that something must be done, for the sake of universal well-being. But what must be done is as complex as the world is, and as we are capable of being. I have already established that in some significant sense we "need" opinions and beliefs about what works and what doesn't by virtue of the fact that our values turn us outward into the social world and toward its improvement. I have also established at the beginning of this chapter that we intervene in the world in a number of ways via our roles as citizens, workers, and consumers, as well as through membership in organizations and participation in social movements.

Hence, we will need to cast a wide net, encompassing remedies global and local, universal and particular. We might be mindful of Karl Popper's injunction that it is better to approach solutions to social problems piecemeal, more as bits of social engineering, than to undertake the world's total redesign.[9] This does not mean, for instance, that we could not finally recommend a global system of universal basic health care, for in the nature of the solution itself, we still have the possibility of estimating benefits, costs, and advantages—in short, we can have an argument about its efficacy with a mix of theoretical inquiry and empirical evidence.

Popper means to caution against erecting utopias—those total visions of another world solely in which the author picks and chooses willy-nilly the assumptions about the living and the dead she wishes to observe. The danger comes in the detachment of the author—and by implication the reader and the follower—from the stubborn materiality of life. In a vision, we might imagine rocks removed; in concrete engagement with reality, we realize that some rocks like mountains are best walked around. The fear arises for Popper, and should arise for us as what Albert Schutz called "wide-awake" persons, that when utopian thoughts are harnessed to state power and empire, people find themselves compelled to move mountains, often causing immeasurable pain and suffering. For Popper, it is the power of putting utopian visions into practice that has been so costly for the human condition over the past 100 years.

Two important caveats are in order. The first concerns the issue of sustainability and the second the question of freedom.

Sustainability as a concept was strongly endorsed in 1987 by the World Commission on Environment and Development,[10] a group convened by authority of the United Nations General Assembly to examine the effects of growing ecological problems on the prospects for further world economic development. The commission argued that development without heed for its environmental costs could lead to a serious world ecological crisis. They argued that development should be "sustainable," which means that our efforts to increase well-being worldwide should not compromise the needs of others in the future seeking to meet their own needs. "The concept of sustainable development," the commission acknowledges, "does imply limits—not absolute limits but limitations imposed by the present state of technology and social organization on environmental resources and by the ability of the biosphere to absorb the effects of human activities." This report was written before global warming and a host of other potentially catastrophic ecological problems became daily concerns, and the commission was relatively optimistic that world poverty could be eliminated, and believed that "technology and social organization can be both managed and improved to make way for a new era of economic growth."[11]

The glow of their guarded optimism has faded since 1987, as further analysis of ecological problems has deepened awareness, and more unforgiving

nvironmental economics have exposed the high costs of unfet-
ic growth when environmental degradation is factored into the
ernational conventions in Rio de Janeiro (1992), Kyoto (1997),
and Johannesburg (2002) have tried to create new, environmentally friendly
norms for economic growth, while attempting to secure agreements that
would regulate some of the more obvious activities that threaten the earth as
one ecozone.

A high degree of environmental concern is warranted and should guide
our exploration of economic alternatives. As such, it is useful to think of sustainability as a material constraint on our actions. Much as the necessity to
show a profit is a requirement of a successful business plan, I would suggest
we adopt some version of environmental sustainability as a criterion that
proposed initiatives should be able to satisfy.

Sustainability is a notoriously fuzzy concept, let us admit that straightaway. The 1987 UN commission implied a number of things, most fundamentally that economic growth must *sustain* a decent standard of living for
the world's poor. It argued for policies that would assure moderate population
growth. It called for the conservation of global resources and the reorientation of technology toward ecological improvement rather than degradation.
It encouraged environmental risk assessment and a new mix of environmental planning with economic analysis.[12]

Think of sustainability as a blunter instrument. If a proposal looks as if it
will significantly degrade the environment, then we can use the constraint
of sustainability to rule it out. Take a concrete instance. In some parts of the
world, vast numbers of people—1.6 billion by some estimates[13]—live with
no electricity, and sometimes these same peoples could generate electric
power by exploiting ample coal reserves. Coal remains the least expensive
fuel one can burn, and in comparison with other more environmentally
sound sources like solar power, it is ten times cheaper.[14] At the same time,
the negative impacts of coal burning are well known. Not only does burning coal contribute huge quantities of carbon dioxide into the atmosphere,
which is believed to add significantly to global warming, but the air pollution it causes is one of the leading causes of preventable death.[15] Though
providing everyone with electricity would be a measurable step toward
greater economic equality, and coal burning the most efficient means, its environmental and health effects would suggest that it is unsustainable as a
strategy for improving well-being.

To be sure, this argument could be put more positively. We could imagine
valuing sustainability as a thing in itself, and encouraging the development
of a kind of environmental economics in which environment-friendly factors

had a priority in our thinking. But I think it is better to use sustainability as a constraint rather than as a value for several reasons. First, it acts as something of a reality principle in our efforts to achieve greater equality. It represents the rough materiality that we have argued is necessary to avoid straying down impractical, even disastrous, paths that we might contrive to cope with such a perfidious foe as inequality. Second, for all of the reasons given earlier, equality is a paramount value, and in our attempts to sort out the complex possibilities and effects of certain courses of action, it is useful to keep it, above all, in mind.

The second caveat: Valuing equality highly can limit an individual's or a people's freedom. The philosopher John Stuart Mill had it right, though he cast the relationship in the negative: Private property, according to Mill, was a person's defense against exploitation.[16] Most proposals we can make here will likely abridge the liberties of someone, particularly her rights to unfettered ownership and control over private property. Why? All of the claims we have made thus far about the direction of economic change suggest that the following two things are true. First, economic growth, however accelerated, is not enough to solve the problems of economic inequality. Second, doing nothing more and hoping for the best mocks our moral commitment to equality for the sake of universal well-being, because the deep-seated problems of inequality will not be solved without positive intervention in our economic affairs. Resources will need to be redistributed from the rich to the poor, both within states and among states.

Property, though it often connotes something stable like a lot or a home to which we have title of ownership, refers to a much broader class of things or resources over which we have control.[17] Our incomes and any accumulated capital in whatever form are also our property, as well as the rights we retain for ourselves through the use of patents and copyrights, among other things. Moreover, it is the freedom with which we are capable of dealing with something called "my property" that is important as well. If you own something, you believe that you also own the ability to sell, give, or use that something largely according to your personal wishes. In the United States, most of us do concede the state's right to a portion of that asset in the form of taxes raised for the common good. Having said that, though, it rather exhausts our usual concept of the limits imposed on our use of what is "ours."

The concession to taxation, however, is an important abridgment of our absolute freedom. It is also the same sort of limit on freedom that can be expected to arise from our work on equality. I think we can expect that, in moving resources from the rich to the poor even via a mechanism as common as taxation, we nonetheless will be limiting the absolute freedom of others to control their resources completely. I think it well, too, that we acknowledge that some ways of life based upon enormous wealth will be harder to pursue, if our projects for equality dramatically increased the amounts of funds that will need to be redistributed for their success.

Some writers, like Ronald Dworkin, argue that equality and liberty are compatible. He says that no one would worry about inequality unless there were liberty in the first place in a society that is based upon his notion of "equal concern." He also believes that no real political world can improve upon the problem of equality by sacrificing liberty because no one would support it.[18]

While Dworkin's attempt to save liberty from equality may or may not have theoretical merit, I would argue that the demands of equality and freedom, or liberty, are not as clearly theoretically incompatible as they are practically incompatible. In this, I would follow Isaiah Berlin, a philosopher who might otherwise choose liberty over equality, who makes it clear that in the world we live in, rather than the one we might fantasize, values as fundamental as liberty and equality are in conflict:

> But if we are not armed with an *a priori* guarantee of the proposition that a total harmony of true values is somewhere to be found—perhaps in some ideal realm the characteristics of which we can, in our finite state, not so much as conceive—we must fall back on the ordinary resources of empirical observation and ordinary human knowledge. And these certainly give us no warrant for supposing (or even understanding what would be meant by saying) that all good things, or all bad things for that matter, are reconcilable with each other. The world we encounter in ordinary experience is one in which we are faced with choices between ends equally ultimate, and claims equally absolute, the realization of some of which must inevitably involve the sacrifice of others.[19]

As sensitive to the practical facts of living as Berlin is, let us concede some loss of liberty as the price of equality. In the practice of robust welfare states, we see this trade-off exactly. In Sweden, Norway, Austria, Denmark, and Belgium, dubbed "high-income, high-equity societies," the tax burden is high and the economic inequality low.[20] These societies transfer wealth from the richer to those who have less. Thus, the parameters of some of what we will propose are less an innovation than the use of a time-honored accommodation—albeit now projected on a worldwide scale.

How Shall We Proceed?

In proposing remedies and measuring them in terms of the degree to which they reduce economic, social, and political equality, we need to align two things. The first is a sensible picture of the world and its dimensions; the second is our own interests and their dimensions. As to the latter, we discussed at the beginning of this chapter the many ways in which we are involved in the world, whether it be as producers, consumers, citizens, or participants in popular movements and public initiatives. Ours is a complex set of attachments that require of us a rather comprehensive and considered view of proposed solutions that involve us in everything from marching against world hunger on a Saturday afternoon, to donating money to humanitarian organizations, to paying our taxes, to pressuring our elected representatives, to electing our elected representatives, including the president. Our rather complete involvement in the world means that we need to evaluate how many actions in many contexts might diminish inequality in the world.

If our personal worlds and attachments are complex, then "the world" itself at times seems unfathomable. Where do we begin? How do we get a handle on this most complex of human realities?

I suggest that at the risk of doing some damage to our ability to see the whole, we must begin to divide the world into workable contexts for evaluating what can be done. Problems, as geographers such as David Harvey and Neil Smith have shown, can be conceptualized as being spatially scalar.[21] That is, one can begin to imagine a problem as contained in or inhabiting one or more planes of experience in space and time. As Harvey points out, we often lump social and economic phenomena into conventional scales from household to community, to nation, to globe, and so on. But behind this seemingly commonsensical classification scheme, a lot of our assignment of scales to problems has to do with how we conceive of their significance, as well as their causes and effects. For instance, now, in contrast to centuries past, poverty, genocide, and war-making—to name a few—are treated as problems on a global scale that come before the world as a community. In the twentieth century, the status inequality of women vaulted from the status of an artifact of households to a global problem of well-being. The aim of this book is also to elevate the problem of inequality to that of a worldwide, and not simply a national or community, concern.

These scales, as Harvey notes, are interrelated contexts for human problems:

> We also know that what happens at one scale cannot be understood outside of the nested relationships that exist across a hierarchy of scales—personal behaviors (e.g., driving cars) produce (when aggregated) local and regional effects that culminate in continent-wide problems of, say, acid deposition or global warming.[22]

As a consequence, we need to propose solutions within and across scales of human activity. We also need to imagine combinations of solutions that are aimed at different scales of the same problem.

Let us take up as a preliminary thought experiment the example of rural poverty worldwide. As we have noted in another context above, three-quarters of the world's poor live in rural areas. Suppose we isolate three key factors related to why agriculture, for instance, does not improve incomes in rural areas. The first fact we encounter is that poor people in poor countries are often deprived of land to work because large landholders monopolize markets for arable land.

Second, if the poor do have land, they find prices depressed for the staples they grow, typically two-thirds of their income, because rich nations such as the United States and those of the European Union subsidize their farmers' staple crops. The farmers in rich nations are thereby encouraged to grow more than they can sell at a profit in the market, picking up the difference from their governments. They dump their staple crops on the world market, depressing world prices, while receiving approximately US$350 billion in subsidies.[23] The World Bank estimates that depressed grain prices, combined with protective import barriers and tariffs levied by northern countries on the agricultural exports of poor countries, costs farmers in poor countries approximately US$100 billion a year in lost income. This is a loss of great magnitude—almost twice the amount of development assistance or "foreign aid" that moves from rich countries to the poor a year.[24]

Third, unlike in the case of the Green Revolution for crops such as rice, wheat, and corn, little technical progress has been made in improving the productivity of such plants as sorghum, yams, and cassava that are basic to the diets of large parts of Africa. Because sorghum, yams, and cassava are not on the same par as wheat, corn, and rice as commodities on the world market, there is less investment, public or private, in improving output.[25]

Using different geographical scales, we see that actions on several planes are necessary. First, on a national scale, there is a need for land reform. Take the case of Brazil. The International Fund for Agriculture and Development (IFAD) reports that Brazil has "one of the highest concentrations of land ownership in the world": 1 percent of the population owns 46 percent of the land. Of the total amount of land in private hands, only 15 percent of it is cultivated; the rest of the land is "either lying idle or given to pasture or held simply for speculative purposes." At the same time, 4.5 million families are landless.[26]

At the national level, therefore, political action is necessary. Moreover, social movements that seek land reform in the countryside deserve support

too. The *Movimento dos Trabalhadores Rurais Sem Terra* (MST, Landless Peasants' Movement) is composed of peasants and landless rural people who have
fought since the 1970s for redistribution and limits on maximum allowable
landholdings. Their platform seeks reforms that will improve the lives of
people in the countryside, Brazil's poorest population, and guarantee food at
an affordable price for all Brazilians. Through their efforts since 1992, 6 million hectares of land has been acquired and redistributed to 140,000 landless
families, many of whom were subsequently organized into rural cooperatives
to support the new cultivators' activities. Wages for cultivators as well as for
workers in agro-industries that process and commercialize their surpluses
have risen significantly.[27]

More can be done at the international level. Rich countries can reform
their agricultural policies, supporting farmers' incomes directly if they
choose, rather than pursue policies that protect their crops at home and encourage them to dump surplus crops for which they have already in effect
been paid via subsidies on the world market. Without reform, their effects
continue to be deadly. The World Bank and the IMF recently estimated that
if world cotton prices were not depressed by subsidies, rural poverty in a
country like Burkina Faso, a cotton exporter, could be cut in half over the
course of six years.[28]

The Green Revolution attempted to relieve rural poverty by increasing
agricultural productivity through irrigation, increased fertilizer use, and the
deployment of high-yielding hybrid varieties of basic staples such as wheat,
corn, and rice. By some measures, it was very successful. Over twenty-five
years, it doubled the food supply in Asia while expanding actual agricultural
acreage by only 4 percent. Poverty rates in affected areas fell significantly. By
other measures, it has been less successful. Rural economic inequality seldom
declined. The technological fix it entailed seems to have reached the point
of diminishing returns, as crop yield growth has declined throughout the
1990s.[29]

Let's look at the three solutions, ranging in scale from national to international planes. A renewed Green Revolution financed by rich nations may be
something good to do, especially as efforts could be concentrated this time on
the neglected staple crops of Africa. But it may not be the place to start, for
equality purposes. On the other hand, land reform remedies the source of rural economic inequality—landlessness on the part of the majority—and social
inequality in the form of stigma and discrimination foisted upon rural people
by an oppressive rural class structure and by states that tilt their efforts, insofar as they make any, toward the satisfaction of the needs of people who have
left the countryside and moved to cities. Importantly, there is a popular social

movement dedicated to the cause of equality and agitating for fundamental social change. Finally, agricultural policy reform on the part of rich nations, to the extent that the experts are correct, could provide as much as US$100 billion in additional income to farmers in poor countries. This would amount to an income transfer and a net gain, since the farmers in poor countries are already producing the goods, but being paid poorly for them.

Let us observe what we have just done using the case of the rural poor and agriculture. First, we have identified distinct planes or scales where solutions could be tried. Second, we have tried to gauge their general relevance and effectiveness. Third, we have applied the criterion of equality to evaluate whether the measures, if taken, would advance human well-being. Given the way we have developed the case, the economic dimension of inequality received our primary, though not sole, attentions.

In the chapters that follow, we will see if we can succeed with this method.

Notes

1. David Brown, "Study: AIDS Shortening Life in 51 Nations," *Washington Post*, July 8, 2002, A2.

2. Geoff Dyer, "Research into Drugs for the Poor 'Virtually Halted,'" *Financial Times*, June 26, 2002, 7.

3. International Fund for Agricultural Development, *The Challenge of Ending Rural Poverty: Rural Poverty Report 2001* (New York: Oxford University Press, 2001), 32.

4. World Bank, *World Bank Development News Press Review*, April 22, 2002, 8.

5. Robert Taylor, "ILO Highlights Lack of Pensions Worldwide," *Financial Times*, April 28, 2000, 3.

6. David Dollar and Paul Collier, *Globalization, Growth and Poverty* (Washington, D.C.: World Bank, 2002), 2–5.

7. International Fund for Agricultural Development, op. cit., 76.

8. United Nations Conference on Trade and Development (UNCTAD), *The Least Developed Countries Report 2002: Escaping the Poverty Trap* (June 2002), available at www.unctad.org/en/pub/ps1ldc02.en.htm, accessed June 27, 2002.

9. Karl Popper, *The Poverty of Historicism* (New York: Harper and Row, 1964), 58.

10. Headed by Gro Harlem Brundtland, then prime minister of Norway, it is often referred to as the Brundtland Commission.

11. The World Commission on Environment and Development, *Our Common Future* (New York: Oxford University Press, 1987), 8.

12. Ibid., 43–65. For a solid analysis of the rise of sustainability as a concept, and as it was used by the Brundtland Commission, see Aidan Davison, *Technology and the Contested Meanings of Sustainability* (Albany: SUNY Press, 2001), 11–36.

13. "Environmental Enemy No. 1," *Economist*, July 6–12, 2002, 11. Rich countries like the United States, while fully cognizant of the risks, rely upon coal burning for a sizable percentage of their power output.

14. Neela Banerjee, "Economic Interests Keep Drive for Renewable Energy Stuck in Neutral," *New York Times*, August 20, 2002, D9.

15. Neela Banerjee, op. cit.

16. Quoted in Saral Sarkar, *Eco-Socialism or Eco-Capitalism: A Critical Analysis of Humanity's Fundamental Choices* (London: Zed Books, 1999), 178.

17. C. M. Hann, "Introduction: The Embeddedness of Property." In *Property Relations: Renewing the Anthropological Tradition* (Cambridge, U.K.: Cambridge University Press, 1998), 34.

18. Ronald Dworkin, *Sovereign Virtue: The Theory and Practice of Equality* (Cambridge, Mass.: Harvard University Press, 2000), 182.

19. *Four Essays on Liberty* (Oxford, U.K.: Oxford University Press, 1969), 168. John Rawls, *Political Liberalism* (New York: Columbia University Press, 1993), 197, cites with agreement Berlin's claim that not all values can be accommodated in one world, remarking that "no society can include within itself all forms of life . . . there is no social world without loss."

20. David Dollar and Paul Collier, op. cit., 122.

21. David Harvey, *Spaces of Hope* (Berkeley: University of California Press, 2000), 75–77.

22. Ibid., 75.

23. World Bank, "U.S. Farm Bill Flouts Consensus on Helping Third World," *Development News Press Review*, May 6, 2002, 2.

24. Hilary French, "Reshaping Global Governance." In Worldwatch Institute, *State of the World Report 2002* (New York: W. W. Norton, 2002), 185.

25. International Fund for Agricultural Development, op. cit., iv, 7, 23; "Special Report: Trade Disputes," *Economist*, May 11, 2002, 66.

26. International Fund for Agricultural Development, ibid., 222.

27. Ibid.

28. World Bank, op. cit., 3.

29. International Fund for Agricultural Development, op. cit., 128–35.

CHAPTER EIGHT

Equality among Nations

Valuing equality weighs upon us straightaway. Let us confess at the outset that few standards in human affairs set the bar as high as does valuing equality. Halting hunger, eliminating poverty—these are daunting goals. But they do not ultimately satisfy the stricter demands of equality. Moreover, we have argued for a fairly stringent application of equality, steering toward equality of outcomes over a guarantee of equality of opportunity wherever possible. This puts the bar higher yet.

At the same time, we confront a world so unequal that no list of remedies offers any immediate prospect of achieving the total result. Our remedies will inevitably be partial, ameliorative, rather than entirely curative. Then, too, the list we could compose will inevitably be incomplete: No one book, no one author, advantaged though she may be by having access to social thought from around the world, can produce a set of efficacious initiatives complete enough to achieve the final result. Following Karl Popper, as we discussed earlier, we should probably mistrust such a list and its promise anyway.

What can we do? We can set about proposing and examining remedies with a single criterion: Does the remedy advance equality in all or any of its several dimensions? Sometimes the remedies upon brief examination appear as clear cases in which an improvement in equality could be readily expected. Other times, the cases will be close and require more detailed analysis and perhaps comparison with other possible remedies to see how valuable one or more of them are. In all, though, since this book is about thinking about economic alternatives, each case we examine enhances our capacity to analyze others with equality in mind. The results should be beneficial for other people's lives and improve our own abilities to work for the greater good.

So let us start with the clear cases, those in which the arguments are fairly clear-cut, and then move on to the close ones. At the same time, we take the vantage point of looking at the world with a global perspective. What can we unlock or unleash at the global scale that will enhance equality in people's everyday lives?

World Governance: One Person, One Vote

The world's governmental institutions do not advance political equality, the absence of which leads them toward less-than-salutary work on the problems of social and economic equality. They are neither formally democratic, nor effectively democratic in the terms we have discussed in earlier chapters.

First to form. Global institutions such as the United Nations (UN), the World Bank, and the International Monetary Fund (IMF), the foundations of our present international order, are not organized democratically. Established by the victors of World War II under the primary though not exclusive tutelage of the United States, they reflected the power politics of their time, not the desire, as we have discussed before, for the "fullest possible participation" of all involved. Thus, the Security Council of the United Nations was installed in addition to the general assembly of all nations to ensure that the world powers of the time had ultimate control over matters of war and peace. The delegation to five permanent members of absolute veto power over UN Security Council actions has drawn repeated criticism, and there is pressure to reform it institutionally too.[1]

Both the World Bank and the IMF also have dual governance structures. At the IMF, each member country receives 250 basic votes; another portion is doled out on the basis of each country's comparative economic power. The effect has been to drastically dilute the share of basic votes in voting power; they now account for only 2 percent of all votes cast for policy decisions and loan agreements.[2] Africa, for instance, by virtue of its small economies, has only 2 percent of the IMF's total voting rights.[3] At the World Bank, each member nation has one vote but, again, the rest are determined by other criteria, in this case by the size of each state's contribution to the World Bank's working capital.

Consequently, committees composed of large shareholders such as the United States, Great Britain, Germany, France, Japan, and Russia make policies and approve loans at both institutions.[4] The IMF and World Bank were meant to operate like banks, and they still do. Their public purposes have not affected their largely "privatized" governance structures, though both organizations have tried since the 1990s to appear more responsive to the needs of poor countries and their peoples. Their bureaucracies are self-perpetuating and in some instances staffed through the use of national quotas that ensure that the powerful nations maintain a secure grasp on the organizations. It is still the case, for example, that a "gentlemen's agreement" allots the directorship of the IMF to a European and the presidency of the World Bank to a U.S. citizen.

Nor, as if by some miracle, are they effectively democratic. As we have discussed in earlier chapters, their missions reflect agendas, whether institutional as banks or political as instruments of foreign policy, of others than poor countries. Their policies, as many leading economists allege, may be more part of the problem than the solution to the vast problems of inequality we have discussed here.

The World Trade Organization (WTO), though a recent addition among world organizations, has also succumbed to processes whereby rich countries rule. It is vital because under its aegis, all world trade occurs. The UN Development Programme (UNDP) describes the WTO policy-making process this way:

> Decisions are based on "one country, one vote" and made by consensus, giving the WTO the appearance of democratic decision-making. . . . But in practice, the WTO is dominated by a few major industrial countries—while the poorest developing countries have little or no representation or negotiation capacity.[5]

"One country, one vote," it seems, may not be enough to have any impact on reducing inequality.

Not surprisingly, many have condemned and called for the dismantling of this spider's stratagem of entangling poor countries in a web of organizations run by the rich countries for their own benefit. The notion is to replace them with new organizations whose charters would be more responsive to the needs of the poor, as opposed to the rich.[6] If the task is to reform existing world organizations such as the IMF, World Bank, and WTO, every attempt should be made to assure that they enhance equality in all of its dimensions. To accomplish this, they will need to more securely guarantee political equality to all of their members. Political equality achieved by making them more democratic in operation would likely trigger shifts in policies and resource allocations that more fully reflect the wishes of poor countries. Though greater political equality is a virtue in itself, it would also seem reasonable to expect that policies would be more specifically directed toward reducing the gnawing economic and social inequalities we have observed worldwide.

Reform proposals like those put forth by the UNDP, for example, often call for increasing the number of votes for each nation, so that the proportion allocated on the basis of economic strength is diminished. In theory, this would improve the prospects of poor nations by increasing their proportion of votes in the total mix of voting.[7] Given the overall discriminatory bias in not only the form but also the actual operation of bodies like the three we have discussed, is this remedy sufficient? Perhaps we should go one step further. Though we could stop at advocating what is essentially a variation on "one nation, one vote" in "one nation, many votes," it would be interesting to consider the effects of "one person, one vote," and its implications for world governance. What if nations in these international bodies had as many votes as they had persons? This would mean that the poor would have a majority in the world's economic decision-making bodies. Their impact, as is true now, would probably be diluted somewhat by the complexities of national rule whereby in many nations, richer minorities lead poorer majorities. But we would be putting democratic powers one step closer to the effective demands of the world's majority who are poor. The poor's leaders, whatever their social stripe, would be shaping world economic policy, and the hope is that they would be responsive to the needs and desires of their poor majorities.

Reforms of this sort inevitably diminish the freedom of rich countries to do as they please, for if effective, reordering governance should lead to greater demands upon their resources by the world's poor majority. The goal is greater equality in which political equality is both a means and an end in itself. To submit to democratic rule, to live with Dworkin's "equal concern" for all, is something we strive for in the United States, however imperfectly we achieve it. The context has shifted: We live or can strive to live in a democratic world.

Free Trade for Poor Nations

The great historian Fernand Braudel always argued that we confused capitalism with free markets. Capitalism is not the ideology capitalists mouth; it is what they do, which is making the most money they can any way they can. Braudel believed that capitalists in fact abhorred competition, which lowered their profits, and ceaselessly sought to fix the game by getting states and other players to help them obtain rules that benefited them and smote their enemies.[8] State connivance, as Karl Polanyi showed even before Braudel, kept capitalism as an economic engine from coming off the rails by absorbing the shocks of worker discontent over chronic bouts of unemployment.[9]

And so it is, at least with world trade—a US$7 trillion business. Rich countries at the behest of people in several economically and politically important sectors of their economies have successfully fixed the rules of world trade to redound in favor of their home producers. Consider this astonishing fact: The poorer you are, the higher tariffs your products face abroad. The effective tariff faced for goods produced by people making less than US$1 a day or for people making less than US$2 a day was 14 percent of the value of the product. Tariffs for goods produced by people making more than US$2 a day averaged 6 percent of the value of the product. This means that poor people face tariff barriers that are on average two and one-third times higher than those faced by people from richer countries. This creates, in effect, an additional tax on the goods of poor people and diminishes their markets.[10]

For poor countries, the losses are catastrophic. It is estimated that poor countries lose US$700 billion annually in potential export earnings, an amount equal to 12 percent of their combined gross domestic product, because of the various devices rich countries deploy to protect their home markets and producers.[11]

Discrimination occurs across the board, but the areas of most serious concern regard agriculture, textiles, and clothing—all bottom-line poor country exports. With respect to agricultural products, the rich countries play the game on both sides of their borders. Inside the borders of the United States, Canada, and the European Union, producers are helped in a number of ways. Farmers may be paid direct subsidies for their agricultural production: for every bushel of corn, wheat, soybeans, or rice, they may be paid a guaranteed fixed amount or an amount consisting of the difference between their costs of production and profit and the market price, the so-called parity price. At the same time, quotas and tariffs are placed on agricultural imports to support higher domestic prices for homegrown goods. Being paid to plant, farmers produce an abundance beyond what the national market can absorb, so they dump the rest of their production on the world market for whatever price it can fetch. Since their surpluses often produce surpluses in world markets, the price of goods plummets. Producers without subsidy or producing at a higher cost of production than the subsidized farmers from the rich countries lose money and market share. Many are driven out of the market entirely.

The stakes are high for rich countries. Aside from the political favor that officeholders curry with voters in agricultural regions, agriculture is a big business. It gives one pause to consider that the United States has a 72 percent share of the world market for corn, 49 percent share of the market for soybeans, 23 percent of the market for wheat, and 11 percent of the market for rice. Production for the market is controlled by large transnational agro-corporations like Archer Daniels Midland and Cargill, both of which are among the largest U.S. campaign contributors to candidates for federal office. The lion's share of the subsidies does not go to the family farmer, but into the hands of grain dealers and corporate farms. The pressure of these powerful forces was so intense that the United States in 2002 passed a farm bill that increases—not decreases—subsidies for growing crops, much of which will eventually be dumped on the world market, causing more pain and failure for small farmers around the world.[12] As noted in the preceding chapter, if we add up all the rich countries' agricultural subsidies, not counting the increases allocated in the U.S. Farm Act, we come up with an estimated US$350 billion a year—seven times the foreign aid that the rich pass to the poor yearly, and equivalent to fully 40 percent of the value of agricultural production in the rich countries. To put this number in perspective, US$350 billion in agricultural subsidies to farmers in rich countries is roughly equivalent to the gross domestic product of all of sub-Saharan Africa.[13]

Outside their borders, the rich countries seek markets for their agricultural goods by forcing poor countries to drop their tariff barriers and quotas on their agricultural imports. Their instrument is the IMF. Oxfam, an international nongovernmental organization with a long record of working for economic development in poor countries, provides some sobering instances of how it works. Haiti, as part of an IMF agreement, reduced its rice import tariff from 35 percent of the price of the product to 3 percent over the course of a year. Oxfam reports that within the space of another year, rice exports from the United States wiped out "tens of thousands of small producers." In Jamaica, the European Community is the benefactor. Under an IMF accord, Oxfam says that Jamaica lowered its tariff on milk, and EU producers selling subsidized milk at cheap prices are driving 3,000 poor Jamaican dairy farmers out of work.[14]

European milk becomes a problem for Indian producers as well, according to Oxfam:

> Consider the Indian dairy sector, now one of the largest milk producers in the world and a potential exporter. Even if it could overcome EU tariffs of 144 percent on butter and 76 percent on milk powder, it could hardly compete in Europe with domestic producers, half of whose income is derived from subsidies. Nor can it compete with EU milk-powder exports, sold at about half the cost of production in third markets such as the Middle East and southern Mediterranean. It is not surprising that Europe is the world's largest exporter of skimmed milk powder. Ironically, the EU was one of the aid donors that supported the development of the Indian industry in the first place.[15]

Thus, rich countries by subsidies, protection, and dumping agricultural products devastate the poor, 70 percent of whom rely on agriculture directly or indirectly for their livelihoods, and who produce precisely those staples that are the specialties of the overproducing rich.[16] Agricultural products comprise a third of poor countries' exports.[17]

For poor countries, so often trapped in discouraging markets for agricultural goods, or producing basic commodities such as unrefined basic metals (also products with uncertain market prospects), the manufacture of clothing, textiles, and footwear is often an important first step. Local handicraft traditions equip local people with know-how. The technology is cheap and easily acquired or transferred—often picked up via second-hand machines from rich countries. And of course, the markets for clothing, textiles, and footwear are enormous.

Yet again, the rich countries refuse to give up markets to poor producers of clothing, textiles, and footwear, areas where, at the low end of these vast markets, the poor producers with lower costs have a comparative advantage. The United States and the European Union, for instance, rely on import quotas to limit the influx of goods from outside, and they levy tariffs on those that they do import. Notwithstanding special concessions granted over the years to Mexican, Central American, Caribbean, and some Latin American producers, the United States still exacts 42 percent of its total tariffs from levies on clothing and textiles. Though a 1994 world trade agreement phases out many of the barriers on textile exports from poor to rich countries, the tariffs will remain high, roughly three times those levied for other industrial goods.[18]

What can rich countries do for poor countries that would reduce worldwide economic inequality? Providing open and unfettered access to their markets for exports from poor countries would be a crucial as well as a clear step toward providing increased economic opportunity. And, if we take any part of the theory of comparative advantage as salient, opening markets to producers in poor countries should significantly raise their incomes and reduce economic inequality between producers in rich countries and producers in poor countries.[19] Thus, we will make some progress toward assuring equality of outcomes with rewards tending toward producers in poor countries.

However, this is not a win-win game if you are a farmer in the United States or the European Union or if you work in a textile plant in a rich country. Losing markets implies losing jobs, and farmers and workers will lose jobs if we are successful in shifting resources via trade to poor countries. But there are several things to say that mitigate the losses. First, agricultural and the textile/clothing sectors in rich countries, despite their production, are economically very ill. This is why the rich countries subsidize them at enormous cost and protect them with quotas and tariffs. Making them healthier depends upon enlightened public policies that support their working populations at the same time they rationalize the industries so that they can compete fairly in international trade. Then, too, the United States could follow the initiative undertaken by the European Union to reorient agricultural production toward domestic consumption, carving out ecologically and economically sound niches for their farming communities.

Second, eliminating a system so damaging to the poor can have equality benefits in rich countries. The farm programs of the rich countries typically reward the large and often corporate farmer, rather than the family farmer. In the United States, a small minority of large farms, 10 percent in 1998, collected up to two-thirds of the farm subsidies. In the European Union, the largest 25 percent of the farms receive 70 percent of the subsidies.[20] The rich countries, in other words, help neither ordinary farmers in their own lands, nor poor farmers in other lands. They could, if they chose, open markets to poor country producers *and* reform their own farm programs, providing small farmers with incentives not to plant or to plant for local markets. This would positively reorient redistribution in rich countries toward greater equality. In the case of the textile and clothing industries, rich countries could make loans available for industrial upgrading of their domestic producers, as well as provide income support and retraining for unemployed workers.

Freer Labor Markets

Labor, too, is traded in markets, and those markets can be just as open or closed as markets for goods. Labor is the bedrock of our economies; through our work, we reproduce our societies. Thus, labor's movement across national borders is an important economic fact for individuals, nations, and the world economy. For instance, immigration was—and remains—one of the foundations of United States economic growth. While other societies, notably the European Union and Japan, experience an aging population and anticipate a decline in their economic prospects because their working-age populations are shrinking, the U.S. labor market grows younger. Immigrants replenish the labor supply and provide the means for further economic expansion. Increasingly, they are highly skilled workers: Some 50 percent of current migrants to the United States have some university training—a remarkable contrast to 100 years ago, when migrants were overwhelmingly composed of agriculturists with limited formal education.[21]

For sending as opposed to recipient countries, migration can be a mixed blessing. Economists in Mexico must wonder what the Mexican economy is losing when they calculate that 10 million Mexicans and Mexican-Americans now live in the United States—a number that is equivalent to 10 percent of Mexico's population. True, a portion of the value their labors create is repatriated in remittances, and the sum is significant. Mexicans and Mexican-Americans working in the United States passed US$6 billion in earnings in 1999 back to Mexico. Remittances for other countries are significant too: US$12 billion for India, US$5 billion for Turkey, US$4 billion for Egypt, and so on.[22] In total, foreign workers worldwide remit on average about US$75 billion to their home countries each year, a sum larger than all the foreign aid sent by rich countries to poor countries.[23] This is good news for poor countries. As the share of migrants from their countries increases, the proportion of the poor population at home decreases. The effect is significant: A World Bank study shows that a 10 percent increase in migration produces roughly a 2 percent decline in the proportion of poor people.[24]

For senders as well as receivers, there are also effects on wages and incomes. Senders, in these cases poor countries, could theoretically feel an updraft in the average wage, though this would depend on the emigration outflow creating tighter labor markets in economies with low unemployment—a situation true for only some of the better-off poor countries with strong economic growth. More typically, senders experience a "brain drain"—the loss of skilled workers who find better wages in rich countries than they do at home. For instance, Mexico, otherwise a winner when we measure only in terms of remittances, has lost 30 percent of its Ph.D.s to the U.S. labor market. Some estimate that African countries such as Ghana and Sierra Leone have lost as much as 30 percent of their highly educated citizens to emigration. Though many of the educated workers are actually trained as students in rich countries, poor countries have often footed the bill for their education. Thus, in effect, they not only lose the value of their skilled workers' future labors, but lose their training investment as well.[25]

The impact of immigration on receivers, in these cases rich countries, is somewhat mixed as well. Some workers in rich countries experience a downdraft in wages, particularly if they are unskilled and semiskilled workers. Increased competition from unskilled migrants in labor markets drives wages down, though the effects of skilled migrants on white-collar, professional and managerial wages are less clear.[26] Here, however, we have one of the probable reasons for increasing economic inequality in the United States, as there is evidence that migrant participation in our labor markets depresses the wages of low-wage workers.[27]

Assuming that the negative effects of migration on poor workers in rich countries can be remedied by government action such as income support and supplement programs, let us entertain a provocative proposal. To reduce worldwide inequality, suppose we encourage freer markets for labor migration. At the outset, let us observe that the overall effects of migration have remained small: Only 130 million, or 2.3 percent, of the world's population lives outside the countries of their birth.[28] Half of the world's migrants find themselves in rich countries, comprising 6 percent of their populations, while the rest find themselves living in other poor countries.[29] Suppose the rich countries marginally enlarged their temporary migration quotas for work, say to include up to 3 percent of their labor forces. The economist Dani Rodrik estimates that this would result in an increased net transfer of at least US$200 billion in remittances to poor countries each year.[30] To put that number in perspective, let us recall once more that total foreign aid flows from the rich to poor countries runs roughly US$60 billion a year. Consequently, liberalizing immigration could help poor countries realize substantial increases in personal income. Unskilled and semiskilled migrants most often pass on savings to their families; housing investments often ensue. Skilled and professional migrants not only pass on funds to families but also increasingly invest in the economic development of their homelands.[31]

As with the trade initiative, opening even marginally migration of temporary workers from poor to rich countries would probably reduce inequality between countries by raising incomes of people in poor countries via remittances. For unskilled worker migrants, higher wages and higher incomes for their households would result. With respect to skilled workers, the case is more complicated. As we noted, migration can become a brain drain of the skilled personnel of poor countries. How do we balance considerations? Or, better put, for whom do we balance considerations—for a society, for a group, or for individuals?

Our efforts to reduce equality began with the motive of enhancing universal well-being, a task that also addresses the need of individuals to enjoy meaningful lives, to fulfill in other words their "human vocation."[32] In this respect, we left open the possibility that proposals for improvement could be aimed at individuals of certain sorts, rather than be aimed always at the aggregate. Though later, for instance, we consider proposals about reducing gender inequality and thus enhancing the well-being of women as a group, we advocate in this case that individuals, skilled or unskilled, be free to find greater fulfillment—and reward—through migration to rich countries. Though this promises to be among the most piecemeal and incremental of our proposals, it reaches directly to the conditions of freedom under which millions of individuals labor as such, and thus, with the other benefits enumerated above weighed in, appears warranted. As a recompense, poor countries could tax remittance income as they tax any other wages earned by their citizens.

Once again, it behooves rich countries to develop policies and programs that support workers whose wages and employment are negatively affected by increased labor migration. They also must take steps to assure that migrant workers enjoy equal protection of the laws, including the right to join trade unions. These two safeguards are necessary to prevent businesses in rich countries—or rich states for that matter—from exploiting the vulnerabilities of foreign workers.

Global Health Care

Thus far, we have asked rich countries to undertake actions that have no costs or have more in the way of indirect costs. Achieving greater political equality in world organizations is not costly per se, but indirectly we could anticipate that resources would shift from rich to poor countries. In the cases of trade in agricultural products and textiles, and in labor markets, the transfers are again not strictly direct. By letting markets for the agricultural products, textiles, and apparel from poor countries grow, or by increasing migration flows from poor to rich countries, rich countries would doubtless feel negative effects. The damage is done to their own citizens by action of the markets. However, by virtue of their experiences in the development of welfare states, rich countries can provide remedies for their citizens who may be hurt by the success of poor countries. Most of them would need to expand services they already provide or make greater investments in training, education, and income support than they now do. The point is that they have the know-how and the resources, and probably the makings of a domestic consensus, to help their own citizens in need.

This is not enough. Redistribution of an indirect sort, consisting essentially of offering poor countries better access to markets for goods and labor in rich countries, could be thought of as the equivalent of providing "equality of opportunity." Under the proposals above, we are offering them the opportunity to compete as effectively as anyone else for resources and rewards in the marketplace. It is a strategy, as we have noted above, highly reminiscent of, if not identical with, the logic underlying programs for the disadvantaged in the United States. We believe in providing people with opportunities, but not guaranteeing outcomes. They should receive the training, but not the job. The latter they must obtain in open competition with others.

This standard—opportunity, not outcomes—is not the whole story, even in the United States. Though the U.S. welfare system is less a safety net than a sieve, it still recognizes that some basic human needs must be guaranteed for the worst off, even if it can't bring itself to guarantee everyone identical benefits as universal rights. Thus, the Medicaid program, for instance, provides complete health care for the eligible poor. The United States also guarantees a portion of its citizenry, the elderly, medical services under Medicare, largely regardless of their economic circumstances. Some equality of outcomes—that the elderly and eligible poor will receive all necessary medical care—is thus provided, even in the least generous of rich-country welfare states.

Suppose we imagine that poor countries stand in the same relation to us as the poor of the United States. What then becomes our obligation? Guaranteeing equality of outcomes finds both its reason and its precedent. And it is particularly in the field of medical care, aside from the protections against hunger that rich nations already provide via world relief agencies, that demands our closest attention. Aside from nourishment, adequate medical care is a fundamental requisite for survival itself. As dear as education, employment, and old age security are to the human vocation, none of these acquires value unless people can function physically with some chance of reaching their maturity.

Let us quickly review once more how deadly economic inequality is. People in poor countries die of treatable medical conditions and diseases in vast numbers. A woman is 100 times more likely to die during pregnancy or in childbirth in sub-Saharan Africa than she is in any rich country. Her children are more vulnerable too. When a child in the United States has an acute respiratory infection, a category that covers everything from the common cold and bronchitis to pneumonia, she sees a doctor, takes an antibiotic if indicated, and receives supportive care from her family consisting of extra nutrition and fluids. Though every mother worries, it is seldom a life-threatening condition. But in poor countries, the same conditions are killers, accounting for 20 percent of child deaths before age five. Supportive family care requires a minimum of human resources, but not having them is what being poor in a poor country means. Moreover, in most poor countries, doctors treat only half the number of children who suffer; in West Africa, doctors see fewer than one in five children.[33]

Assuming children survive to age five, other major killers await them. Malaria infects 500 million persons a year, and kills 1 million persons a year. Tuberculosis kills 2 million persons a year. AIDS has infected 42 million persons and kills 3 million persons a year. Most of the victims of these catastrophic diseases live in poor countries where therapies are few and death more certain than in rich countries.[34]

Yet therapies for these conditions exist in rich countries. For fifty years, doctors have been successfully treating most tuberculosis cases with drugs. In rich countries, we may be on the verge of transforming AIDS from a certain killer to a chronic disease. Effective supportive therapies and drugs have given sufferers hope and access to many more precious years of their lives. Even malaria, the least tractable of these three diseases worldwide, is preventable if you come from a rich country. For instance, when you travel from the United States to a malarial zone outside the country, your doctor's prescription of quinine is usually enough to prevent infection.[35]

People in poor countries do not have access to the medical care they need to combat these killers. They neither have the resources—read money—to devote to the necessary care, nor the medical infrastructure, that is, the doctors, nurses, health aides, drugs, health centers, and health education programs, to deliver it.

Poor health creates a vicious cycle: People in poor countries are poorer because they cannot get healthier. The reason is that a sick population produces less. Imagine if even just 10 percent of the adult population of your society suffered from untreated AIDS, tuberculosis, and/or malaria. The victims would suffer chronic fevers, anemia, and fatigue—all symptoms that would drastically reduce or eliminate their productivity as workers. Higher death rates would take their toll on the work force. Economists estimate that the sick and dying populations of poor countries result in a total of US$186 billion a year in lost production, goods, and services that could better feed their populations and help them build sustainable economies. And these societies pay the final price, experiencing the untimely and unnecessary deaths of 8 million persons a year.[36]

Suppose, then, we envision a system of basic health care for all poor citizens of the world. Perhaps this seems too daunting a prospect. But let us remind ourselves again that the world we live in knows for the first time in history the depth, distribution, and scope of human problems. We can locate and map the human battle with disease worldwide, down to the level of the province and the county, and often even the village. If anything, it is the mismatch of our age between what we know and what we are doing that incites greater and more profound moral reflection on the need to ensure well-being for all under conditions of greater equality.

We can also be encouraged by the fact that people have begun to imagine what such a system would look like, how much the first installment of it might cost, and how it could be constructed. The World Health Organization organized the Commission on Macroeconomics and Health in 1999 with the mission of studying the feasibility of a basic system of worldwide medical care. It argues that such a system should concentrate on the cata-strophic killers we have described above, and also focus on providing care for mothers, infants, and young children. In its view, these are the conditions that are most economically and socially costly. They are also those for which basic medical treatments have been developed and routinized through trial and error in millions of cases all over the world.[37]

The commission proposes that community health centers be established in every locality where none exists, and that care be supported, focused, and streamlined along lines it suggests in areas where they do exist. The audacity of its proposal lies in prescribing a world health care system—not in the modality that it chooses. If you think for a moment about the public health system in the United States, and you subtract the costly acute care infra-structure represented by our hospitals and urban medical centers, then you begin to see what the commission is after. The community health centers in the United States, for instance, deliver care to help people cope with diseases perceived as public health threats. In addition, the federal government sub-sidizes care and nutrition for poor mothers and children.

This, in a rough sense, is the commission's proposal. Once the centers are established worldwide, the commission envisions that people with other chronic diseases for which simple treatment regimes can be devised would also receive care. Treatment for diseases like hypertension, heart disease, and diabetes could be added to the centers' competencies. These diseases would become a treatment focus once the big killers were out of the way, allowing local populations to age and thereby became more liable to them.

This approach is not unprecedented. In fact, as the commission points out, it builds upon efforts since the 1950s that have undertaken interna-tional campaigns to eliminate specific diseases. Worldwide vaccination against scourges like polio and smallpox has eliminated them almost en-tirely. Initiatives against leprosy, guinea worm, Chagas' disease, and schisto-somiasis are beginning to show positive results. A global attack on AIDS has through fits and starts finally begun. Each of these attempts tells us more about how to help people effectively, even in the most unfavorable circum-stances.[38]

Centers such as those proposed by the commission are not as costly as one might assume. In fact, they estimate that it would cost around US$34 per year per patient to deliver the services discussed above. Poor countries now spend US$13 per year per person on health care. In total, the global program would cost in new monies US$57 billion in 2007, and rise with full imple-mentation to US$94 billion a year.[39] If rich countries undertook full funding of the program, it would effectively double their current foreign aid contributions of US$60 billion in 2007 and increase their commitment in 2015 again by another 60 percent of their current foreign aid.[40]

This is not a lot of money for rich countries. Their current foreign aid contributions amount to less than one-quarter of 1 percent of their gross domestic product. Doubling their commitment would increase their liability to one-half of 1 percent in 2007. Given that their economies are likely to grow at least marginally, the more money in aid needed for 2015 could probably be met out of income without increasing the percentage commitment of their gross domestic product.[41]

A proposal of this sort seems an obvious good thing. But we need to ask the question of how it meets our requirements for greater equality. To begin with, it provides equality of resources for some basic human killers. No dumbed-down or discount solutions are being contemplated here. The treatments offered are those that would be applied to people in rich countries should they be at risk of tuberculosis, malaria, and AIDS, or should mothers or their children need supportive care. It offers the prospect that people in poor countries will substantially improve their longevity and their overall health so that they, too, can appreciate the virtues of life after sixty—and in some cases fifty. As Amartya Sen would put it, helping people be healthy increases their capabilities for creating a life with more chances for well-being. And the costs of poor health—8 million dead yearly and US$186 billion in lost income—become gains.

The community health center focus also evens up the equality score among people in poor countries. The poor generally do not have much access to the health care that already exists in poor countries. Just as in rich countries, money is poured into maintaining acute care hospitals in the cities that offer little to residents of the countryside and little more to poor people living in nearby squatter settlements. The middle and upper classes, though a fraction of the population of poor countries, consume the lion's share of medical care and health services. As we noted in an earlier chapter, the top 20 percent of households in eight of twelve countries surveyed in a 1999 World Bank study got more than their statistical share of medical care. Shifting resources to where poor people are, and emphasizing the treatable conditions that can severely damage or end their lives, via the community medical center enhances the well-being of those who most need it. Studies of who is treated at existing community health centers confirms that the poor would be the most likely beneficiaries of services delivered in this rather direct and simple—when compared with hospital services—way.[42]

For these reasons, a global system that can deliver specific kinds of health care in this way shows significant promise of remedying existing inequality and foreclosing on the future inequalities that arise through the poor health of poor people.

Are There Other, Better Options?

Are there other, better options to the remedies advocated above? To be sure, there are other options, and perhaps some better ones. One thinks immediately of a worldwide progressive income tax that would redistribute the world's riches to the poor, a prominent and largely forgotten proposal of the 1980 North-South Development Commission headed by the late Willy Brandt.[43] It has been estimated, for instance, that with 2 percent of the gross domestic product of rich countries, the 1.2 billion poorest of the world's poor could move from a US$1 a day to a US$2 a day subsistence level.[44] At the same time, there are absolute limits to the good that redistribution can do. The deficit between North and South is so vast that a simple transfer of rich-country wealth would not automatically resolve the problem of equality.[45] This insight will lead us in a subsequent chapter to discuss the appropriate role of economic growth in tandem with distribution as part of the answer to persistent inequality.

New ideas are finding their way into earnest discussion. One of the most interesting, put forward by economist Robert Schiller, is a process whereby poor countries could lay off some of the downside risks of the development process—in this case, the real possibilities of economic failure—by selling bonds in an international market consisting of all other sovereign nations. Under this scheme, poor countries would sell securities for which, at the end of a determined period, the buyer, another sovereign nation, would pay the poor country if it could not meet its development goals. If the poor country met or exceeded its development goals, it would pay the bondholders a premium on their money. If a country succeeded, the premium would return more for the cost of capital borrowed, though it would be a small cost, since important economic growth would have sustained with the bonds. If the country could not succeed, then it would receive recompense from the bondholders that would help it sustain its society even as the economy floundered.[46] When we recall that according to the UNDP, fifty-four poor nations did not grow at all economically during the 1990s and are thus poorer now than before, the virtue of Schiller's idea becomes plain.[47] Had such a bond market as he advocates existed, these countries would have received significant transfer payments to help ameliorate the misery of their people.

Schiller's is an intriguing proposal, but may not be enough for our purposes. Though on initial inspection, it would in practice appear to transfer resources from rich to poor countries, its overall impact on narrowing huge gaps between rich and poor nations is uncertain. It would pay poor countries when they failed to grow economically. Under this condition, unless the rich countries failed to grow, too, the compensation would be unlikely to match the lost economic growth, and poor nations would either be falling further behind the rich or not making up ground. Within poor countries, the bond scheme might provide some economic protection as well as an incentive among the political and economic elite not to fail with their economic plans. But, as we have seen many times above, unless one acts directly to increase equality, one doesn't get it. Economic growth can lessen poverty, but it does not disproportionately reward the poor. In the best of circumstances, it acts evenly across social classes, raising the standard of living of each stratum in the rough proportion of the country's rate of economic growth. With growth, the poor may be better off, but they don't catch up with the rest of society. Hence, Schiller's proposal as it presently stands doesn't fully meet our equality needs.[48]

Our highly restricted selection of remedies—from democratizing global governance and freeing trade and migrant labor to funding global health care—helps us in the thought experiment of learning how we might refashion the world with equality as our guide. Then, too, the ambition of this book is to help us freshly imagine what can be done now that the world is set up as it is. Part of the challenge to our imaginations is extensional: We need to consider the implications of our beliefs in other, newer, broader contexts. Thus, as consistent with our beliefs, extension of democratic principles and procedures to world organizations becomes an inescapable commitment for which excessive "shaving," or modification of democratic processes for the comfort of the comfortable is difficult to countenance.

Another aspect of the challenge is to redefine our social obligations so that the "social" in the expression now connotes a worldwide responsibility for equality of opportunity. For instance, the sort of free trade and free labor proposals we have entertained imply that we assume an interest in equity or fairness in our transactions with all others, and especially with relatively powerless poor countries. Of course, rich countries could continue to subsidize their agricultural producers, protect traditional industries, and shut out migrant labor—or exploit that labor in the most base ways through the tool of illegality, as occurs in both the United States and Europe. But this would mean that we were unwilling to absorb the costs of providing rather minimal sorts of equality of opportunity for people in poor countries. It would also overlook some self-interested reasons that could still be adduced for extending our concerns: Agricultural goods and apparel would become cheaper with rich-country protection withdrawn, and the utilization of legal labor migrants adds real and significant taxable wealth to the coffers of host countries.

Accepting these costs would lighten poor nations' burdens while signifying our participation in a global network of economic support and reciprocity. But moving toward the provision of equality of resources worldwide represents perhaps the greatest extension of our concerns and beliefs. For if the transfers of resources are significant enough that we experience our wealth lessened at the cost of providing for people in poor countries, then we have loosed the bonds of strict reciprocity over our actions and embraced something remarkably similar to justice in world affairs.

Still, though our thought experiment rests upon the extension of our moral beliefs and our social responsibilities, some of the argument presented here must inevitably rely for support upon a pillar, however slender, of plausibility. Such questions as how would something work, do we have the resources at present to do it, can we foresee some prospect for an idea's acceptance, and so on, create the conditions whereby we can begin to take up a proposal seriously. It then invokes and tests our own beliefs and moral convictions. Dwelling exclusively on the implausible creates a discussion without real moral consequences. Ideas need to have consequences. And putting values in practice signifies that real choices must be made, if only at first to extend our view of the possible.

Notes

1. See United Nations Development Programme, *Human Development Report 2002: Deepening Democracy in a Fragmented World* (New York: Oxford University Press, 2002), 117–18, for a discussion of grievances about UN governance and of possible reforms.

2. Ibid., 114.

3. World Bank, *World Development News*, March 13, 3000, 2.

4. Ibid., 113.

5. Ibid., 121. For more commentary, see Hilary French, "Reshaping Global Governance." In Worldwatch Institute, *State of the World Report 2002* (New York: W. W. Norton, 2002), 194–95.

6. Walden Bello, *Deglobalization: Ideas for a New World Economy* (London: Zed Books, 2002), 104–12.

7. Hilary French, op. cit.,114.

8. Fernand Braudel, *The Wheels of Commerce: Civilization and Capitalism, 15–18th Century, Volume 2* (New York: Harper and Row, 1982).

9. Karl Polanyi, *The Great Transformation: The Political and Economic Origins of Our Time* (Boston: Beacon Press, 1944).

10. World Bank, "Global Economic Prospects and the Developing Countries," 2002, available at www.worldbank.org, quoted in Martin Wolf, "Broken Promises to the Poor," *Financial Times*, November 21, 2001, 13.

11. Oxfam, "Harnessing Trade for Development," *Oxfam Briefing Paper #1*, August 2001, 12, 7. Available at www.oxfam.org.uk/what_we_do/issues/key-papers.htm, accessed June 15, 2004.

12. Elizabeth Becker, "Raising Farm Subsidies, U.S. Widens International Rift," *New York Times*, June 15, 2002, A3. Oxfam, ibid., 33, reports that 70 percent of the world trade in agricultural commodities is controlled by no more than six transnational corporations, including those named in the text.

13. World Bank, "Agricultural Subsidies Must Be Cut, Nations Say," *World Bank Press Review*, August 28, 2002, 3. Oxfam, op. cit., 27.

14. Oxfam, "Europe's Double Standards: How the EU Should Reform Its Trade Policies with the Developing World," *Oxfam Briefing Paper 22*, April 2, 2002, 5. Available at www.oxfam.org.uk/what_we_do/issues/key-papers.htm, accessed June 15, 2004.

15. Ibid., 11.

16. World Bank, op. cit. International Fund for Agricultural Development, *The Challenge of Ending Rural Poverty: Rural Poverty Report 2001* (Oxford: Oxford University Press, 2001), 23.

17. Oxfam, "Harnessing," op. cit., 26.

18. Oxfam, "Europe's," op. cit., 14, 45.

19. Paul Krugman, *Pop Internationalism* (Cambridge, Mass.: MIT Press, 1996), 47–68.

20. Oxfam, "Harnessing," op. cit., 27–28.

21. World Bank, *World Development Report: Sustainable Development in a Dynamic World, Transforming Institutions, Growth, and Quality of Life* (New York: Oxford University Press, 2003), available at http://econ.worldbank.org/wdr/wdr2003/text-17926, accessed August 23, 2002.

22. David Dollar and Paul Collier, *Globalization, Growth and Poverty* (Washington, D.C.: World Bank, 2002), 44–47.

23. Ibid., 44–47. World Bank, *World Development Report 1999/2000: Entering the 21st Century* (New York: Oxford University Press, 2000), 39.

24. Richard Adams Jr. and John Page, "International Migration, Remittances and Poverty in Developing Countries," *World Bank Policy Research Working Paper 3179* (December 2003), available at http://econ.worldbank.org/view.php?type=5&id= 31999, accessed December 30, 2003.

25. "Outward Bound: Do Developing Countries Gain or Lose When Their Brightest Talents Go Abroad?" *Economist*, September 28, 2002, 24–26.

26. David Dollar and Paul Collier, ibid., 151.

27. Christopher Jencks, "Who Should Get In?" *New York Review of Books*, November 29, 2001, available at www.nybooks.com/articles/14868, accessed September 9, 2002.

28. World Bank, op. cit., 38.

29. David Dollar and Paul Collier, op. cit., 44.

30. Dani Rodrik, "Mobilising the World's Labour Assets," *Financial Times*, December 12, 2001, 14.

31. World Bank, op. cit., 39.

32. Ethan Kapstein, arguing for increased freedom of labor to migrate, asserts that otherwise "There is little reason for an individual to invest in education, training, and self-improvement if no jobs are available." See "Distributive Justice as an International Public Good: A Historical Perspective." In *Global Public Goods: International Cooperation in the 21st Century*, edited by I. Kaul, I. Grunberg, and M. Stern (New York: Oxford University Press, 1999), 104.

33. United Nations Development Programme, *Human Development Report 2003, Millennium Development: Goals: A Compact among Nations to End Human Poverty* (New York: Oxford University Press, 2003), available at www.undp.org/hdr2003, accessed July 9, 2003, 97–99.

34. Ibid., 97–100.

35. Ibid.

36. World Health Organization Commission on Macroeconomics and Health, *Macroeconomics and Health: Investing in Health for Economic Development*, December 20, 2001, www.who.int/macrohealth/en, accessed June 15, 2004, 12–13.

37. Ibid., 6–9.

38. Ibid.

39. The commission recommends a form of burden-sharing whereby poor countries increase their spending by 1 percent of the GDP in 2007 and 2 percent in 2015, an amount that would reduce the funding liabilities of rich countries to US$22 billion and US$31 billion, respectively, for those years. The commission foresees a planning process whereby national governments work their own special needs and capabilities into the mix of services provided. Ibid., 6, 11.

40. United Nations Development Programme, *Human Development Report 2003*, op. cit., 145–46.

41. Ibid.

42. World Bank, *World Development Report, 2000/2001: Attacking Poverty* (New York: Oxford University Press, 2001), 80–82. See also Dominique van de Walle, "Incidence and Targeting: An Overview of Implications for Research and Policy." In *Public Spending and the Poor: Theory and Evidence*, edited by D. van de Walle and K. Nead (Baltimore: Johns Hopkins University Press, 1995), 601–15.

43. Independent Commission on International Development Issues, *North-South: A Programme for Survival* (Cambridge, Mass.: MIT Press, 1980), 22.

44. Martin Wolf, "Spreading the World's Wealth," *Financial Times*, December 20, 2000, 15.

45. Anthony Giddens, *The Third Way and Its Critics* (Cambridge, U.K.: Polity Press, 2000), 129.

46. Robert Schiller, *The New Financial Order: Risk in the 21st Century* (Princeton, N.J.: Princeton University Press, 2003), 175–85.

47. United Nations Development Programme, *Human Development Report 2003*, op. cit., 2.

48. Schiller, in another equally interesting section of his book, proposes that the U.S. tax system be insured for not increasing economic inequality. He proposes that Congress set a limit to economic inequality via the measurement of the Gini index. Tax rates would adjust automatically to assure that economic inequality did not rise. Perhaps his international growth bond proposal could include an improvement in equality as part of the criteria for compensation. See Schiller, op. cit., 149–64.

CHAPTER NINE

Equality and Disadvantage Abroad

We must redress the balance of equality among nations. In the last chapter, we discussed how we might begin. In this chapter, we ask how we might apply the imperative of greater equality to aid populations throughout the world that are characterized by systematic disadvantage. Taking up the challenge of the deplorable condition of women in many situations worldwide, we try to discover what remedies now in use can assist them in achieving greater equality—and which are unlikely to achieve the objective.

Let us start from a standpoint where a contemporary market-friendly World Bank economist might begin. When faced with a problem that markets cannot readily solve, the economist speaks of "market failure." What she means is that one or more of a variety of circumstances can prevent markets from satisfying a buyer or a seller's need. Often, a lack of information separates buyer from seller. Someone needs coal and doesn't know who has it; someone has coal and doesn't know who needs it. The result is that neither party's need is satisfied, and presumably there is a missed opportunity for increased economic utility shared by society at large.[1]

We have made enormous strides in mastering the art of information-gathering, and this greatly improved access to information has helped markets expand dramatically, and in many cases to operate more efficiently. More coal buyers are finding coal sellers, one expects. New markets are also emerging. Consider the homely example of eBay: Who would have imagined ten years ago that someone could make markets that electronically connect buyers and sellers of everything from one-of-a-kind heirlooms like Grand-mother's Steinway baby grand piano to Barbie Doll paraphernalia?

There are, of course, cases that cut closer to the bone. For instance, artisans in poor countries throughout North Africa and the Middle East are now linked by Internet with craft buyers all over the world. The virtual souk, or market, has helped them increase their production and get better prices by dealing directly with the end buyers of their goods.[2] In Bangladesh, the organization of a network of individual women providing poor villages with cell phone service thanks to the ingenuity of the Grameen Bank enables small-scale women producers to get better prices for their goods. A quick call to a market center helps women keep track of prices for their goods and aids them in getting better prices from the itinerant wholesalers who move their produce to market.[3]

Economists have also helped nations and the international community make new markets in rather surprising commodities, such as pollution. Following the earlier success of creating a voluntary market for pollution permits among coal-burning industries in the United States, the international community, meeting in Kyoto, Japan, in 1997, framed an accord under which global pollution caused by carbon-burning of all sorts would be steadily reduced by assigning nations more limited pollution quotas. Should a nation exceed its quota, it would need to go on to the "pollution permit market" and purchase the right-to-pollute permits of other countries that had not exceeded their quotas, and thus had excess "pollution capacity" to sell. The price of pollution permits would fluctuate on an open market, much like the price of corn, stocks, and other commodities do in exchanges around the world.[4] Parenthetically, a pollution permit market would redistribute significant financial resources from rich to poor nations, as the world's prime carbon-burning polluters are rich countries, with the exception of China and Russia.

Markets of all of these sorts—from Barbie Dolls, North African artisan ceramics, and Bangladeshi cell phone calls to pollution—are possible because we are able to calculate the magnitude of world outputs with the irreplaceable aid of the products of the information revolution.[5] This astonishing capacity can help us improve the human condition.

Alas, information isn't everything. There is plenty of information, understood and accepted as fact by everyone from the social scientist to the person on the street about the greatest "market failure" of them all: the structures of inequality that deprive a majority of the world's population of some significant portion of their well-being. This in turn deprives the rest of the world from the benefits that derive from the full participation of disadvantaged peoples in the ongoing project of social life.

As we have noted in earlier chapters, situations of ethnic and racial as well as caste and caste-like disadvantage abound throughout the world. The consequences for those victimized are damaging to their well-being and degrading to their fundamental human dignity. Which among the many measures contemplated or already undertaken will bring more equality, and thereby, we believe, improve their lives? Taking up the case of improving the prospects for women may tell us a lot about what might be usefully done.

If women weren't a numerical majority of the world's citizens, we would probably best describe them in terms of a despised minority. Violence is visited upon them as if they were. The World Bank estimates that 20 percent of the world's women have been physically abused or sexually assaulted.[6] The facts of women's inferior status begin at—and in some cases—before birth. The abortion of female fetuses, the selective neglect of female newborns, the underfeeding of female young, all take their toll, so that demographers estimate that the world's population is between 60 million and 100 million women shy of what would be the likely world population, given human reproductive probabilities. Women's reduced educational and economic capabilities lead to stunted economic growth in poor countries. Women's low domestic autonomy and their poor educational and economic opportunities are all highly correlated with higher birthrates as well as higher rates of infant and child mortality.[7] Moreover, worldwide, women's wages, when compared with men's, continue to be significantly undervalued—the equivalent of 70 percent of that earned by men. "Women's work," their social reproduction of the population, is all but completely uncompensated, except in those few instances where nations indirectly subsidize mothers' child-rearing labors with grants for child support.[8]

Of course, first things first: nations need to assure equal rights for women as full citizens in their societies. Taking care to see that women are accorded the rights enumerated in the United Nations Declaration on Human Rights (discussed at length in an earlier chapter) would be an ideal starting place. Then, it is no doubt prudent, as the World Bank indicates, to encourage economic growth, as there is clear evidence that women benefit no less than men do from increasing national wealth. Once again, though, we learn that economic growth will not create enough equality, in this case for women, or, as the World Bank in its extensive analysis of gender in the development process puts it:

[E]conomic development and income growth tend to promote gender equality. But the positive effects of economic development can take a long time to play out. And they are not sufficient to eliminate gender disparities. Nor are they automatic. For these reasons governments and development organizations need to take a more integrated approach to promoting gender equality.[9]

At least since the first United Nations conference on women held in Mexico City in 1975, policy makers around the world have devoted a great deal of attention to the problem of gender equality in the distribution of economic rewards and resources. They have produced programs that try to increase women's educational attainment, employment, and access to financial resources.

Two programs have become significant options in trying to remove the burden of disadvantage by gender in local societies. A new approach is emerging in the development community. International organizations such as the World Bank, nongovernmental organizations (NGOs), foreign aid donors such as the United States Agency for International Development, and poor nations themselves have sponsored programs that offer women small loans to support small business development. They have also tried to encourage increased educational attainment among women by subsidizing the elementary and, in some cases, secondary education of young girls, on the theory that more education for women means higher earnings and faster economic development as a whole.[10]

Our question in each case is not whether each succeeds on its own terms. That is, whether the microlending program we are about to examine can get money to women, help their businesses flourish, successfully recoup its loans to poor women, loan the money out to others, and so on. It can be a success by the standards that we would ordinarily expect if we were purely interested in program effectiveness. The same would be true of educational efforts: Did the money reach the participants, did female school attendance go up, and so forth. While these questions are reasonable for our World Bank economist to ask, our overriding interest here, instead, is whether either program has any effect on reducing economic inequality that arises from gender differences.

Improving Equality for Women: The Case of Microlending

Poverty, as one wag once put it, is the absence of money. Poor people don't have money, and they don't typically have access to it via banks and credit unions. This does not mean that people are idle. Quite the contrary, people in poor countries spend enormous amounts of time scraping together a living, working in the market stalls, garages, alleyways, and kitchen tables of what is rather ambiguously referred to as "the informal economy." Few transactions are recorded, few taxes paid, and little money made in these kinds of economic environments.[11] Though illegal or unregulated labor makes up a significant portion of most informal economies, people put an enormous amount of energy into their own small businesses. Their activities—everything from selling farm goods and reselling household items to producing crafts and small services—consist for the most part of eking out a living selling to poor people like themselves. Their businesses often need credit to turn profitable or to at least become capable of supporting a person and part of her household. Since people without capital are people without collateral, banks generally eschew doing business in poor communities. The risks are too great, and the prospects for profit slim.

For a variety of reasons, poor women are well represented, but not over-represented, among small businesspeople in informal economies around the world.[12] As women focused the attention of the international community on the conditions of their disadvantage, especially as it negatively affected the economic development of poor countries, women's local self-help activities received particular scrutiny. It was discovered in the 1970s that poor women were lending each other small amounts of money, or working with local non-governmental institutions to establish microcredit lending among themselves, to help their small businesses survive and, where possible, to grow. The concept was simple. If outside money from a credit bank or nongovernmental organization were involved, women would be gathered into a lending circle, and all of its members became responsible for paying off the loans of all others in the circle. In this way social support—as well as pressure—helped assure that loans were repaid. The presumption was that if a woman could pay off her microloan, she was achieving some success with her business. Where these programs succeeded, they soon became part of the action programs of women's self-help organizations and developed strong roots in their communities.

Microlending began to find external support in the 1980s from nation-states and NGOs as policy makers sought ways of supporting economic change initiated by local people themselves. The result is that microlending became a key policy strategy for addressing the manifest economic disadvantages of women in poor countries, more now than ever. For instance, a policy maker like John Williamson, the author of the set of policy prescriptions strongly recommended by the International Monetary Fund (IMF) and the World Bank for adoption by poor countries that became known as the "Washington consensus," and formerly a firm believer in exclusively macroeconomic solutions such as budget-balancing, currency devaluation, privatization, and so on, now concedes the importance of microeconomic solutions. His leading candidate for part of the new "Washington consensus" prescription is microlending.[13]

Because it has become such a key economic intervention, it is important that we critically examine microlending's effects on equality. It would also provide an excellent instance for attempting to evaluate a social policy by a yardstick other than the instrumental one of market efficiency. If we followed the latter, for instance, we would be concerned with whether microlending overcame an obvious market failure in poor countries, where banks fail to provide small businesspeople with liquidity. In contrast, let us ask whether microlending to women's small business enterprises reduces or eliminates economic inequality among women and/or men.

"With Little Loans, Mexican Women Overcome," the headline of a *New York Times* story reads.[14] Tim Weiner, a highly experienced liberal reporter, leads off his article with the following story:

> Guadalupe Castille Urena was widowed at 31, left alone with five children when her husband died trying to get to the United States from their hut here in the foothills of Mexico's southern Sierras. She was among the poorest of the poor—scraping by, like half the people in Mexico, and half the world's six billion people, on $2 a day or less, barely surviving. Then an organization called Finca came to the village. It asked the women there—and only the women— whether they would be interested in borrowing a little money, at the stiff interest rate of 6 percent a month, to start their own businesses. Change came. With a loan of about $250, Ms. Urena, now 35, started making hundreds of clay pots this winter. With Finca's help, they were sold in bulk to a wholesaler, who sells them in the city. She pocketed $15 to $20 a week in profit. That sum, the first real money she had ever earned, was enough to help feed her children and pay their school expenses. "It's exhausting," she said, kneading the mud, stoking the kiln. "But it's something. An opportunity."[15]

Microlending, Weiner argues, "is producing wealth in some of the world's poorest countries."[16]

In addition to providing poor women with small-business loans, Weiner notes that the NGOs involved in lending have also begun providing other financial services, effectively becoming the banks of the poor. "The fact is that poor people can save money," one World Bank expert who had been involved in microcredit start-ups tells Weiner, who also observes that this fact was "something of a revelation to economists."[17]

The high interest rates of microlenders do catch Weiner's eye. The article ends with the story of another client, Escolatica Medina, who had borrowed the equivalent of US$500 from the Finca microlenders. The sales of the clay pots she produced with the loan amounted to US$800. The US$300 "profit" calculated as the difference between the loan and the sales—and not counting her labor as a cost of production—was split between her and the microlender. She received US$190 and Finca received US$110, the latter a consequence of what Weiner describes as an interest rate "about five times higher than any United States credit card company could legally charge."[18]

As a result of her loan-assisted business, Escolatica Medina and her children could probably not be said to be living richly. "A little money for when my children need something—enough for food, for school, for their health," is how she puts it. Consistent with the upbeat character of the article, though, Weiner concludes by quoting Medina's very positive sentiments about the effects of microlending on her life: "Now I feel equal to anyone."[19]

Though perhaps with less skill than that of Weiner, this story has been told time and again in development and political circles. Microlending, and through it the fostering of microenterprises, works for women otherwise weighed down by child care and household labor and beaten down by males in patriarchal societies. The microlending movement, dating roughly to the establishment of Bangladesh's Grameen Bank in 1974, has quickly become one of the premier development interventions designed to wrest disadvantage from the shoulders of women around the world. The World Bank estimates that 7,000 microlending institutions have made loans to 25 million people, 75 percent of them women, in more than forty countries.[20] In Bangladesh alone, owing to the success of Grameen Bank, 7 million people, largely women, have received small loans. Grameen has branched out as a bank and as a nongovernmental organization into a variety of income-generating businesses, including dairies, fisheries, textiles, and telecommunications. In the case of the last, it can now boast of being the largest mobile phone company in Asia, using its links with local lending circles to distribute handheld cellular telephone service operated by women microentrepreneurs throughout poor rural villages in Bangladesh. We noted above how this phone network had helped a poor woman get a better price for her goods from a wholesaler.[21] Other credit banks engaged in microlending have reported similar successes in Latin America, and of late in the United States.[22]

Microlending is popular among policy makers and politicians, locally and internationally, for several reasons. First, it makes a market for poor people where the private banking sector has failed. Second, it does so without relying on state intervention, as the solution involves setting in motion at most some NGOs, themselves voluntary and private entities. These two points support a conclusion that a market-based approach, albeit assisted a bit by the visible hand of organized charity, is still the best solution to economic problems. Third, the rationale for microlending fits the prevailing welfare presupppositions of many rich countries. The new approach to development, as World Bank president James Wolfensohn puts it, is analogous to that underlying the reformed U.S. welfare system: "It is about scaling up—moving from individual projects to programs, building on and then replicating, for example, micro-credit for women or community-driven development *where the poor are at the center of the solution, not the end of a handout*."[23]

Women become the solution, rather than the problem. This is an attractive slogan. If women can do something for themselves, a greater moral dignity is attached to them and some change in their character is inferred. They are, in a word, *empowered*. That is, women exercise more everyday autonomy over their bodies, their labor, their associations, and their time, and they have greater access to and control over material resources in their environments.

But what are the results? Looking at the question of empowerment rather than taking the sterner measure of equality, microlending has a mixed record. Putting money in women's hands through loans in Bangladesh, for instance, is highly associated with improving children's nutritional status, an outcome not typically found when money is given to men.[24] As one Salvadorian woman told a microlending researcher, microloans beat depending upon the local loan shark: Instead of "feeding the fat man," the loan shark, she could feed her children.[25] However, there is contradictory evidence as to whether microlending helps women overcome the practical conditions of patriarchy at home. In one Bangladesh study, women microloaners as compared with nonloaners did increase their say in household decision making.[26] Another study, once more from Bangladesh, suggests the opposite, except that it notes that women do have access to more financial resources and do acquire more control over fertility decisions in family planning.[27]

However, microlending may also have unintended negative effects on participating women. It appears that men advantage themselves from programs otherwise directed toward improving the lot of women relative to their men. While evidence from Bolivia suggests that women were able to put the loan money to good use and maintain control over their businesses,[28] a detailed Bangladeshi study of households to whom loans in the name of the senior woman were made revealed that in about half of the cases, men—not women—controlled the loan monies.[29] It also is reported that women experience enormous peer pressure from their co-loan recipients, the other women in their lending circles, to pay off their loans. More vulnerability, rather than the expected empowerment, can be the result.[30]

But what of the equality effects? That is, do microlending programs create greater economic equality? In actuality, this is presently impossible because microlending is but an economic drop in the bucket, even in nations where it is highly diffused. The Grameen Bank is not only a pioneering microlender, but can boast of loan operations in 40,000 of Bangladesh's 68,000 villages. Yet, its turnover, the amount of money it contributes on an annual basis to the country's gross domestic product, varies between 1 percent and 1.5 percent a year.[31] Perhaps the dilemma of BancoSol, a successful Bolivian microlender, illustrates the point best: despite providing 40 percent of all bank loans in Bolivia, BancoSol holds only 2 percent of the country's banking assets.[32]

However, based upon the evidence of how microlending has been working in local situations, we can get some measure of its impact on reducing economic inequality. We can begin to get some idea of whether it is an intervention to be promoted in achieving greater economic equality, or whether the present and future assets devoted to it might be better placed elsewhere. To develop our assessment, we must take and adapt the findings of studies for which the question of equality was not directly evaluated. First, we can review studies analyzing the degree to which microlending has reduced poverty among its client populations, a focus of much current research.

Several international aid agencies, having analyzed the results of a wide range of empirical studies, conclude that microlending is not directly effective in reducing poverty. Noting that while some research has highlighted microlending's potential for significant poverty reduction, while others have found minimal impact on poverty reduction, the International Fund for Agricultural Development argues:

> It is now increasingly recognized that microfinance alone is not a magic bullet for poverty reduction, but only one of the many factors that may contribute to it. In fact, in an effort to dispel the impression that microfinance is a cure for poverty, it is argued that the claims that microfinance assists "the poorest" and "the poorest of the poor" are unfounded within national contexts. Microfinance institutions virtually never work with the poorest . . . and many microfinance institutions have high proportions of clients who are non-poor, using national poverty lines.[33]

The World Bank in similar fashion concludes that microlending is "no panacea for poverty," noting, too, that studies suggest participants living at or above the national poverty line derive significantly greater benefits than do those below the poverty line.[34]

Based upon these findings, another question would seem warranted: Is microlending *increasing* rather than decreasing economic inequality? The question needs to be qualified in two ways. On the one hand, has microlending, a program historically targeted at women, reduced their inequality vis-à-vis men? Discussion above of the data related to research on women's empowerment suggests that women do get access to money to which they would otherwise not have access, but the research also notes that women in some contexts lose control over the loan money to male residents of their households. Aside from the softer measures of "empowerment," there is not much evidence available to confirm or deny that women's equality vis-à-vis men in their immediate surroundings or in areas with lively microlending programs has increased.[35] If a positive equality effect compared with men were significant, it would likely be noted widely. Perhaps all we can infer is that in the matter of men versus women, microlending neither increases nor decreases equality.

On the other hand, analysis does suggest that microlending increases economic inequality among women as a whole in contexts where it is prevalent. We have just noted above that reviews by large international development agencies such as the World Bank and the International Fund for Agricultural Development found that more advantaged women, relative to their surroundings, do better in microlending programs, and that as a consequence, poorer women are underserved. Several ethnographic studies show that microlending can actually deepen class differences among women by providing limited social mobility for a better-off minority that is able to capture microloans as a new local resource. A field study of the activities of three microlending NGOs in Bangladesh shows that women of the local elite monopolized receipt of microloans. They did so in part because of their superior social connections, and in part because NGOs, both desiring elite participation and needing lending successes for their own institutional reasons, favored them. Microenterprises funded by microlending, the author argues, reinforce existing inequality.[36]

An ethnographic inquiry outside La Paz, Bolivia, reveals much the same thing, except that the pattern discovered by the research suggests something far more insidious. NGOs outside La Paz also recruit economically advantaged women whose more likely successes make the organizations and their programs look good. Microlending participation also connects women more closely with NGOs and avails them of greater access to local financial and political power, which becomes itself a creator of more inequality.[37]

But Lesley Gill, the author of the La Paz study, also posits that the growing involvement of a microlender like BancoSol, which has become a for-profit business, signals that microlending is being transformed into another circuit for the capitalist exploitation of the poor through the extension of small loans at rates little lower than offered by the local loan shark. Like the U.S. banking giant Citicorp that has dipped down through acquisitions of "consumer finance" corporations (a.k.a. usurious lenders) to lend to "substandard" (a.k.a. poor) clients at high rates, Gill sees an agency like BancoSol leading the way in the transformation of grass roots microlending into a profitable, private banking business.

Whether microlending will take the route spotted by Gill in the case of BancoSol or whether it will remain largely the province of NGOs interested in self-sufficiency rather than, strictly speaking, a profit, one cannot at this point say.

If one, however, were interested in increasing equality, specifically in this case economic equality—and one would be expectant about increasing social equality as well if one succeeded—then microlending would not be a wise intervention. It appears to have no measurable effect in narrowing the economic inequalities between men and women. It would also seem less than efficacious in reducing the social inequalities that arise between men and women in households, as suggested by the empowerment studies that attempt to capture precisely the closing of social status differentials at home.

Supporting microlending for women may be virtuous when seen in the light of other values. Surely it supports the development of petty capitalism, and may ease the impact of market failures to provide credit at reasonable prices for women in small enterprises. To the degree that petty bourgeois values such as thrift and hard work are associated with small business, microlending may strengthen these kinds of value orientations among women entrepreneurs. Many ascribe additional value to people "making something of themselves," and "pulling themselves up by their bootstraps," no less than the persons trying to do it for themselves.

Those valuing equality, particularly economic equality in this case, however, will probably not find in microlending a highly congenial solution. With respect to the condition of women and the poor, for instance, there is some evidence suggesting that public works programs, education, and job training programs provide more concrete support for people's earnings, and thus eat away at income inequality more directly.[38]

Paying for Educational Opportunity

In our vision of the good life, education ranks highly—so highly, in fact, that a recent, very disparaging study provocatively entitled "Does Education Matter?" caused nary a blip on the collective radar screen.[39] We simply take for granted that education is a virtue, and that more of it is good—and probably related to having more wealth. As we have accepted Aristotle's view of human life as the development of a kind of practical mastery in the pursuit of happiness, education is a conventional way of building up our capacities for skilled accomplishments of which a good life is made.

It is apparently also of crucial significance in our economic outcomes as well. Seldom, if ever, have daily beliefs received such ringing empirical support from social research, especially as applied to the problems of gender equality and poverty. Economist Lawrence Summers, president of Harvard University (2001–), argued based upon empirical analysis of data from three large poor countries that educating young females was the best single development investment a poor society could make.[40] There are abundant reasons. First, the more women's educational attainment approximated that of men, the faster the poor country's rate of economic growth.[41] Providing women with more education increases a society's labor productivity and its personal income. In fact, one study in Kenya shows that giving women farmers the same education and inputs as men receive increases total agricultural yields by 22 percent; a study in Burkina Faso shows similar results.[42]

Second, improving education opportunities for girls and women has many additional benefits to the well-being of society as a whole. Better-educated women have children who live longer, are better fed, and experience better cognitive development. Their children are more likely to be immunized against basic infectious diseases. The more education channels more income into women's hands, the more likely children are to be the direct recipients than if the same money were in the hands of their men.[43]

Third, and very important for our consideration, increasing educational levels among poor people significantly increases their overall income share. One recent cross-national study showed that increasing the number of high school graduates by just 1 percent among the bottom 40 percent of the population in poor countries increases their share of the national income by 6 percent. This would seem a very important equality effect, and it is suggestive of how directly more education could raise women's incomes significantly.[44]

Though universal public education is spreading throughout the world, there is still a long way to go for both men and women in poor countries. Primary school education is most widely diffused in poor countries, but it is still the case that one-quarter of primary age schoolchildren in poor countries in 1997 were not going to school. Only half of those children eligible in poor countries in 1997 were attending a secondary school. These numbers contrast rather smartly with the experience of children in rich countries, where 100 percent primary school and 96 percent secondary school attendance has been the norm for at least a generation.[45]

If we add gender to our analysis of educational opportunity, we find girls and women at a disadvantage generally, but especially so in the poorest regions of the world. Women in poor countries spend little actual time in school. By 1990, for instance, women were averaging just two years of primary school in South Asia and sub-Saharan Africa, and about three and a half years in the Middle East and North Africa. In East Asia, Latin America, and the Caribbean, women did better, having averaged about five years of primary schooling. By contrast, women in rich countries finished nine years of school.[46] The educational opportunities made available to women in poor countries leave a great deal to be desired.

But the situation, when we take up the question of gender equality and educational opportunity, becomes particularly dramatic in specific regions among the world's poor countries. In South Asia, women in 1990 were receiving only half as much schooling as were men. In sub-Saharan Africa, the Middle East, and North Africa, the figure is 60 percent.[47] To put this gender deficit in perspective, these regions comprise 38 percent of the world's population, and in rough numbers, the same proportion of the world's women.[48] So, we might put it this way: The problem of gender equity in education is enormous, even if it is most severe in particular places and populations.

As we noted earlier in this chapter, economic growth alone will not bring gender equality in education with all its advantages. Recognizing this, policy planners and governments have designed programs that offer households financial incentives for putting their daughters in school. Results from around the world suggest that the programs work well: girls' primary and secondary school attendance improves significantly. The strategy, essentially, is to make girls' education more valuable to their households or communities or, at minimum, less of an expense to their kin.

Let us look at several different programs and their results. In 1982, Bangladesh experimented with a school stipend program that subsidized expenses that girls incurred attending secondary school in several areas of the country. After five years, the proportion of girls enrolled in secondary schools increased from 27 percent to 44 percent. The Bangladeshi government then went a step further by eliminating secondary school tuition for girls and expanding the stipend program for expenses to all of its rural areas. The result is that nationally the proportion of all girls enrolled in secondary school by 1992 had reached one-half, high school completion rates increased, and many more young women went on to postsecondary education.[49]

In the Balochistan region of Pakistan, government, NGOs, and neighborhoods tried a different approach to improved gender equity in education. NGOs would build primary schools and subsidize their operation on the condition that the school enrollment of boys was less than half of the school's roster. This was an interesting experiment in reversing incentives.

Even if communities had a prior and/or greater incentive to educate their boys—following the logic of gender discrimination in the first place—their possibility was conditioned on educating more girls in order to increase educational opportunities for their boys. The program worked out well. Girls' primary school enrollment rose by one-third in the city and by almost one-fourth in the countryside, and boys' primary school enrollments rose also.[50]

More recently, Mexico has tried to fine-tune a stipend program to encourage school attendance among the children of its poorest rural communities. As part of its PROGRESA program beginning in 1997, it offered poor households a grant for every child enrolled between the third grade of primary school and the third year of secondary school. Grants for girls' attendance were slightly higher, and grants grew in size the older a child became, so that by the third year in secondary school, a family would receive a monthly grant equaling 46 percent of an agricultural worker's average monthly earnings. Enrollments have increased across the board, in some cases as much as 17 percent in crucial grades, when children ordinarily drop out for low-wage agricultural work.[51] Overall, students completed two-thirds of a year more of schooling than they might have if they had not been enrolled in the program.[52] Girls' middle school attendance grew from 67 percent to 75 percent, while boys' attendance rose from 73 percent to 78 percent.[53] The PROGRESA program is another instance of how states and policy makers are remedying gender discrimination in their attempts to strengthen educational opportunities for poor people.

Taking all the cases into account, the results are encouraging. More girls and young women are going to school, and going for longer periods of time. The programs appear to significantly reduce their educational disadvantage when compared with boys and young men. The programs also strengthen the educational capacities of poor people in societies with high class divisions. Comparing the three programs, it probably makes sense to follow the example of Bangladesh in supporting girls directly or that of Pakistan in creating incentives for serving girls first. It seems to improve boys' prospects as well but, most important, does more to assure equality for girls.

Greater gender equality in education is not a magical intervention that can knock out gender disadvantage in one decisive move. However, these kinds of programs seem to go a long way to eliminate gender disadvantage in schooling, thus providing directly the equality of outcomes that we have argued is necessary to solve the problem of inequality. They would also contribute to increased equality of economic opportunity, assuming their widespread adoption and success, and assuming for our purposes that education improves economic outcomes for the educated. Finally, an indirect, if wanted, consequence in the case of stipend programs is that they transfer re-sources—money—directly into the hands of poor people through the eco-nomic support of their daughters.

Programs and the Pursuit of Equality

Microlending and girls' schooling are programs that politicians and policy makers around the world hope will lessen the disadvantages of gender for women and foster economic growth. They reason that a healthy entrepre-neurial sector and an educated labor force, both with the full participation of women, will improve well-being in poor countries. We have seen, however, that their consequences for equality are different. Microlending neither low-ers economic equality at large nor between the sexes. Empowerment, often described as the goal of microlending, is not equality, and there is even an open question as to whether microlending meets its own lesser goal. In con-trast, increasing educational attainment among girls and young women re-dresses the problem of equality on two grounds. First, they pull even with men in obtaining a resource valuable in itself. Second, the girls and young women as adults have better prospects of garnering the higher earnings often attached to educational qualifications—another equality effect, though ad-mittedly long-term.

The point of our comparison here is to show how our equality concerns change our evaluations of what we should be doing to improve human well-being. In this chapter, we have taken up two now "standard" development community initiatives that comprise part of the package of remedies cur-rently finding their way into the national plans of poor countries, non-governmental organizations, and lending agencies like the World Bank. Mi-crolending, from this perspective, seems fundamentally flawed. On the contrary, girls' schooling seems promising. Remembering that equality is paramount, however, may lead us to conclude upon further examination that other remedies, whether discussed in other chapters of the book or lying out-side our scope, may be superior if they provide more equality than do efforts to increase girls' schooling.

Notes

1. For useful discussions of market failures, see Joseph Stiglitz, *Whither Socialism?* (Cambridge, Mass.: MIT Press, 1994), 42; Robert Kuttner, *Everything for Sale: The Virtues and Limits of Markets* (New York: Alfred A. Knopf, 1997), 328–62; and Mary Douglas, *Risk and Blame: Essays in Cultural Theory* (London: Routledge, 1992), 128–47.

2. World Bank, *World Development Report 2000/2001: Attacking Poverty* (New York: Oxford University Press, 2001), 73. You can explore the virtual souk online at www.elsouk.com/.

3. Ibid.

4. Seth Dunn and Christopher Flavin, "Moving the Climate Change Agenda Forward." In *State of the World, 2002: A Worldwatch Institute Report on Progress toward a Sustainable Society*, edited by L. Starke (New York: W. W. Norton, 2002), 24–50. Countries exceeding their pollution quotas would also be allowed to spend the amount equivalent to a pollution permit to cover their liability by funding emission control projects in poor countries with surplus pollution permits. For example, Denmark, as a participating signatory of the Kyoto agreement, purchased Romania's excess pollution permits by installing pollution control systems on power plants throughout Romania. See Vanessa Houlder and Phelim MacAleer, "Romania Looks at Ways to Improve Its Climate," *Financial Times*, June 26, 2003, 5. For careful discussion of Kyoto, see World Bank, *Entering the 21st Century: World Development Report 1999/2000* (New York: Oxford University Press, 2000), 96–101.

5. Manuel Castells, *The Rise of the Network Society* (Cambridge, Mass.: Blackwell, 1996).

6. Cited in Amnesty International, *Broken Bodies, Shattered Minds: Torture and Ill-Treatment of Women*, March 6, 2001, available at www.amnesty.org, accessed March 6, 2001.

7. World Bank, *World Development Report 2000/2001*, op. cit., 118–19.

8. World Bank, *Engendering Development through Gender Equality in Rights, Resources, and Voice* (New York: Oxford University Press, 2001), 55, 152–53.

9. Ibid., 231–32.

10. Ibid., 251–52.

11. See Alejandro Portes, Manuel Castells, and Lauren Benton, editors, *The Informal Economy: Studies in Advanced and Less Developed Countries* (Baltimore: Johns Hopkins University Press, 1989).

12. World Bank, *Engendering Development*, op. cit., 136–39.

13. John Williamson, "The Poor Need a Stake in Developing Countries," *Financial Times*, April 8, 2003, 15.

14. Tim Weiner, "With Little Loans, Mexican Women Overcome," *New York Times*, March 19, 2003, A8.

15. Ibid.

16. Ibid.

17. Ibid.

18. Ibid.

19. Ibid.

20. *World Bank Development News Press Review*, March 18, 2002, 9.

21. Alastair Lawson-Tancred, "Micro-Credit System Comes Under Fire," *Financial Times*, May 21, 2002, 6. See also Women's World Banking website, available at

www.swwb.org. Women's World Banking accounts for roughly half of the microcredit loans being given to women through its forty agents throughout the world.

22. ACCION International, a network of credit banks operating in thirteen Latin American countries, as well as in Africa and the United States, served 2.7 million clients between 1999 and 2002 and disbursed US$4.6 billion in loans with a loan loss rate of 3 percent. See www.accion.org, accessed April 7, 2003.

23. *World Bank Development New Press Review*, April 2, 2002, 4. Emphasis added.

24. World Bank, *World Development Report 2000/2001: Attacking Poverty* (New York: Oxford University Press, 2001), 119.

25. Serena Cosgrove, "Guadalupe's Story: The Complexities of Microcredit," *Grassroots Development: Journal of the Inter-American Foundation* 22, no. 1 (1999), 46–47. Reduced dependence on local loan sharks is also reported in Hans Buechler, Judith-Maria Buechler, Simone Buechler, and Stephanie Buechler, "Financing Small-Scale Enterprises in Bolivia." In *The Third Wave of Modernization in Latin America: Cultural Perspectives on Neoliberalism*, edited by Lynne Phillips (Wilmington, Del.: SR Books, 1998), 102.

26. Rurul Amin, Stan Becker, and Abdul Bayes, "NGO-Promoted Microcredit Programs and Women's Empowerment in Rural Bangladesh: Quantitative and Qualitative Evidence," *Journal of Developing Areas* 32, no. 2 (Winter 1998), 221–36.

27. Lutfun Khan Osmani, "Impact of Credit on the Relative Well-Being of Women: Evidence from the Grameen Bank," *Institute for Development Studies Bulletin* 29, no. 4 (October 1998), 31–38.

28. Hans Buechler, et al., op. cit., 101.

29. Annemarie Goetz and Rina Sen Gupta, "Who Takes the Credit? Gender, Power, and Control over Loan Use in Rural Credit Programs in Bangladesh," *World Development* 24, no. 1 (1995), 45–63; Aminur Rahman, "Micro-credit Initiatives for Equitable and Sustainable Development: Who Pays?" *World Development* 27, no. 1 (January 1999), 67–82.

30. Rahman, ibid.; Jude Fernando, "Nongovernmental Organizations, Micro-Credit, and Empowerment of Women," *Annals of the American Academy of Political and Social Science* 554 (November 1997), 150–77.

31. See fact page of Grameen Bank, available at www.grameen-info.org/bank, accessed April 4, 2003.

32. See www.accion.org, accessed April 7, 2003.

33. International Fund for Agricultural Development, *The Challenge of Ending Rural Poverty: Rural Poverty Report 2001* (New York: Oxford University Press, 2001), 209.

34. World Bank, *World Development Report 2000/2001*, op. cit., 75.

35. Ware Newaz, "Impact of NGO Credit Programs on the Empowerment of Rural Women in Bangladesh: A Case of UTTARAN" (Dublin: International Society for Third-Sector Research Conference, July 5–8, 2000), reports that no women in her sample of twenty microlenders were able to purchase land with their increased earnings. In this context, property ownership would probably figure as a significant measure of economic equality.

36. Fernando, op. cit.

37. Lesley Gill, *Teetering on the Rim* (New York: Columbia University Press, 2000), 146–49.

38. David Dollar and Paul Collier, *Globalization, Growth, and Poverty* (Washington, D.C.: World Bank, 2002).

39. Alison Wolf, *Does Education Matter? Myths about Education and Economic Growth* (London: Penguin Books, 2002).

40. Cited in World Bank, *Engendering Development*, op. cit., 256.

41. Ibid., 88–92.

42. Ibid., 84–85; World Bank, *World Development Report 2000/2001*, op. cit., 118–19.

43. Ibid., 78–82.

44. Frances Stewart, "Income Distribution and Development," *UNCTAD X: High-Level Round Table on Trade and Development: Directions for the 21st Century*, Bangkok, February 12, 2000, available at www.unctad.org, accessed January 17, 2003.

45. World Bank, *World Development Report 2000/2001*, op. cit., table 6: Education, 284–85.

46. World Bank, *Engendering Development*, op. cit., 43.

47. Ibid.

48. World Bank, *World Development Report 2000/2001*, table 1: Size of the Economy, 274–75. The very rough number used is the sum of the populations of the three regions as grouped by the World Bank. The groupings are the same as used in World Bank, *Engendering Development*, ibid.

49. World Bank, *Engendering Development*, ibid., 168.

50. Ibid.

51. World Bank, *World Development Report 2000/2001*, op. cit., 84.

52. Jere Behrman, Piyali Sengupta, and Petra Todd, "Progressing through PROGRESA: An Impact Assessment of a School Subsidy Experiment (Washington, D.C.: International Food Policy Research Institution, 2001), accessed via the World Bank's Poverty Net, available at http://poverty.worldbank.org/library/view/5643, accessed June 29, 2003.

53. World Bank, *World Development Report 2004: Making Services Work for Poor People* (Washington, D.C.: Oxford University Press, 2003), 30–31.

CHAPTER TEN

Equality at Home

As it is abroad, so it is, too, at home: Economic inequality is the single most iniquitous condition affecting the health of U.S. society. This land of plenty, this producer of 30 percent of the world's economy, provides more and more for its wealthy and less and less for its poor. We have embarked on creating a society very different from the kind we once shared with other rich countries, one that featured much less absolute inequality between rich and poor. Instead, we find ourselves joining the grim company of poor countries such as Cambodia, China, Ethiopia, Tunisia, and Turkmenistan whose economic inequality matches ours, despite our superior economic performance.[1]

Our colleagues in the "unequal camp" have much to do with few resources. That is why in earlier chapters we have shown how important it is for rich countries to shift significant portions of their resources to poor countries so as to reduce inequality worldwide. We have also demonstrated that some programs will increase economic equality within countries and between countries, and others will not.

In contrast, we in the United States, while also having a lot to do, at least have a lot of resources with which to do it. A quick review of the facts about the distribution of income and wealth in the United States, however, makes for bracing reading. The top 20 percent of U.S. households in 1997 captured 56 percent of all the income generated by the U.S. economy, and the bottom 40 percent of U.S. households received 11 percent of all U.S. income. The overall "take" for the rich is skewed heavily toward the top families: Just the top 5 percent of U.S. households accounted for 31 percent of all U.S. income in 1997. These proportions remained stable throughout the 1990s, a period of historically unprecedented U.S. economic growth. The poor, in other words, did not make up lost ground during the boom years. Rather, their incomes stagnated.[2]

As striking as these facts are, and as unequal as incomes among Americans are, the picture becomes more disheartening still when we examine the distribution of wealth. Again, the top 20 percent of U.S. households does well, but this time their hold is quite remarkable: They owned in 1998 fully 83 percent of the nation's wealth. If you subtract the value of people's homes from their net worth, you get some idea of how little wealth outside of their homes most Americans possess; for then, the top 20 percent of the households in 1998 own 91 percent of America's wealth. Small investors may be noteworthy new citizens of Wall Street, but their holdings, looking at the big picture of America's liquid wealth consisting of the bank deposits, stocks, and bonds and other negotiable instruments that can be readily converted to cash, are minuscule when compared with those of the top families. And again, these results are tilted toward the very rich, as the top 5 percent of U.S. households owned 59 percent of America's wealth, an amount that becomes 68 percent when you take out homes as readily cashable financial assets.[3]

Looking at the bottom 40 percent, this time for net worth and liquid assets, we find out what really makes one poor in the United States, aside from low incomes. The bottom 40 percent of U.S. households in 1998 held *less than 1 percent* of America's wealth. When the value of homes is deducted from net worth, they become net debtors. That is, what savings they have does not surmount their debts.[4] This means that four out of ten U.S. households have no funds to see them through even a three-month spell of unemployment, a serious illness, or a family emergency where money is involved. In real terms, they have nothing to fall back on in difficult times.[5] Using figurative language, economist Richard Freeman argues that we are becoming an "apartheid economy—in which the successful upper and upper-middle classes live fundamentally differently from the working classes and the poor."[6]

But in the United States, the term "apartheid" is never merely a metaphor. For its fundamental meanings—that a society is in fact separated into two racially different and economically unequal societies—are never far from being at least a partial description of our world. Integration of public facilities and friendship groups, the growth of culturally diverse large firms, professions, and public bureaucracies, as well as the success of federally mandated affirmative action programs, have created the warranted impression that people of color have made economic and social progress since the 1970s.

Their relative success has been celebrated by many throughout society at large.

This era of better, if not completely good, feelings should not fool us, though, about the gross economic inequality between people of color and white Americans. If you are African American or Latino/a, your income, financial assets, and net worth are a fraction of those held by your white counterpart. For African-American households in 1998, average income was 49 percent of white income, and net worth was 18 percent that of whites. When houses are subtracted from net worth, African-American financial assets amounted to 15 percent of that of whites.[7]

For Hispanics, a category that conceals groups of different ethnicities and national origins, the comparison with white Americans was somewhat, but not much better than found for African Americans. Hispanic households garnered an average income equal to 54 percent that of white income in 1998. Their net worth was 25 percent that of whites, but when homes were subtracted, they figured for only 20 percent what whites possessed in financial assets.[8]

In the United States, therefore, we have a situation in which rather dramatic economic inequality between rich and poor is further exaggerated by persistent racial and ethnic disadvantage. Given these circumstances, reducing inequality at home, then, suggests that we analyze remedies in terms of how they address both problems. Given the depths of disadvantage faced by people of color, it would be hard to recommend remedies that were not likely to advantage them greatly. It may also be the case that some remedies may meet our demands for greater equality *and* be largely, even solely, dedicated to improving the condition of people of color. If, however, we can achieve greater equality for people of color and the millions of Americans who suffer the effects of inequality more generally, so much the better. In fact, perhaps this goal will point the way to better solutions overall to the problems we have enumerated.

Shifting Assets for Equality

Once more, as we have seen in the case of the world economy and global economic inequality, we in the United States cannot grow our way to equality. Though this would seem obvious from the income and wealth figures reported above, it needs to be said again. If a decade of sustained economic growth such as the 1990s, itself a period without precedent since World War II, cannot bring it, the reasonable inference to draw is that something must be done to change economic opportunities for what is roughly a majority of U.S. citizens.

Redistribution, shifting resources from the rich to the poor, is the answer, and the U.S. federal government is the only agency with the means and legitimacy to accomplish the task successfully. In fact, it is an elemental function of the federal government to redistribute tax monies generated by our economy to finance national needs like defense, welfare, education, social security, and so on. It also transfers monies to groups or categories of citizens whom we, through our representatives in Congress, believe deserving of additional compensation. For instance, the federal government redirected resources via the G.I. Bill to support economic success for almost 10 million former members of the armed services who served in either World War II or the Korean War. Veterans received support for their higher education, mortgages for their first houses, and start-up loans for businesses. Congress estimated that it had spent more than US$80 billion in 1988 dollars over the life of these programs to support veterans.[9] These figures do not include the billions yearly spent by the Veterans Administration on its national system of hospitals that provide for the medical needs of veterans.

As a society, we have also made significant commitments to other groups, such as farmers, homeowners, retirement savers, and holders of financial capital. We have noted in earlier chapters that the U.S. government spends upwards of US$100 billion a year supporting farmers. People paying off a home can deduct the mortgage interest charged to them; if they sell the property, the first US$125,000 of any gain they make over its original cost is tax free. These subsidies to homeowners in fiscal year 2000 cost the government an estimated US$75 billion. During the same year, taxpayers saving money for retirement received effectively a US$124 billion subsidy, because no tax was levied on the money put away. Tax forgiveness for business investments, exclusions of some financial gains from the capital gains tax, and making government bond income tax-free passed on US$289 billion to the holders of capital.[10] In all, then, the federal government redistributes significant sums of money to designated beneficiaries by legislation.

Often, we overlook this fact and neglect its obvious impact on economic inequality. To get the mortgage interest deduction and/or profit from a home sale, one must have a house in the first place. To set aside money in savings for retirement, one must have an income that offers some surplus above one's cost of living. To benefit from reductions in the capital gains tax, the tax exemption of government bonds, and so on, one must have capital. Counterintuitive to our notion that the more money you make, the more tax you pay, those with more money get more tax breaks, and ultimately more money back engaging in these activities. Between one-half and two-thirds of these benefits in 1998 went to households making more than US$100,000 a year.[11]

In light of our quest for greater economic equality, these redistributive efforts must give us pause. Let us set aside the question of veterans' benefits, for it could well be argued that they are a form of deferred compensation and in some cases an indemnity for disabilities suffered during the course of service in the armed forces. Looking at the other government expenditures, I would argue that they are manifestly unequal in their effects, and by their operation recreate economic inequality by giving more to those who have more, and leaving out those who don't possess the assets for which the federal government gives the holder a reward. What should we recommend? The elimination of these benefits?

We could. In each case, we might find grounds for doing so. There would seem in some of these schemes plenty of injustice to correct. Tax policies such as these are unlikely to meet our demand for equality and thus warrant elimination. Following the recommendation of the late economist James Tobin, the other sensible thing to do is return to and increase the progressive taxation of individual income, and recoup a much greater portion of the wealth of the wealthy, estimated to be about US$25 trillion, an amount three and a half times the size of the annual gross domestic product, by an equally progressive tax on wealth itself.[12] There is little doubt that these two initiatives along with abolition of tax breaks described above would lower economic inequality in the United States. As a consequence, our economic inequality as measured by the ratio of the top earners to bottom earners might look more like Sweden's, where the ratio is four to one, instead of the twelve to one now characteristic of the United States.[13]

Thus, taxation itself is our first instrument of greater economic equality. It clips income and wealth from the top of the population and lowers inequality ratios. But we need to address the question of greater equality in light of our major theme of enhancing human well-being. Would progressive taxation enhance well-being? The answer would have to be no. Unless we dramatically enhance the well-being of those in the bottom half of the U.S. population, the equality we claim is simply a bookkeeping effect we achieve by lowering through taxes the income and wealth of the top, not a transformation of people's lives. Enabling people to save for their security, own a home, invest in a small business, and have an education and health care—these are things inscribed in the American dream. When we think about what equality would mean in the United States, this vision, all technical calculations aside, is probably about as close as we can get to operationally defining "equality," and about as close as we need to get for the purposes of our argument here.

Once again, redistribution is the necessary next step. The federal government, whom we have made flush with funds setting it to progressively tax income and wealth, needs to put the wealth to work among the people comprising the struggling half of U.S. society. It needs also to assure a solution that deals with the special equality deficits of people of color and other disadvantaged populations, such as women and handicapped persons.

Perhaps it would be easier, more economical, and pragmatically more acceptable if we strengthened and expanded a highly successful ongoing government program, the Earned Income Tax Credit (EITC). Passed into law with the support of both political parties in 1975, the EITC is a very simple and effective way to put money into the hands of poor people who have earned it by their hard work. Up to US$3,800 in federal taxes are returned as tax refunds to low-income household heads yearly. By this means, the federal government redistributes more than US$30 billion a year to 15 million working poor, more than under any other federal program targeting poor people.[14]

Expanding the EITC has many advantages as social policy. High on the list of its virtues is that it rewards people for working.[15] In the argot of the day, it is a hand up to poor people—not a handout. In addition, it can get money directly into the hands of poor people. Sociologists Fred Block and Jeff Manza have calculated that if all the resources the federal government now devotes to a variety of social programs designed to help poor people were funneled into a robust national incomes program, we could bring all of the U.S. poor above the poverty line.[16] The expansion of the EITC on its own merits is something we should do.[17]

As a parenthesis, the same could be said—without, I hope, discussing the topic at length—for devising a scheme for universal health care in the United States. As we showed in the chapter on equality among nations, good health is crucial to a person's well-being. Without it, the development of one's full capabilities is difficult, often impossible. We saw that this had significant effects on society as a whole, including a lower potential for producing the goods and services everyone needs to survive. If we are agreed on the premise, then let it be noted, but not argued here, that part of the redistributive task is to provide equality of resources in health care.

Turning back to the EITC, there are several reasons why it falls short of the equality mark. First, getting people over the poverty line only marginally reduces the vast disparities of income and wealth. Supposing, as we did just above, that well-being in the context of the United States was equivalent for argument's sake to the American dream, then people will need more resources to achieve it than the EITC could provide.

Second, the EITC, though a simple, almost elegant, way of redistributing income via the tax return, rewards only people who are working and provides money based upon the extent to which they work. Many people don't work:

They are too young, too old, or disabled. They may be unemployed due to layoffs or skill deficits, or only able to find part-time work. They may be caring for family, friends, children, and/or working at home to maintain a household. They may be going to school to strengthen their skill bases. They may be working "off the books," making untaxed income taking care of people's children, cleaning their houses, or engaging in the myriad tasks of living for themselves or toiling for others that occur outside the purview of the federal government. If you think of the EITC as a wage subsidy of about US$2 an hour presently for low-income workers, then poor people working illegally, a growing proportion of our labor markets, are actually working at a US$2 hourly discount.[18]

Third, one of the unintended consequences of the EITC is that it actually supports the continued existence of low-wage jobs and low-wage labor markets. It "works" for workers because it is in effect a wage subsidy based upon the hours they work. But this also means that it is in effect an employer subsidy because it allows bosses to pay workers less out of their pockets than they might otherwise have had to pay.

Fourth, and perhaps the most important for our argument here, is that the EITC, for all of its value, enters the picture after the damage has already been done. People are already poor, their cognitive and vocational skills weak, and their health neglected and perhaps already significantly compromised. By early adulthood, new and often lasting economic inequality has been produced, and people find themselves ensnared in the traps of bad labor markets, substandard and expensive housing, awful education, and inadequate and costly health care. They seek what little relief they can find in our ungenerous and unforgiving welfare state that is little more than a poorhouse without portals.[19]

For this reason, many have begun to think about what economist Richard Freeman and Ronald Dworkin call "starting-gate equality." By this they mean that we should "front-load" our welfare state so that it intervenes effectively in the lives of all children. For illustrative purposes, let's see what Freeman lists among the essential activities:

> We'd need things like full insurance and counseling on prenatal and maternal care; paid time off at birth for either parent (which would encourage both work and the two-parent family); health insurance for the child up to maturity; child-care subsidies sufficient to get all kids into safe and responsible care by qualified caregivers earning a living wage; child allowances to keep all kids out of poverty; and increased investment in schooling such as intensive and extensive use of technology, more teacher training and more demanding standards on teacher performance, and an extension of the school year.[20]

Freeman's proposal is a paean to early intervention, a kind of comprehensive Head Start program that he offers because he believes that "most Americans would . . . prefer generating equality 'naturally,' from more equal labor-market endowments, to generating it 'unnaturally' by correcting market outcomes through taxes and transfers."[21]

Despite the robust intervention Freeman advocates, there is something austere, even chaste about his proposal. Reminiscent of the old Protestant cast of mind that a person must earn her own salvation and therefore must be cast into the world to make her own fortune, so too Freeman can tolerate, even encourage a welfare state from the cradle through the high school. But there will be no cradle-to-the-grave notions to be heard from him. He abjures further interference: "But once government accomplishes a basic redistribution," by which he means starting-gate equality, "I believe it should step aside and let us all compete fairly in the market (with some modest social insurance for those who fare poorly)."[22]

As in the case of the EITC, let us suppose that the federal government did everything that Freeman asks of it. They are good ideas, and probably deserve adoption. Like the EITC, they are another way to spend the resources the federal government would recoup through progressive taxes on income and wealth and the elimination of tax breaks for the rich. But would this initiative advance economic equality sufficiently? Freeman's faith in the necessity, even the virtue, of free competition in the marketplace tips us that this is a proposal for equality of opportunity—not of resources. Recall the statistics with which we opened this chapter. What is the meaning of opportunity when you have no resources and those of your competitors are overwhelming? Without a transfer of resources, how can the competition ever be fair? This is not starting-gate equality, because Freeman's proposals don't make the participants equal. The poor with this strategy will always be in the position of catching up. They will be smarter, healthier, more skilled, and perhaps more integrated with their families. But most will most likely lag behind in the fundamentals that make up the notion of well-being we have adopted in the American dream.

An Algorithm of Equality

Let us see what we can do to achieve real starting-gate equality. To make the game equal, we will need to handicap the players and redistribute resources with those differences in mind. To whom would we award handicaps if we were organizing a fair competition? Let us start with persons of color, for whom we have made a case above. Let us add women. In another chapter, we explore how women worldwide find themselves profoundly disadvantaged. At home, though the facts have improved since the 1970s, they are still deeply disquieting. Women's wages are 70 percent those of men. At the same time, their economic burdens have increased. They now head one-quarter of all households with children and 60 percent of all poor households with children.[23] Thus, we will need to handicap women for the race too.

We should also add persons with developmental disabilities and handicaps. They suffer on two scores. Their needs are great, and they often require additional resources to develop and exercise their capabilities. At the same time, their economic means as measured by earnings potential is often lower by virtue of their disadvantage.

Our selection here is not arbitrary. Every set of persons whom we have marked for handicapping in the race is a legally protected category of persons. In our constitution and laws, and their interpretations by courts, we have explicitly declared that the United States has a special interest in their well-being. And we have already charted the depths of disadvantage suffered by poor and working-class people in the United States. Being on the short side of the yawning disparities in wealth and income, we have claimed, is at the core of the diminishment of their capabilities for well-being.

Thus, our proposal must meet the equality needs of all economically disadvantaged persons, and also accommodate the particular needs of categories of persons whom we have shown to be more profoundly disadvantaged. One solution, advocated by Bruce Ackerman and Anne Alstott, is to give every person at age eighteen a personal stake of US$80,000, payable in installments over four years. The only eligibility requirement is that a person has successfully completed high school. Recipients are free to spend the money in any way they choose. The authors imagine that many persons will spend their stake on higher education, but they foresee that it might be just as rational for others to finance a house purchase. They estimated that their proposal would have cost US$255 billion in 1997, and that it could have been financed by a 2 percent wealth tax on the top 40 percent of U.S. households. The authors also provided that recipients would pay back their stake in small increments over the course of their work lives.[24]

The "stake-providing" proposal has pluses and minuses. On the plus side, it countenances a significant transfer of resources to support people's pursuits of their well-being. It also does not restrict how people use the money, in contrast to other proposals that insist that a social endowment of this sort be used for education and training.[25] Nor does it reward people with funds according to the extent to which they invest or save in projects preferred by the government.[26] This is important because we have shown that well-being is fundamental to individual happiness, as well as perceptible as a group characteristic. Insofar as it is possible, we have argued that persons should be able to plot their own courses according to their own designs for living. Hence, the absence of restrictions on choice is admirable.

The minuses, however, overwhelm the good sense of this proposal. To repeat our earlier objection to simply supporting people through the EITC, stake-provision at age eighteen is too late. Second, by provisioning everyone equally, the proposal actually increases inequality, for it confers the same resources on rich and poor alike. Nothing is leveled save the resource provided. Consequently the proposal fails in a third respect: Namely, it does not provide a remedy to the problem of the depth of disadvantage suffered by the categories of persons we have nominated above. As we have argued, some persons need more resources than others for economic equality to take on concrete meaning.

Let us fashion our own plan. Our criticism of the "starting-gate" and "stake-provisioning" proposals provides our first two dimensions. First, resources should flow to persons from birth forward. Second, resources should be redistributed progressively. Third, distribution of resources should reflect the specific disadvantages of protected categories of persons as well as the general disadvantage of being poor. Fourth, a program should offer both surety *and* flexibility. For people to thrive in their projects of well-being, it is helpful for them to know that the support they receive is a constant of their condition. At the same time, any program should be flexible enough to support households caught in situations of disadvantage that may be more acute and short-lived than chronic.

With these points in mind, suppose we imagine an algorithm of equality composed of two steps. First, we address the general problem of income inequality with a guaranteed annual income. Second, we envision additional compensation for disadvantages that persons acquire at birth by virtue of their sex, color, or disability.

As an initial step, we need to establish a baseline of support. Let us suppose that our unit of redistribution is the amount of money it takes annually to support the subsistence needs of one person in a household living at the level of the national median. We can calculate the necessary amount in the roughest sense for illustrative purposes if we take US$43,000, the 2003 median income of a U.S. family,[27] and, assuming the household is composed of four persons, divide that amount by four, yielding US$10,750. This sum becomes what can be called a *redistribution unit*—the basic annual income guaranteed to every person living in the United States. Though this figure can be adjusted or calculated anew when a proposal of this nature begins its trek toward becoming a law, the principle of providing an adequate income guarantee must be retained if we are to meet the general imperative of providing economic equality. Since every person will now have an income, and thus either filing an income tax form or being part of a household filing, we can assure that each person receives the total amount of the minimum guaranteed by raising the standard deduction to US$10,750, thus rendering the income tax-free. Tax refunds can serve as the device for delivering the guaranteed income. So that we do not re-create inequality by giving every person the same amount, and thereby providing well-off persons with an additional income subsidy, we need to assume that income above the minimum level is taxed progressively. This means that the federal government will tax higher incomes at higher rates, not simply as a means of financing government expenditures, but as a social policy designed to redistribute the national income more equally.

Now the second step: Suppose we apportion additional amounts of the *redistribution unit* based upon the degree(s) of disadvantage. There is an ongoing, specific economic cost to being a person of color, a woman, and/or a handicapped person, as comparisons of their income and wealth with that of their counterparts who are white, male, and/or not affected by disability or handicap have shown. From the ratio of the differences in income and wealth between those disadvantaged by one of these factors and those who are not, we can begin to compile additional sums, portions of the *redistribution unit*, that indemnify those marked by disadvantage and provide them with additional support.

This notion that there should be an indemnity for disadvantage parallels philosopher Ronald Dworkin's criticism of and amendments to John Rawls's landmark theory of justice. As we discussed in earlier chapters, Rawls argued that all individuals should be provided with a given quantity of primary social goods, and that any social differences that arise must ultimately redound to the favor of the disadvantaged. Dworkin's proposal is that a society can establish a kind of insurance against the effects of disadvantage that provides people with, in effect, disability policies. The amount of compensation for particular disadvantages could be recalculated by democratic means as circumstances indicate.[28]

We have the capability to calculate disadvantage fairly. Our skills in estimating future income and earnings, as well as lost income and earnings because of various disadvantages, have advanced greatly over the past half-century of social research. Consider how very skilled we have become. For instance, labor economist Joshua Angrist was able to show how just one event—being drafted in the 1969 Vietnam War lottery—could change the life chances of an otherwise random group of individuals. He proved that those men with low numbers who were drafted subsequently earned 15 percent less in income than those with high lottery numbers who were not drafted—even ten years after discharge from the military.[29] Though Angrist's work demonstrates how sophisticated our statistical tool kit has become, the ability to derive ratios for disadvantages will not probably depend upon such fine-grained analysis. There is already a good amount of national data aggregated on the impact of disadvantages on earnings, as our thumbnail sketch above and the data sources upon which they were based suggest.

Let us remember, too, that both public and private sectors have been tracking income and its differential distribution for a long time. Insurance companies with the help of actuaries and other statisticians are routinely developing and revising the probabilities and costs of losses of income and livelihood on the part of their policyholders. This assures that they can pay off disability and other income claims and still make a profit. Their techniques must stand the test of constant scrutiny, as business survival depends upon their accuracy. The federal government's Social Security Administration also possesses the actuarial capability to predict changing rates of mortality among its current and future senior citizen clients. Their estimates of growing demand for old age pensions since the early 1970s have been largely accurate, if ignored by the nation's politicians. In all, then, the technical means exist to develop an algorithm of equality.

Our next move—to remedy the problem of profound disadvantage—departs from the standard formulas. As we noted earlier in the chapter, African-American household income is 49 percent that of white income; for Hispanics, the income ratio to that of whites was 54 percent. Taking these as the roughest of indicators of income inequality, for every African American residing in a household with an income of less than US$43,000, we would award them 1.51 *redistribution units*, or US$16,233, annually; for every Hispanic under the same circumstances, we would award them 1.46 *redistribution units*, or US$15,695, annually. Since women are members of the overwhelming majority of households, we cannot derive directly the ratio of disadvantage by comparisons among households, dividing the data between those with and those without women. We can, however, take the data presented above showing that a woman earns approximately 70 percent of what a man does, and award her 1.3 *redistribution units*, or US$13,975, annually. With respect to persons with handicaps and disabilities, suitable ratios could be found as well. To assure that persons receiving additional *redistribution units* based upon disadvantage obtain the whole amount that is their due, additions to their standard deductions will render their income guarantees tax-free.

Let us sum up the practical consequences these two proposals would have for people residing in the United States. The following list illustrates what the guaranteed household minimum incomes of various household types composed of four persons would look like:

Guaranteed Minimum	US$43,000
Household with two females	US$49,450
African-American household	US$64,932
Hispanic household	US$62,780

These results are merely approximate sketches of the results we derive from guaranteeing each person a decent living standard and compensating disadvantaged persons with additional resources.

Problems arise. First, to whom would the money be given in the case of a minor? Like other disbursements made to minors, the parent or guardian would receive the funds on behalf of the child until she reaches her legal majority. There is ample precedent. Parents and guardians are entrusted with Social Security survivor benefits, which a child receives upon the death of a parent. Private insurance indemnities of many kinds, including inheritances, for minors are superintended by parents and guardians.

Second, for how long shall a person receive a redistribution award? Here it is important that we part company with the "starting-gate" and "stake-provisioning" proposals that have helped us thus far in constructing a new proposal. Here, too, we join company with proponents of the negative income tax or guaranteed annual income. The observation that must guide us is that disadvantage does not disappear at age eighteen, twenty-five, or thirty-five—and sometimes never at all. For persons in the protected categories whom we have identified above, disadvantage is a lifelong condition. The U.S. economic slowdown in the first years of the twenty-first century provides dismal reconfirmation, for instance, that people of color suffer disproportionately the effects of layoffs and earnings declines of business recessions. Though we look forward to the day when this is no longer true, we argue that a proposal like the one put forward here is needed to create the avenue for exodus. In addition, as the great American experiment continues, people should be held harmless for stigmatizing conditions not of their making and able to pursue well-being of their choosing.

More generally, we know that people can be born poor or fall into poverty at any point in their lives. We have seen above how the lower 40 percent of the U.S. population is especially vulnerable to the effects of one-time economic crises for lack of savings. The same fate can befall households just above the median income line via unemployment, a business failure, illness, or just a string of bad luck. To be sure, the disadvantage experienced in acute crises such as these can be temporary, a drastic income slip of a year or two. These households also deserve support, as a slip can become an inarrestable slide if people find themselves vulnerable and unaided. Being born into a poor family confers an initial disadvantage that may—or may not be—overcome in time. Once again, lifting people's household incomes to the national family median is a direct answer to their needs. It provides them with a decent means of living and improves their prospects for being able to pursue their personal projects.

Putting a Proposal into Perspective

Despite our proposal's expansive scope and size, it is important to confront its limitations in light of the equality problems we have discussed.

Most importantly, it does not magically end economic inequality. Progressive taxation of income and wealth is crucial. Redistribution following our suggestions is necessary in a long journey toward greater economic equality. It shifts substantial resources to economically disadvantaged persons whom we have defined as those residing in households making less than the median household income. It also takes care to assure that persons belonging to constitutionally protected groups that nonetheless find themselves profoundly disadvantaged receive additional resources.

The plan we have sketched also has an important progressive feature. The plan funnels resources to households below the median, thus causing the median household income to rise steadily over time. As the median household income rose over time, the value of the basic *redistribution unit* would too. This would be in addition to the increase in median household income that often accompanies economic growth. What this means, at least in theory, is that the ratio of total income devoted to the bottom half of society should increase incrementally. Our society, by this device, would become progressively more economically equal.

That said, the plan does not solve the wealth and savings deficits that a substantial majority of American households suffer, as we observed above. Increased income could perhaps provide people with more possibilities for saving, but the redistribution contemplated would probably find its way toward purchases of goods like housing, education, and health care that people cannot presently afford. The federal government could find ways to encourage small savings in the same spirit in which it has supported accumulation via savings and investment among the rich. It could sort out its housing policies, taking care to assure that its subsidies for home ownership support these same desires among the disadvantaged rather than simply reward the rich for purchases they would have made anyway. It could also levy higher taxes on inheritances, thus reducing the starting-gate inequality in the first place.

Finally, it is good to recognize that proposals such as the one we have constructed above have been around before, as generations of persons concerned with the pernicious inequalities of industrial capitalism have tried to envision remedies. Perhaps the "algorithm of equality" that drives this attempt will lead to justice more directly.

The politics of such a transformation of U.S. society as of this writing are unfathomable. It is important to recall from an earlier chapter that Sweden, for instance, has gone much further along the lines of economic equality than we have, with fewer objective resources per person than we possess. This suggests technical feasibility, to be sure. But it will take substantial political protest and revitalization of the U.S. democratic process for the majority to express its will, which, one hopes, would be in favor of a new politics of equality.

Notes

1. World Bank, *World Development Report 2000/2001: Attacking Poverty* (New York: Oxford University Press, 2001), table 5: Distribution of Income or Consumption, 282–83. The five countries listed score forty on the Gini index, as does the United States. There are many whose indexes indicate higher economic inequality than the United States and these five. In contrast, the European Union and Scandinavian countries score below the United States and others, often finding themselves between the mid-twenties and thirty on the scale. The United Kingdom is the exception at thirty-six.

2. Edward Wolff, "Recent Trends in Wealth Ownership from 1983 to 1998." In *Assets for the Poor: The Benefits of Spreading Asset Ownership*, edited by T. Shapiro and E. Wolff (New York: Russell Sage Foundation, 2001), table 2.2, 40–41.

3. Ibid.

4. Ibid.

5. Thomas Shapiro, "The Importance of Assets." In *Assets for the Poor: The Benefits of Spreading Asset Ownership*, 16.

6. Richard Freeman, *The New Inequality: Creating Solutions for Poor America* (Boston: Beacon Press, 1999), 4.

7. Wolff, op. cit., table 2.7, 50–51.

8. Ibid., table 2.8, 52–53.

9. Shapiro, op. cit., 14.

10. Michael Sherraden, "Asset-Building Policy and Programs for the Poor." In *Assets for the Poor: The Benefits of Spreading Asset Ownership*, 303–4.

11. Ibid.

12. James Tobin, "A Liberal Agenda." In R. Freeman, *The New Inequality*, op. cit., 58. See also Frances Fox Piven's contribution to the same volume titled "New Ideas?" in which she also advocates a wealth tax. In R. Freeman, *The New Inequality*, op. cit., 54.

13. Gosta Esping-Andersen, *Social Foundations of Postindustrial Economies* (Cambridge, U.K.: Cambridge University Press, 1999), 7.

14. "The People Left Behind," *Economist*, September 30, 2000, 28.

15. James Heckman, "Old Problem, New Despair." In R. Freeman, *The New Inequality*, op. cit., 65.

16. Fred Block and Jeff Manza, "Could We End Poverty in a Postindustrial Society? The Case for a Progressive Negative Income Tax," *Politics & Society* 25, no. 4 (December 1997), 473–511.

17. See Paul Krugman, "What Consensus?" In R. Freeman, *The New Inequality*, op. cit., 41, for advocacy of increasing the EITC precisely because it is politically more feasible.

18. "Out of Sight, Out of Mind," *Economist*, May 20, 2000, 28.

19. This is why Block and Manza propose converting the EITC into a negative income tax, a proposal close in many respects to that offered here.

20. Richard Freeman, op. cit., 18–19.

21. Ibid. James Tobin had offered a program he called "youth endowments" that also focused on building capabilities for economic success at young ages. See James Tobin, "Raising Incomes for the Poor." In *Agenda for the Nation*, edited by K. Gordon (Washington, D.C.: Brookings Institution, 1968). Interesting also is Roberto Unger's call for social endowment accounts in *What Should Legal Analysis Become?* (London: Verso, 1996).

22. Ibid., 76.

23. Heidi Hartmann, *Through a Gendered Lens*. In R. Freeman, *The New Inequality*, op. cit., 33–34. See also Leslie McCall, *Complex Inequality: Gender, Class, and Race in the New Economy* (New York: Routledge, 2001), 106.

24. Bruce Ackerman and Anne Alstott, *The Stakeholder Society* (New Haven, Conn.: Yale University Press, 1999), 4–77.

25. See Tobin, "Raising," op. cit.; Unger, op. cit.

26. Asset-matching savings accounts that have been sponsored by foundations to support asset-building among the poor often provide incentives for activities like home-buying. See Sherraden, op. cit., 314–16.

27. Kimberly Blanton, "Numbers of Poor, Uninsured Rise," *Boston Globe*, August 27, 2004, C1.

28. Ronald Dworkin, *Sovereign Virtue: The Theory and Practice of Equality* (Cambridge, Mass.: Harvard University Press, 2000).

29. Reported in Schiller, op. cit., 62.

CHAPTER ELEVEN

A Good-Enough Economy

Two regions sit side by side, facing the Indian Ocean from the coast of the Asian subcontinent. Kerala and Karnataka are two of India's twenty-eight states. And they are two regions whose economic development, or lack thereof, has drawn worldwide attention.

Kerala is perhaps the more famous of the two, probably because the region is such an exception to every rule that development economists have propounded. Its well-earned reputation derives from the observation that it has achieved by its efforts as a region of 31 million persons since the 1960s substantial well-being for its population *without significant economic growth*. In fact, its record is quite astonishing. Average life expectancy for men and women approximates the averages of rich countries; it is universally literate; and its birthrate conforms to rich-country norms. Its infant mortality rate, a key measure of well-being as a whole, was twelve per 1,000 persons in 1997, contrasting with India's sixty-five per 1,000, and again comparing favorably with high-income countries. All this was done on a per capita income of less than US$1.25 a day.[1]

The Kerala accomplishment's admirers, among them Amartya Sen, attribute its success to enlightened civic action and wise regional planning. An active, alternating party democracy, mass organizations involving a third of the population, and popular struggle were key ingredients. Land reform, unemployment insurance, a pension system, subsidized rice and local feeding programs for children and infants were some of the ways that Kerala achieved dramatic improvements in economic equality.[2] Important, too, was the reforming

181

vision summarized by two proponents of Kerala's social mobilization in these past years. Kerala's experience, Thomas Isaac and Richard Franke write, "shows that even at low levels of economic development, basic needs can be met through appropriate redistribution strategies, a paradigm that has come to be called the 'Kerala Model.'"[3]

Opponents criticize the Kerala Model for discouraging capital investment and entrepreneurial activities. They note the region's chronic unemployment and its inability to capitalize on its highly literate potential workforce. They argue that the Kerala economy has stagnated and relies now upon remittances (some US$2 billion a year) from the 3.5 million Keralites whose work it exports abroad because it can't occupy them at home. In the mid-1990s, one of the reform leaders most responsible for the redistribution politics of Kerala's regional government acknowledged the value of what many of the critics believe:

> Let not the praise that scholars shower on Kerala for its achievements divert attention from the intense economic crisis that we face. We are behind other states of India in respect of economic growth, and a solution to this crisis brooks no delay. We can ignore our backwardness in respect of employment and production only at our own peril.[4]

Perhaps for Keralites, an anxious glance northward to Karnataka reveals for them the path not taken, for better or worse. Karnataka, with its population of 53 million people, figures itself to be India's future. Bangalore, the state's capital, is the headquarters of India's information industry. Since the 1980s, it has become one of the premier computer software production sites in the world. Its productive dimensions are measured in billions, whether it be output or investment. Like California's Silicon Valley, it is a beehive of development, employing 80,000 software professionals in more than 1,000 firms, large and small, foreign and domestic. The industry's clients include Fortune 500 firms, its growth rate is phenomenal, and its economic direction is decidedly upward bound.[5]

Yet, while Karnataka surpasses Kerala in production and technology, finding itself at the leading edge of the world's leading industry, it lags—and then some—in well-being. Only two-thirds of its population is literate, and this proportion drops substantially for women, of whom only 58 percent are literate. These figures are equivalent to the overall Indian average, and significantly less than Kerala's virtually universal literacy.[6] Though Karnataka's poverty rate is slightly less than that for India as a whole, it still amounts to one-third of the population. Despite the economic boom in information, Karnataka's per capita gross domestic product in 1997, though more than that of Kerala, was still only 82 percent of the US$430 Indian average. Its infant mortality rate of fifty-three per 1,000 persons compares favorably with India's sixty-five per 1,000 persons, but poorly with Kerala's twelve per 1,000 persons.[7]

Despite widespread external praise, as Nicholas Stern, former chief economist of the World Bank, put it, for "driving the dynamic India," there is also unease with the evident unevenness of Karnataka's economic growth and the resultant economic inequality. The state's chief minister, S. M. Krishna, has noted that regional development without equity and justice is a lopsided development. Especially vexing are the economic inequalities between town and countryside, between men and women, and between scheduled castes and tribes and the rest of the population. Recall that despite its success, the information industry employs only 80,000 professionals—not much of a lever to lift a population of 53 million people. The state remains overwhelmingly committed to a rather impecunious agriculture, which absorbs 70 percent of the working population, but produces only about 37 percent of the state's domestic product.[8]

The cases of Kerala and Karnataka are not just opposite; they are also apposite. To be sure, there is the surface contrast between Kerala, the state that gets welfare at least minimally right but can't succeed at economic growth of any sort, and Karnataka, which succeeds in creating a world-class industry but doesn't produce much welfare. But there is more here than meets the eye. Taken together, their plights tell us just how hard it is to enhance well-being and run at least a modestly successful economy that can support your welfare proposals.

This is why, after focusing on creating more equality so as to enhance human well-being, we turn in this chapter to the economy. We need an economy for provisioning and for redistribution. We have established that the world cannot grow its way to economic equality. Not even the United States, with all of its resources, can grow its way to economic equality. The reason, we have seen, is that economic growth at its best rewards everyone in a society equally. And precisely because it rewards everyone equally, those starting behind can never catch up. They can sometimes escape poverty, but they remain economically disadvantaged—a condition that damages their well-being in every other sense. Without economic equality, the social and political dimensions of equality are hard, typically impossible to attain. Social and political deprivation then become means by which economic inequality—even with economic growth—becomes once more a grim fact of life for the disadvantaged. Thus, our prescription is economic redistribution from rich to poor, at home and abroad.

But lurking beneath our efforts all along has been an assumption that our economies will continue to produce the goods and services we need to provision ourselves more equally. Because equality is not pegged to growth, we did not put forth remedies designed to speed up our economies in hope of closing the gap between rich and poor. Yet it must be admitted that we have assumed that the world economy and its national constituents could produce adequately enough to support the world's population and its incremental increase. We also accepted that the world economy should produce only what it could within the accepted limits of environmental sustainability.

But what must that economy be? A continuation of what we have now? An acceleration of what we have now, if we take the advice of many development economists? You will recall from an earlier chapter that the United Nations Conference on Trade and Development (UNCTAD) estimates that if poor countries could boost their annual growth rates to 7 percent, they could reduce extreme poverty, that is, the number of people living on less than a US$1 a day, by one-half by the year 2015. This would mean that if the thirty-three countries in their sample, taken from the poorest countries for which there are reliable data, were able to sustain a 7 percent growth rate between now and 2015 instead of the average 3.5 percent growth rate they sustained for the 1990s, they would still have 200 million extremely poor people instead of 400 million without accelerated economic growth.[9]

Never say never, of course, but we noted that only China had achieved a growth rate of this magnitude in the 1990s. While it could be reasonable to assume that one or more economies—even including a giant like China—could grow at an accelerated rate simultaneously, we also argued that *it was unlikely that the world as a whole could sustain that rate*. The more typical pattern, looking around the world today, is for one country or region to run ahead, while the others lag or are pulled along by the leadership of the economically quicker. Thus, no new, remarkable global economic run seems likely to arise and fix our problem. And it also bears repeating that even an accelerated growth rate like that of China's would not eliminate poverty. Even doing so supports but does not at all win the battle to achieve economic equality.

So, what is an economy "good enough" to support our equality project and enhance well-being? Once again, a caveat is warranted. As we observed in earlier chapters, official economic advice either from rich countries or their surrogates such as the World Bank and the International Monetary Fund should not be taken at face value. The information they supply and the policy prescriptions they provide emanate from their own highly interested stance as economic top dogs. At the very least, it must be said that they read economic experience from their point of view and with their own desire to remain top dogs commingled with their conclusions. Given the need to choose between believing and saying what is true about the world and what is to their advantage, the latter looms large, particularly in the policy discussions that revolve around economic development and growth. The rich countries' combination of selective vision and overweening economic and political power can misdirect policy in poor countries and deeply damage their peoples. Poor states and their ruling groups, either led by rich-country policy directives or up to no good on their own, can contribute mightily to their peoples' miseries.[10]

Inside rich countries, perhaps much the same process is at work. Ideas can be just as self-serving, information distorted, and policy prescriptions tipped in favor of the top dogs on home grounds like the United States. Here the rich seek to capitalize on their accumulated national advantages. Through political representation, business pressure, and policy development itself, they try to move the complicated process of democratic governance along the lines that they favor. The facts are often the first casualties in a not-so-subtle struggle for control over the policy directions of the nation. Because of the economic and political hegemony of the United States in the world today, the game of the nation's rich also includes maintaining its top-dog status in the world economy.

With this caveat in place, we can reenter our discussion of what is a good-enough economy to support our goal of economic equality. First, let us look at the foundations for our approach: What is implied by "good enough"? The key here is to make room in our thinking for other values, such as equality, in what is otherwise a standard economic rationality dominated by efficiency and maximizing the gains of every transaction. The incomparable German sociologist Max Weber argued that an instrumental rationality, one in which economic actors calculate the most efficient means to achieve the greatest reward, lay at the heart of modern capitalism. Instrumental rationality was thus both the work and the basic belief system of modern capitalism. There were, Weber countered, possible rationalities other than simply the economic calculation of means and ends, including those that arose out of a person's concerns with what he called "ultimate ends." These beliefs about the cosmos, human nature, and virtue that most often, though not exclusively, found their outlets in religion, provided alternative justifications for taking one course of action over another. They implied a different measure of value for human experiences than did instrumental rationality. Though Weber thought that capitalism's instrumental rationality would dominate the modern age, one can infer from his studies of religion and charisma that some future potential for rejecting altogether the means-ends economic rationality remained.[11]

Our devotion to equality and human well-being is thereby a commitment to a rationality of ultimate ends that does not rely upon instrumental rationality for its justification. It is important to recall from an earlier chapter, however, that several serious researchers have empirically linked greater equality in its economic, social, and political dimensions with greater economic growth.[12] Because the root of our concern lies elsewhere, we won't make the argument directly. It also should be freely acknowledged that creating greater equality may decrease strictly economic efficiency. Equality, as we have seen in our chapters on remedies, entails costs. Meddling with markets, imposing higher tax burdens, transferring economic "rewards," (that is, resources) from rich-country "winners" to rich-country and poor-country "losers," in the parlance of mistrustful rich-country economists—these and other notions proposed in earlier chapters can interfere with the basic function of markets to efficiently distribute resources based upon supply and demand.[13] One could respond immediately: What about the cost of a poorly trained and unhealthy army of unemployed persons in our midst? What is the cost of discrimination in potential output lost by inefficient economic utilization of disadvantaged people? Like the question of whether equality fosters growth, a comparison of the strictly economic value of redistribution or repairing discrimination with the costs of not doing so on overall economic efficiency is not an argument we can resolve here. The evidence is mixed, so much so that the eminent economist Robert Solow speculates that the costs of redistribution to economic efficiency are probably not very high at all.[14] But it is prudent not to pick and choose our assumptions with an eye toward greater convenience.

So, let us just assume for argument's sake that it costs something in extra economic potential to move ahead with our equality project. Our goal, instead of chasing optimal economic functioning, is to capture resources for redistribution without triggering economic decline. We may slow the economy down, but our success could be measured by whether we managed to produce a "good enough" economy for our needs.[15]

It would also be useful to take another look at the economy itself to discover the degree to which economic processes could produce in their operation more egalitarian outcomes. In a world that takes the nature of the firm to be inviolate, as a kind of institution with the social valence of the family, if not its respectability, are there ways in which we can advance various dimensions of equality in the day-to-day activities that constitute our economies? We take up this question in the following and final chapter, where we address how we can become engaged in moving economic actions into more promising directions.

Thus, the issue of creating a good-enough economy occupies us for the remainder of the chapter.

A Poor People's Guide to a "Good-Enough" Economy

We have observed with a mix of fascination and mistrust our present-day capacity to plan, and commented on whether mendacity or hubris could explain the ease with which rich governments and their international surrogates could produce remedies for economic privation that were themselves more depriving. Our position has been that gathering relevant data and devising solutions that involved assembling something called "a plan" was not in itself a bad thing. Its virtue depended instead on who was doing it and by what democratic authority.

Having said that, though, it is important to recognize that plans have their place in a context where a set of participants is embarked upon taking concrete actions in pursuit of a remedy. The very particular embedding of people in a given environment, replete with its potentials as well as problems, diminishes the value of the tidy, one-size-fits-all type of policy prescriptions for poor countries that have flowed from the leadership of rich countries and their surrogates since the end of World War II. More appropriate, perhaps, would be a set of heuristics or orientations under which alternatives in which we have interest might be discussed. This is especially true for us in the context of this book, where the objective is to create the conditions for thought experiments that would aid us in understanding what might be done.

An Open Economy—But Only Partially

The first heuristic is that an open economy—*with important qualifications*—is better than a closed one. The beliefs that an economy can delink from the world economy, and poor economies should delink, are alluring but neither possible nor wise.[16] Autarky, the notion of autonomous, self-reliant development, doesn't seem possible, given the present stage of worldwide economic integration: What society today is disconnected from the world economy? Looking at the post–World War II period, Eastern Europe and the former Soviet Union with the onset of the Cold War ran their own collective world economy separate and apart from Western capitalist countries and their postwar dependencies. By the 1970s, however, trade, aid, and bank loans connected the two economic blocs back together. Only Albania and

North Korea sought continued economic independence from capitalist economies, with rather self-evident results, though North Korea remained dependent upon China for important economic exchanges. The case of con-temporary Cuba is instructive as well: Despite the best attempts of the United States to starve Cuba into submission by preventing its integration into the world economy, the Cuban government has realized that opening its economy to exchanges with others is important to its survival. The open-ing is helping Cuba cope economically but, rather predictably, it appears to be increasing economic inequality.

Supposing, then, that all economies in the world are already integrated to a greater or lesser degree with others in a larger world economy, how would a society disembed its economy from the countless connections that form the everyday basis of material life? How does one pull the millions of little plugs that literally as well as figuratively connect one economy to others? It doesn't seem practicable.

If it is not readily possible, we should still pursue the question of whether it is advantageous. Many argue that it is desirable as well as necessary for poor countries to escape the clutches of the rich via deglobalization. The promi-nent intellectual and political deglobalization activist Walden Bello has put together perhaps the most complete proposal for at least a partial delinking of poor from rich economies that advances more concretely the concept of deglobalization. It consists of seven points:

1. Gathering capital from within poor countries rather than depending upon external sources;
2. Creating a strong local market through land reform and income redis-tribution;
3. Reducing environmental despoilation by deemphasizing growth and stressing equity;
4. Making more democratic instead of market-based decisions;
5. Monitoring both state and private sectors by civil society;
6. Creating an economy that includes more community cooperatives, pri-vate and state enterprises, and excludes transnational corporations; and
7. Producing as much as possible for local needs with community and na-tional resources.[17]

Though other deglobalization activists share parts of Bello's proposal, his is by far the most carefully balanced and articulated.[18] There is much to ad-mire in it. Bello emphasizes local production with local capital for local needs, and stresses redistributing land and other resources to create greater equity. He envisions an economy that is subject to democratic control and composed of a mix of actors: state, private, and cooperative. As such, it appeals very much to the sentiments of many that the world has grown too big, too complicated, too "Jurassic," to paraphrase Bello,[19] to reproduce livelihood for all and to do it democratically and equitably. The bigger the economic sphere for Bello, the greater chance that the rich will outrun democratic controls and get richer, and the poor will get poorer.

Bello's proposal is a compendium of good sense, but suffers from a mix of timidity and ambition. Its timidity lies in Bello's underestimation of the degree to which poorer countries can control foreign capital. During the 1997–98 Asian financial panic, countries such as Korea, Indonesia, Thailand, and the Philippines largely succumbed to the dictates of the International Monetary Fund, the World Bank, and the U.S. Treasury Department. Malaysia more successfully managed the crisis by instituting currency controls that limited the damage caused in other countries when investors withdrew their money from local economies.[20] The 2002 financial collapse of Argentina should have been a knockout blow to that country's national autonomy and made its subjection to international authorities and foreign investors complete. Instead, new political leadership elected in 2003 reasserted Argentina's national autonomy by insisting that foreign creditors assume a significant share of the financial burden involved in paying off its national debt. Arguing that foreign creditors had received high-interest-rate returns on Argentinean bonds precisely because the country was in acute financial distress and was thus a risky investment by any standard, the government is resolved to pay off the debt at much less than its face value.[21]

Moreover, countries have also demonstrated the capacity to control the rate and behavior of foreign investments. After a serious banking crisis, Chile, for instance, resolved to insulate its economy from the ill effects of "hot money" investment flows into its financial system by requiring foreign investors in Chilean stocks and bonds to deposit a fixed amount of their capital in an interest-free bank account for a year. Investors forfeited this bank capital if they withdrew their investments from Chile before the year was up. This rule enforces a certain seriousness on foreign investors, in effect discouraging them from shifting their money willy-nilly out of the country wherever a point or two extra of profit might be gained. It also potentially sets aside low-cost capital for loans to Chilean lenders.[22]

China, anyone's candidate for most successful developing country of the 1990s, prudently controlled from the beginning the terms for foreign investment in its economy. Though China encouraged capital flows from Hong Kong and Taiwan that were destined for the small and medium industrial enterprises in its southern regions, it insisted during the crucial first decade of its economic takeoff that large-scale investments in sectors like automobiles be joint ventures with Chinese companies. This maneuver guaranteed ultimate Chinese control over business decisions and assured the transfer of complex manufacturing technologies to Chinese industries. Further, in the first years of its economic rise, China refused to allow free conversion of its currency into the currency of other nations, thus ensuring that it could control its value both at home and to some extent abroad. As of this writing, China is the only major nation that still controls the value of its currency. The value of all other currencies is fixed in the daily transactions of foreign exchange markets.

Surely China has exploited its enormous size and potential to control the terms of its economic relations with the rest of the world. But Malaysia, Chile, and even Argentina are not blessed with great size or wealth when compared with rich countries, nor even when stacked up against such countries as Brazil and Indonesia, which have succumbed to greater international discipline over their economic decisions. Their success, albeit modest, suggests that poor countries need not disengage from the world economy the extent to which Bello might prefer.

Moreover, if Bello exhibits a bit of timidity on behalf of poor countries when confronted with the powers of the international system, his ambitions for locally created capital, production, and technologies seem also to overshoot the mark. Foreign capital and technology can be very useful, indeed instrumental, in supporting local development. Rich countries like the United States are huge capital importers. One need only think of the U.S. auto industry. U.S.-based manufacturing plants for such firms as Toyota, Honda, Nissan, Mazda, Volkswagen, and Mercedes-Benz, to name a few, produce almost half of the United States's autos, provide jobs for thousands of persons in regions that are otherwise in deep economic decline, and have stimulated via competition the technological renewal of American firms like General Motors. The United States also succeeds in protecting domestic ownership from takeover in what it deems strategic industries, such as airlines, communications media, and defense. A similar scenario could be sketched for the effects of foreign investment and technology transfer on the relative success of the post–World War II European economy.

Why should poor countries choose at some cost to their own economic growth to be exceptions to these historically rather routine economic practices? If there is a lesson to be found in the collapse of the Russian and Eastern European economies in the 1990s, it is that their relative isolation from the technological innovations produced in the West, combined with restricted access to foreign capital for industrial renewal, left them unable to contend with their newfound Western competition.[23] Bello's expectations for local production of capital and technological innovation are not only overly ambitious, given the general sense of how economic development goes, but also onerous for poor countries that lack capital, technology, and the experience of linking them together effectively. Foreign investment and technology transfer are not the only answers to economic growth in poor countries, but they are several of the answers necessary for success.

This realization must be used carefully. It is not a recipe for unfettered openness. Rather, it is a recommendation for a wide-awake, even hard-nosed control over a national economy's exposure to the world market. As Fred Block astutely remarks in developing his notion of a more egalitarian "practical utopia," every country needs a few key industries that can earn it export earnings and track the technological progress being introduced into the world market by other economies.[24] If your nation is poor, you need the world market. It reminds me of what a famous bank robber is said to have replied when asked why he robbed banks: "That's where the money is." The world market and, particularly, rich-country markets are where the money is. Thus, in addition to importing capital and technology, export-oriented production from poor countries makes sense for many reasons, not the least of which is that it represents the transfer of real resources from rich to poor countries.

Important, too, is that irreducible dyad in capitalism, the relationship between buyer and seller. To capture markets, one needs to find buyers and produce what they want to buy and at the price they are willing to pay. If one succeeds, then one can extend production lines, lower costs, develop or purchase technology, increase efficiency, and capture more market share. Poor countries need access to world markets and the money through production that they provide. Without the markets and the money of rich countries, you have the situation that Max Weber once offhandedly claimed was true of nineteenth-century Naples: a group of poor people working very hard every day, trading, haggling, and scampering about, only to find at the end of the day that all of their efforts boiled down to exchanging the equivalent of the same dollar, and finding themselves both exhausted and poorer for it.

Fair Trade, not Free Trade

Rich countries can sniff out the poor countries' gambit, and they resist free trade. In earlier chapters, we have documented, for instance, how rich countries close their markets to agricultural commodities and textiles from poor countries, areas where poor countries because they are poor should have a comparative advantage. Further, we have seen that rich countries compound the problem they create for poor countries by subsidizing their producers of the same goods, thereby providing them with the opportunity to dump their products on the world market at prices below their cost of production, and at both a rate and price that destroys the market possibilities of poor-country producers.

Should free trade be freely reciprocal? That is, should poor-country economies be as open to imports as those of rich countries? From the poor-country perspective, the best answer, and our second heuristic, is not completely, and certainly not right away. There is both positive and negative evidence for this stance. On the positive side, the performance of several of the highly successful East Asian economies, starting with Japan and including Taiwan and Korea, relied initially on protecting certain of their industries and markets while they developed exportable products, often based upon technologies licensed from U.S. firms. To maintain and expand its post–World War II footprint in Asia, the United States provided markets for their exports and allowed them to run up large trade surpluses that financed their highly successful industrial growth, while receiving very limited access to their domestic markets in return. This relationship would come to grief in Japan during the 1980s, as U.S. industrial producers suffered greatly from Japanese competition, and U.S. policy makers decided to obtain trade reciprocity from Japan.[25] But initial nonreciprocity paid off, and it offers empirical support for poor-country resistance to wholesale trade reciprocity.[26]

There is negative evidence as well, and it comes via Mexico. Sitting next to the largest national market in the world, a succession of Mexican governments attempted to tap its productive potential by encouraging U.S. businesses to produce their final goods across the border in Mexico, tariff-free and with inexpensive Mexican labor. The subsequent boom in *maquiladora*, or assembly production, further enticed the Mexican elite to risk national development in the great leap forward crystallized in 1994's North American Free Trade Agreement (NAFTA), which created a continental free trade zone that included Canada.

A decade later, U.S. farmers, with their highly subsidized products and increased access to the Mexican market, have run small farmers off the land and converted them into migrant laborers bound for the United States, rather than helping create through competition a much-hoped-for upgrading of Mexican agriculture. Mexican tolerance, even encouragement initially of the final assembly export production process on the border, has not created in the new NAFTA environment the complex industrial production chains of subcontractors, parts producers and on-site design and production technologists that sustain long-term industrial development. An astonishing 99 percent of the value of the inputs that go into Mexico's export production are produced outside Mexico. The only component Mexico is producing in many circumstances is the labor in the last manufacturing stage. Low Mexican wages were Mexico's initial comparative advantage vis-à-vis the U.S. market. Now that China is open for business and its average wage is one-fourth that of Mexico's, U.S. and other foreign businesses are off to China. Unemployment in northern Mexico, once an area of labor shortage, is now common.[27]

The lessons to be drawn from Mexico's experience with the United States are several. Once again, absolute reciprocity, in many cases, was probably too dangerous for the damage that unmediated competition with an industrial behemoth like the United States could cause. In the case of agriculture, the dismantling of the U.S. protection and subsidy system for its farmers should have been the quid pro quo for even the partial opening of other Mexican markets to U.S. business. With respect to manufacturing, Mexico would have been wise to continue to insist on substantial foreign investments in production infrastructure and local content requirements for complex industrial goods, strategies that helped it build a successful automobile industry in the pre-NAFTA days.

Mexico's loss has become China's gain, as we have seen, and the case of China is again highly instructive. China began its commercial opening to the world market with its significant size advantage, figuring correctly that foreign businesses and their governments would concede much in return for access to its enormous untapped market. Owing to its size and complexity, many different kinds of commercial opportunities have been created in its territory, including a more laissez-faire, export-oriented industrialization zone between Hong Kong and Shanghai. That said, it has succeeded in insisting on local-foreign joint ownership and production partnerships in many basic industries with an eye to appropriate the technology and technology-based learning as well as capital facilities for the rapid expansion of its industrial base. Its object is to build internationally competitive industries in most major fields of production by its controlled involvement with more sophisticated and resourceful foreign firms.

Obviously there is only one China,[28] but that is at least nominally true of every poor country. Each has its assets and liabilities and therefore its own special requirements for economic development. Economist Joseph Stiglitz puts the point well:

> The policy issue is not "to globalize or not to globalize" or "to grow or not to grow." In some cases it is not even "to liberalize or not to liberalize." Instead

the issues are: To liberalize short-term capital accounts—and if so, how? At what pace to liberalize trade, and what policies should accompany it? Are there pro-poor growth strategies that do more to reduce poverty as they promote growth? And are there growth strategies that increase poverty as they promote growth—strategies that should be shunned?[29]

Careful linkage with the world market, judicious trading relations with an eye toward export production—these can get the economic motor running at a much faster clip than autarky.

But there is a final and conclusive reason for treading carefully. Opening markets to trade can be especially harmful to poor people. There is some good evidence that income growth among the bottom 40 percent of populations in poor countries slows as an initial consequence of trade openness.[30] Any attempts to expose domestic markets to foreign competition need to be accompanied by strong redistributive programs to the poor.

Equality Programs

This leads to our third heuristic: Poor states need to undertake equality programs while building good-enough economies. The World Bank and the International Monetary Fund (IMF) have instituted a policy process whereby all aid-receiving countries must develop an explicit poverty reduction strategy.[31] This is an interesting initiative—to get countries to spell out how and by how much they will reduce poverty over time—but again poverty reduction is not equality production. Having learned that growth alone won't bring equality, we can nonetheless gather up the surplus generated by growth, even in poor countries, to redistribute creatively to poor people.

Providing adequate public education and health care is a good start. These services can be targeted toward the poor and improve their incomes and quality of life. They are not particularly complicated interventions, and perhaps do not create much of a glimmer in a planner's eye. In fact, there is a distinct lack of artifice in setting out to provide health care and subsidize education. We discussed earlier how a network of basic health care could enhance the well-being of poor people significantly. Education, too, has a big payoff for poor people, particularly, as we have seen, when women succeed in getting more schooling. We have also argued that subsidizing the education of girls and young women by direct payments to their families not only gets women more education, but gets money directly to poor families on a regular basis. In another instance, via a school attendance subsidy, the Brazilian government of Luis Inácio Lula da Silva will be delivering a family grant of US$24 a month to a quarter of his country's population. In addition, basic medical services will be delivered to the children in school.[32] The long-term effects of the education itself are extremely favorable for poor people. As previously stated, one cross-national analysis of educational attainment of both men and women in poor societies suggests that for every 1 percent increase in the number of poor high school graduates, the income share of the bottom 40 percent of households increases by 6 percent.[33]

Targeting resources and thinking about how to provide them effectively is important. Devoting resources exclusively to poor and working-class people in poor countries does respond to our interest in providing equality of resources. Providing universal access to resources, rich or poor, does not. For instance, subsidizing primary and secondary education is pro-poor; spending the money instead on higher education is pro-rich, as analyst Dominique van de Walle plainly puts it. Brazil provides a fine illustration of this point. It spends 25 percent of its education funding on higher education for the 2 percent of all students who attend college, a funding level that amounts to three and one-half times Brazil's per capita gross domestic product per student. Meanwhile, 13 percent of the population is illiterate, and only one-third of the teenage population attends secondary school.[34] Providing basic health care through community centers in rural areas and poor sections of cities gets medical care to poor people. Building highly capital-intensive hospitals in urban areas and providing "universal" access to health generally aids the rich. They have the networks and connections to capture the resources in amounts greater than their numbers.[35]

Thus, the more one can get the services and the money directly to poor people, the better. The necessary administrative costs of sophisticated interventions—those, for instance, that are elaborately targeted at specific subgroups or are extensively means-tested—can eat up funds that could go to the poor. Direct grants get more of the money to the poor.[36]

This is what makes public works employment and job training so useful. Amartya Sen has argued that jobs programs in areas struck by natural disasters or succumbing to famine such as India, Botswana, and Zimbabwe have been a highly effective way of getting money into economies undergoing these kinds of stresses.[37] Other research, in Latin America, has shown that jobs and job training programs are superior to unemployment insurance and savings accounts programs in reaching the poorest workers. The problem with the insurance and savings programs is that they already assume that workers are regularly employed. In poor countries, poor workers are most likely employed (if at all) in the informal sector. Offering a job or training places no prior constraints on eligibility. The only negative features of these programs, it would seem, is that they are not more widely in place, and that they often offer a wage less than the prevailing average in a given area to assure that only the really needy will have the incentive to take the posts. Self-selection thus replaces a formal means test of the sort with which we in this country are familiar, but the cost is that less income is transferred to poor workers. This can prevent these kinds of programs from significantly reducing poverty.[38]

This is especially important when we consider another important possible initiative for equality in poor countries—the development of incomes policies. Though poor countries are probably unable to mount as robust an income redistribution scheme as we proposed in an earlier chapter for the United States, they can attack inequality through a pension system. The need is great. Just 16 percent of workers in poor countries have pension coverage, a proportion that drops to 10 percent in South Asia and sub-Saharan Africa. Should we succeed even modestly to improve well-being in poor countries, life expectancy will rise, thus compounding the problem of income support for the elderly. Moreover, since most pensioned persons in poor countries are tied to work in the formal economy, there is an uncounted number, perhaps four or five times as many persons working in the informal economy, who have no access to pensions whatsoever.[39] We have just discussed how Kerala, as poor as it is, instituted a pension system that helped enhance the well-being of its poor people.[40] Marc Edelman shows how a very good Costa Rican welfare system including state pensions and land reform that had dramatically improved the quality of life over forty years was deeply wounded by the impact of a structural adjustment plan imposed by the World Bank and the IMF from 1985 onward.[41] Namibia provides universal old age pensions, and it is estimated that the program reaches 88 percent of those eligible. Studies also show that the pensions contribute significantly to poverty reduction, serving as the main source of income for 14 percent of rural households and 7 percent of urban households.[42] Pensions, by redistributing significant sums to the elderly, can keep people out of poverty and increase economic equality, as the Kerala and Namibia cases show.[43]

States in poor countries can also help poor people gain legal title to lands they have worked and houses they have built or improved. This idea has been promoted by the economist Hernando De Soto as a solution to the problem that poor people lack capital to function successfully in the economy. By titling their houses, now held informally or illegally in barrios and favelas in the burgeoning cities of poor countries throughout the world, De Soto believes that poor people will discover in their homes the collateral for financing entrepreneurial initiatives.[44] His position is increasingly sanctioned and supported by the major development interests, including the United Nations and the World Bank.[45]

Poor people should be able to own property protected by law and to gain sweat equity from their labors as, in so many ways, they should find equal protection under the law. As precedent, De Soto offers that United States law during the nineteenth century recognized deeds based upon people's use and improvement of land.[46] Though converting a small plot or a one-room house into titled property does not significantly increase poor people's prospects for equality of resources, it does support equality of opportunity, and thus is worth doing. The verdict does not depend on how effective property titling is in lifting poor people's prospects, though the World Bank itself questions how fungible housing assets in poor neighborhoods will be, absent viable real estate markets and banks to service them.[47] Common sense suggests, I think, that it will not prove to be the magic bullet De Soto or his supporters believe it to be. One has only to ask oneself some basic questions. How many of us would risk our house to finance a small business? Having gained a roof over our heads through enormous sacrifice and sweat, how many would gamble it in the quicksilver stability of a poor-country economy? More to the point: Why should poor people need to risk in all probability all they have when none of us with more means would? Though many poor people in Lima, Rio de Janeiro, and other places will and should achieve a piece of security through home titling, the effort will not yield a cornucopia of "hidden capital" that will propel poor people out of poverty and toward economic equality.[48]

Pluralism in Building the Good-Enough Economy

This speculation on the prospects of building assets among poor people suggests the fourth and final rubric that might guide the construction of a good-enough economy in poor countries. That is, a good-enough economy can be built in a variety of ways, so beware of fads and formulas. Since the early 1990s, international and nongovernmental agencies that comprise the "development community" have devoted increasing amounts of rhetorical energy as well as funds to stimulating the growth of microenterprises among the poor. We have already examined how microlending for small businesses has become a primary strategy for supporting the growth of women's economic and social equality. Now the focus is on all people in poor societies, male and female. As Paul Martin, Canadian prime minister and United Nations cochair of an elite commission formed by UN Secretary Kofi Annan in 2003 to develop ways of supporting microentrepreneurship, puts it, the poor "want a hand up, not a hand out" in lifting themselves up from their desperate straits.[49] Sound familiar? The locution, "a hand up" rather than a "hand out," echoes the words spoken a year earlier by World Bank president James Wolfenson and quoted in our earlier discussion of microloans for women. We observed then, too, that the slogan bore a strong resemblance to the "welfare reform" rhetoric in circulation when the Clinton administration changed the Aid for Dependent Children program of the Social Security Act to a mix of temporary income support, job training, and employment. This should tip us off a bit that we are in the midst of something of a marketing and sales campaign pitching small-scale entrepreneurialism. It is becoming the newest "new thing" in a string of solutions that the rich have offered the poor since the end of World War II.

We have noted in an earlier chapter how appealing microentrepreneurial talk is in a world economic climate that is dominated by market-friendly rhetoric. If only poor people could find a channel for their protocapitalist energies, which they surely have, probably naturally, we can hear Paul Martin, UN commission cochair, say:

> Whatever else we do to help the poor, local entrepreneurs have the power to create the greatest change for their countries. The entrepreneurial spirit is everywhere. It does not have to be imported. Visit the smallest town in the poorest country on market day and you will see the private sector at work.[50]

This magical belief in the powers of peoples in markets to spin gold from the straw of their impoverished existences needs a dose of De Soto's "magical realist" belief that poor people's capital, their gold, was actually beneath their feet in the trillions of dollars of unrealized value in their squatter homes. De Soto was right about one big thing: Poor people need capital for small enterprises. Unless an economic program dedicated to small business entrepreneurship delivers it, we have Max Weber's Naples all over again, a situation where poor people trade their poverty with each other.

A good-enough economy needs small businesses, entrepreneurialism, innovation, and so on. As an anthropological field researcher, I have been following since 1981 the economic development and social impact of an Italian region that has become a beehive of small-scale entrepreneurial activity since the 1960s. I can report that microindustries producing such export goods as shoes, fashion clothing, furniture, and machine tools have brought a high standard of living to entrepreneurs and workers alike, and thus I am not immune to its "small and beautiful" charms. It has served as a model for regions in other countries that are trying to produce prosperity with small industries and family-run firms.[51]

It can work, as I have found out. But it depends upon a number of factors. It relies upon injections of capital, whether loaned at home by banks or states or garnered abroad through export earnings. It relies upon state (or regional) support and sometimes even direct guidance. William Easterly, an utterly committed market-oriented development economist for the World Bank, nonetheless argues that states need to take a leading role very often in subsidizing the research and development that enables poor countries to establish internationally competitive industries. He notes, as have many, that state involvement in the research process and its financial support of technological innovation were highly important in the East Asian economic successes of the 1970s, 1980s, and 1990s.[52]

But before we are carried off by rather romantic notions of entrepreneurialism, expressed well above by UN Commissioner Martin and believed by many others, it is important to acknowledge that there are upper limits on the degree to which entrepreneurialism can transform poor societies. First, there is significant doubt even among World Bank development economists that small and medium-sized enterprises advance economic growth. Both small and medium-sized firms in goodly numbers and economic growth are found together in a sophisticated statistical survey of economic development in seventy-six countries, but there is no evidence of a causal link between the two. That is, a good-growing economy has small and medium-size enterprises, but there is no surety that the small and medium-sized firm sector helped the economy get there. In addition, they found once more, as we noted in the case of microenterprises and women, that *small and medium-sized firms do not reduce poverty in any way*. This is a significant finding, if only to warn us of the doubts that should replace the commonplace certainties of the development community noted immediately above.[53]

Second, let us recall that three-fourths of the world's poor live in rural areas; by 2025, one-half will still live in rural areas. Industrial development is important, but to be especially beneficial it needs to occur in countrysides where poverty is greater and labor underutilized. To that end, it is important to acknowledge that nonfarm activity already provides a significant proportion of rural income, as the agricultural economy supports needs for trade, transport, and construction. For these nonfarm activities to grow, a healthy farm economy is necessary. And the answer to the agrarian question of how a society sustains its nutritional life and ordinary persons might wrest a living from the land is not simply to dissolve the agricultural into the industrial and hope there is no residue. Farmers need their capital—land—and need working capital no less than do microindustrialists.

Land reform—by redistributing land and making smallholders out of the landless and by providing adequate agricultural credits—diminishes poverty by enabling agriculturalists to feed themselves. For instance, the redistribution in the late 1970s of agricultural lands to the Chinese peasantry eliminated food poverty in the Chinese countryside. Dividing big agricultural plots into small plots also improves productivity, sometimes doubling yields because small farmers use the lands more intensively.[54] Recall that land reform preceded industrial development of both the small and large sorts in East Asian countries such as Taiwan and Korea as well.[55] A good-enough economy has to make significant progress in agriculture no less than in industry, and perhaps must do so as a sort of precondition for industrial success in areas that are still predominantly agricultural.

The third limit to microentrepreneurship as development's new saving grace is that the world economy allots a significantly smaller space to its practitioners. It is important to bear in mind the rather sobering fact that four-fifths of the world's industrial output is a product, directly or indirectly, of the world's 1,000 largest companies.[56] Let us suppose that 20 percent of the world's industrial output of US$10 trillion dollars, or US$2 trillion, flows through the productive capacities of entrepreneurial small and medium-sized firms.[57] While this is certainly not small change, brief contemplation of these facts helps one to keep in perspective the actuality of the kind of world in which petty capitalists live and compete. Large firms dominate world industrial production. In addition, the progressive incorporation of the output of small businesses into the production chains organized by the world's megafirms is fortunate for those who find themselves inside the production chain and unfortunate for those who are newcomers.[58]

Does it make sense for the overwhelming majority of the world's population to confine its economic prospects to garnering a portion of one-fifth of the world's economic production? Again the example of China is instructive, for its industrial leap forward incorporates big and small firms, multinational giants and township microenterprises, foreign investment and local capital accumulation. On the one hand, the emplacements of foreign capital and domestic labor can be truly gargantuan: Consider that in Dongguan, a city in the Guangdong region of southern China, one factory employs 80,000 workers making upward of 100 million running shoes per year.[59] The River Rouge–like dimensions of some of China's capitalist development is a reminder that firms can still build great factories and manufacturing facilities that would make even Henry Ford envious, when the circumstances are suitable. Too, these industrial behemoths can still find customers for their long runs of standardized goods, even though they have mastered flexible manufacturing with its speedy changeovers, just-in-time supply systems, and reprogrammable machines. Large firms have no trouble finding markets for this factory's enormous output, nor do they encounter difficulties financing plant, equipment, and the working capital necessary to make a year's run.

On the other hand, the Chinese regions located north of Hong Kong are the homes of hundreds of thousands of small firms, privately or publicly owned, either guided by Hong Kong capital or dealing directly with firms in Japan, the United States, and Europe, that are producing a great deal of merchandise and making China the new center of the industrial world. Their success, and the rapidity with which they have transformed the Chinese as well as the world economy, is testimony to UN commissioner Martin's wish: that the entrepreneurial energies of every local marketplace can be released for economic development.

However, these same industrial giants that make the enormous investments in China as reflected in the Dongguan shoe factory may subcontract to hundreds, even thousands of small entrepreneurial firms to produce the same output. Or, the running shoes made in Dongguan are also made simultaneously in Taiwan, Brazil, Mauritius, and Albania. A megaproducer might even produce an enormous quantity in Dongguan *and* the same quantity or more all over the rest of the world. What this means for poor countries is the single-minded pursuit of local entrepreneurialism needs to be amended to take into account the continuing role of transnational firms and their mix of production chains. As in Dongguan, they may aggregate labor and capital in massive quantities, or they may subcontract shoes to the more than 800 smaller producers in the same Chinese region. All said, some accommodation to the facts of how they operate the 80 percent of the world market they control is necessary.

Too often, this "accommodation" is a one-sided affair. The Fortune 500 firm dictates the terms, investments are made, and the poor country perforce accepts the accord with the firm as the best available. This was certainly the dominant impression fifteen, even ten years ago. We have already noted in this chapter how China attempted to blunt the transnational firms' powers, and sought capital and skill investments that would help the country build its own core industries on an international scale. There is something else to observe: Large, transnational production endeavors like an 80,000-worker shoe plant may be no greater exploiters of human labor than small firms run by a stranger, a townsperson, a neighbor, or even kin. Sometimes, one is better off in a big, bureaucratic firm, and sometimes one is better off in the familial, neighborly entrepreneurial firm. It is an empirical question: Neither is inherently virtuous.[60] These are issues that poor people, their communities, and their states can in part determine through negotiation and struggle with large *and* small firms.

It also should be pointed out that the welfare states of rich countries were deeply indebted for their existence to the struggle and power of organized labor, which was typically stronger and more effective when lodged in large firms, rather than in small firms where it was often weak.[61] In countries that have created robust industrial capacities over the past 25 years, such as Korea and Brazil, labor movements have been instrumental in advancing wages, improving working conditions, and challenging the governments of conservative, probusiness elites.[62] Aggregating capital and labor is still necessary in heavy industries like metals, chemicals, and auto manufacturing, for instance, and this can confer greater opportunities for worker gains. Again, there is no guarantee whatsoever that greater factory size and increasing the capital intensity of the plant will put the lever for a politics of equality in the hands of workers. It may, but it is an empirical matter, rather than some universal imperative.

Bello raises legitimate fears, as the empirical evidence we have analyzed shows, about the overweening power of transnational corporations in the world economy. However, keeping them at bay by denying them entry to poor countries seems a cure worse than the disease. If they are the current purveyors of most of the world's commodities, then does one expect poor countries, or perhaps each poor country so as to avoid recreating transnationals among poor countries, to produce replacements for all of these types of goods, from toothpaste to tractors? This seems an impossible task and yet another grand burden to impose on poor countries. It also seems a great waste of human potential, if the efficiencies of mass production, however minimal they might be in some cases, were wasted in duplication and costly production processes.

Rather, in sympathy with Bello's concerns here, it is the *power*, both economic and political, of the transnationals that must be curbed. Two things need to happen. One, corporate power can be curbed in basic industries through nationalization, a remedy currently out of favor but worth a revisit. Power, energy, and sanitation—areas that have been targeted by the IMF and World Bank as necessary candidates for privatization in poor countries around the world—could be considered once again public utilities and operated in the public interest as government entities or public trusts. A moment's reflection on the costs, chaos, and hardship that arose from the enormous power and fraudulent practices of Enron in the United States suggest that nations need to rethink the role of states in guaranteeing public safety, instead of leaving basic services to the whims of profit. As Joseph Stiglitz points out, part of Chile's economic success since 1994 owes to the fact that it did not privatize some key industries, including copper mining, that returned important financial dividends to the Chilean economy.[63] Second, the international community must build institutions that can do the job of effective regulation. In line with earlier recommendations for expanded and more powerful global government, it is time to do so. For example, the succession of sanctions regimes executed through the United Nations were successful in controlling commerce to a degree that suggests that curbing the sales and distribution networks of transgressing transnational corporations might be a fruitful means for enforcing effective international regulation of their conduct.

So Far, So Good?

The four rubrics we suggest could guide the making of a good-enough economy—an economy open to investment and technology but protected from free trade, state efforts to end inequality, and an eclectic economic mix to assure some growth and limiting the power of transnationals—may seem, in retrospect, just so much good sense. All to the good, for the closer we hone our remedies to the realities of the everyday lives of people in poor countries, the greater the prospect that the notions might be useful and efficacious.

So far, though, we have dealt largely with making economies grow and focused on production and redistribution. We have not considered what might be done inside economic institutions such as firms and markets to advance the goals of economic equality.

In the final chapter, we take up the issue of ways we might improve the process of economic production to aid in our struggle for equality, as well as reflect finally on how people can take action for the sorts of equality that are the concern of this book.

Notes

1. For life expectancy and per capita income data, see Amartya Sen, *Development as Freedom* (New York: Alfred A. Knopf, 1999), 21–24, 46–47. For literacy data, see Census of India 2001, *Provisional Totals: Kerala*, available at www.cyberjournalist.org.in/census/census.html, accessed September 7, 2002. For birthrate reduction, see Joseph Tharamangalam, "The Perils of Social Development without Economic Growth: The Development Debacle of Kerala, India," *Bulletin of Concerned Asian Scholars*, available at http://www.bcasnet.org, accessed June 15, 2004. For infant mortality rates, see T. M.

Thomas Isaac and Richard Franke, *Local Democracy and Development: People's Campaign for Decentralized Planning in Kerala* (New Delhi: LeftWord Books, 2000), 3–4.

2. See Patrick Heller, *The Labor of Development: Workers and the Transformation of Capitalism in Kerala, India* (Ithaca, N.Y.: Cornell University Press, 1999) for a detailed analysis of how labor and political struggles helped achieve significant victories for Kerala's poor and disadvantaged.

3. T. M. Thomas Isaac and Richard Franke, ibid. For an incisive discussion of the practical impact of the Kerala reform program at the village level, see Richard Franke, *Life Is a Little Better: Redistribution as a Development Strategy in Nadur Village, Kerala* (Boulder, Colo.: Westview Press, 1993).

4. E. M. S. Namboothiripad, quoted in Joseph Tharamangalam, op. cit., 2. Data for remittances cited in David Gardner, "Kerala Set for Push on Economy," *Financial Times*, June 1, 2001, 3.

5. William Easterly, *The Elusive Quest for Growth: Economists' Adventures and Misadventures in the Tropics* (Cambridge, Mass.: MIT Press, 2001), 186–87; Department of Information Technology, Government of Karnataka, *IT Scenario Karnataka*, available at www.bangaloreit.com, accessed June 15, 2004.

6. Directorate of Census Operations, Karnataka, *Figures at a Glance: Karnataka, Census of India*, 2001, available at www.bangaloreit.com, accessed June 15, 2004.

7. World Bank, *Karnataka at a Glance*, available at www.worldbank.org/SAR/sa.nsf/Attachments/KnData/$File/KN.pdf, accessed September 7, 2002.

8. "Development Debate Gets Underway in Bangalore," *World Bank Development News*, May 23, 2003, 4.

9. United Nations Conference on Trade and Development (UNCTAD), *The Least Developed Countries Report 2002: Escaping the Poverty Trap* (June 2002), available at www.unctad.org/templates/countries.asp?intitemID=1676, accessed June 15, 2004.

10. For serious discussions of the causes and consequences of rich-country domination of the economic development discourse, as well as accounts of how states and local planners become involved in the process, see James Ferguson, *The Anti-Politics Machine: "Development," Depoliticization, and Bureaucratic Power in Lesotho* (Minneapolis: University of Minnesota, 1994 [1990]); Arturo Escobar, *Encountering Development: The Making and Unmaking of the Third World* (Princeton, N.J.: Princeton University Press, 1995); and James Scott, *Seeing Like a State: How Certain Schemes to Improve the Human Condition Have Failed* (New Haven, Conn.: Yale University Press, 1998).

11. Max Weber, *Economy and Society* (Berkeley: University of California Press, 1978), 24–26.

12. There is a significant body of economic literature discussing how equality improves development. See Frances Stewart, "Income Distribution and Development," (UNCTAD X: High-Level Round Table on Trade and Development Directions for the 21st Century, Bangkok, February 12, 2000), available at www.unctad.org, accessed January 10, 2000; Andres Solimano, "Beyond Unequal Development: An

Overview," in *Distributive Justice and Economic Development: The Case of Chile and Developing Countries*, edited by A. Solimano, E. Aninat, and N. Birdsall (Ann Arbor: University of Michigan Press, 2000), 24; and William Easterly, op. cit., 265. Policy organizations have also begun making the connections between equality and greater economic growth. See, for instance, Oxfam, "Growth with Equity is Good for the Poor" (June 2000), available at www.oxfam.org.uk/what-we-do/issues/key_papers. htm, accessed June 15, 2004.

13. See William Easterly, op. cit., 264, for a hypothetical discussion of how redistribution lowers national growth rates, and notice how taken-for-granted the relationship in normal economic circles is.

14. Robert Solow, "Welfare: The Cheapest Country," *New York Review of Books*, March 23, 2000, 20–23.

15. It is worthwhile noting that Sweden, perhaps the premier redistribution state among rich countries, has grown economically at an annual rate of 2.1 percent since the 1970s, while the European Union countries have grown at a 2.6 percent rate and the United States at a 3.1 percent for the same period. This comparison, as it reflects precisely the higher degree of redistribution effort from Sweden to the European Union to the United States, in that order, is highly suggestive of the kind of trade-off implied by a "good-enough" economy. See Christopher Brown-Humes, "Sweden's Ageing Model," *Financial Times*, August 30, 2002, 10.

16. Arturo Escobar, op. cit., 99, reviews the importance of delinking in Samir Amin's conception of autocentric development.

17. Walden Bello, *Deglobalization: Ideas for a New World Economy* (London: Zed Books, 2002), 112–14.

18. See also proposals made by the International Forum on Globalization via www.ifg.org for documents and speeches outlining some of their thoughts.

19. Walden Bello, op. cit., 115.

20. Joseph Stiglitz, *The Roaring Nineties: A New History of the World's Most Prosperous Decade* (New York: W. W. Norton, 2003), 217–18.

21. Gianni Beretta, "L'Argentina di mister K. sfida i creditori," *Il Manifesto*, February 21, 2004, 9.

22. Joseph Stiglitz, op. cit., 230; Walden Bello, op. cit., 96. Bello points out in a footnote (no. 9, 105), that the Chileans dropped the requirement in 1998 when the Asian financial crisis reduced significantly the circulation of footloose "hot money" in stock and bond portfolio investment around the world.

23. See Janos Kornai, *The Socialist System: The Political Economy of Communism* (Princeton, N.J.: Princeton University Press, 1992); Joseph Stiglitz, *Whither Socialism?* (Cambridge, Mass.: MIT Press, 1994); and Katherine Verdery, *What Was Socialism, and What Comes Next?* (Princeton, N.J.: Princeton University Press, 1996).

24. Fred Block, *The Vampire State and Other Myths About the U.S. Economy* (New York: The New Press, 1996), 234.

25. In 1992, I found myself in the Japanese countryside, sitting in the conference room of a highly successful small producer of women's sweaters. Above me on the

wall was a picture of the owner with the legendary U.S. ambassador to Japan, Edwin Reischauer, congratulating my host for being the outstanding Japanese exporter to the United States in 1967. How times—and our foreign economic policy—have changed. Shortly after my visit, the Clinton administration came into office and embarked on a no-holds-barred campaign to push open Japanese markets to U.S. goods.

26. For a comprehensive account of the fusion of U.S. economic and foreign policies in the postwar incorporation and protection of Japan, Korea, and Taiwan in a new East Asian "co-prosperity sphere," see Bruce Cumings, "The Origins and Development of the Northeast Asian Political Economy: Industrial Sectors, Product Cycles, and Political Consequences," *The Political Economy of the New Asian Industrialism*, edited by F. Deyo (Ithaca, N.Y.: Cornell University Press, 1987), 44–83. For the practical impacts, see Robert Brenner, "The Economics of Global Turbulence: A Special Report on the World Economy, 1950–1998," *New Left Review* 229 (May–June 1998); and Saskia Sassen, *The Mobility of Labor and Capital: A Study in International Investment and Labor Flow* (New York: Cambridge University Press, 1988).

27. "The Sucking Sound from the East," *Economist*, July 26, 2003, 35–36; John Authers and Sara Silver, "Mexico's Lost Decade: As Investment Switches to China, the Opportunities Created by NAFTA Are under Attack," *Financial Times*, July 1, 2003, 13. Oxfam, *Agricultural Trade and the Livelihoods of Small Farmers*, March 2000, available at www.oxfam.org.uk/policy/papers/agricultural_trade/agric.htm, accessed May 15, 2003, argues that half a million Mexican small farmers have lost their livelihood since NAFTA put them in competition with U.S. farmers. Diana Alarcon Gonzalez, *Changes in the Distribution of Income in Mexico and Trade Liberalization* (Tijuana, Mexico: El Colegio de la Frontera Norte, 1994), provides a detailed discussion of Mexico's shift from import substitution industrialization to trade openness and its impact on the national distribution of income.

28. To be sure, there is only one China. To wit, its currency as of 2004 is not yet freely convertible, and therefore, the Chinese government can raise or lower its value to suit its domestic economic priorities, something other governments, including the United States, cannot do. In the twenty-first century, China has chosen to keep the value of its currency artificially low to stimulate foreign investment, export production, and thereby ensure a high continued rate of economic growth.

29. Joseph Stiglitz, "Poverty, Globalization, and Growth: Perspectives on Some of the Statistical Links." In United Nations Development Programme, *Human Development Report 2003: Millennium Development Goals, A Compact among Nations to End Human Poverty* (New York: Oxford University Press, 2003), 80.

30. Mattias Lundberg and Lyn Squire, quoted in Martin Wolf, "The Big Lie of Global Inequality," *Financial Times*, February 25, 2000, 13.

31. World Bank, *World Development Report, 2000–2001: Attacking Poverty* (New York: Oxford University Press, 2001), 195.

32. World Bank, *World Bank Press Review*, December 25, 2003, 3.

33. Frances Stewart, op. cit., 10.

34. Peter Collins, "Make or Break: A Survey of Brazil," *Economist*, February 22, 2003, 13.

35. Dominique van de Walle, "Incidence and Targeting: An Overview of Implications for Research and Policy." In *Public Spending and the Poor: Theory and Evidence*, edited by D. van de Walle and K. Nead (Baltimore: Johns Hopkins University Press, 1995), 601–16.

36. For specific cases of the costs versus the benefits of targeting, see essays collected in D. van de Walle and K. Nead, ibid.

37. Amartya Sen, op. cit., 177–78.

38. David Dollar and Paul Collier, *Globalization, Growth, and Poverty* (Washington, D.C.: World Bank, 2002); World Bank, *World Development Report, 2000–2001*, op. cit., 155–56. Martin Ravallion and Gaurav Datt in "Is Targeting through a Work Requirement Efficient? Evidence from Rural India," in D. van de Walle and K. Nead, op. cit., 435, evaluate the Maharashtra employment guarantee program and find that the program does reach the poor, but does not lift them out of poverty. Given administrative costs of targeting that involve assuring eligibility, they argue that it may better reduce poverty to simply provide direct grants to poor people.

39. World Bank, *World Development Report, 2000–2001*, op. cit., 153.

40. Richard Franke, op. cit., 179.

41. Marc Edelman, *Peasants against Globalization* (Stanford, Calif.: Stanford University Press, 1999), 46–87.

42. World Bank, *World Development Report, 2000–2001*, op. cit., 154.

43. Richard Franke, op. cit.

44. Hernando De Soto, *The Mystery of Capital: Why Capitalism Triumphs in the West and Fails Everywhere Else* (New York: Basic Books, 2000).

45. De Soto was named on July 25, 2003, to an elite UN commission headed by former Mexican president Ernesto Zedillo and former Canadian finance minister Paul Martin that will explore capital formation and small enterprise development among the poor of poor nations. See Felicity Barringer, "UN Will Back Entrepreneurs in Bid to Lift Poor Nations," *New York Times*, July 27, 2003, 5. John Williamson, the author of the Washington consensus, now calls for property titling as one of the major new initiatives for international development assistance. See his "The Poor Need a Stake in Developing Countries," *Financial Times*, April 8, 2003, 15.

46. Hernando De Soto, op. cit., 130.

47. World Bank, *World Development Report 2003, Sustainable Development in a Dynamic World: Transforming Institutions, Growth, and Quality of Life* (New York: Oxford University Press, 2003), 125.

48. Brazil is launching a titling program for poor people's housing in the favelas of its big cities, but it is also spending US$1.7 billion to build 250,000 new homes for low-income families as well. See Larry Rohter, "Brazil to Let Squatters Own Homes," *New York Times*, April 19, 2003, A7.

49. "Secretary-General Kofi Annan Launches Commission on Private Sector and Development," News Bulletin, United Nations Development Programme, July 25, 2003, available at www.undp.org/dpa/pressrelease/releases/2003/july/25jul03.html, accessed August 11, 2003. Prominent members of the commission include Robert Rubin, former U.S. Treasury secretary and executive committee chair of Citigroup; Rajat Gupta, senior partner worldwide of McKinsey, and Carleton Fiorina, chief executive officer, Hewlett Packard, as well as Hernando De Soto, among others.

50. Felicity Barringer, "UN Will Back Entrepreneurs," op. cit.

51. See Michael Blim, Made in Italy: Small-scale Industrialization and Its Consequences (New York: Praeger, 1990).

52. William Easterly, op. cit., 192.

53. Thorsten Beck, Asli Demirguc-Kunt, and Ross Levine, "Small and Medium Enterprises, Growth and Poverty: Cross-Country Evidence," World Bank Policy Research Working Paper 3178 (December 2003), available at http://econ.worldbank.org, accessed December 30, 2003, 1–26.

54. International Fund for Agricultural Development, The Challenge of Ending Rural Poverty: Rural Poverty Report 2001 (New York: Oxford University Press, 2001), 76, 79. However, the Chinese central government created hardship in other ways by shifting funding for health and education to local taxing authorities, and some of this increase in the cost of living in the countryside has led to massive emigration and the development of a "floating population" consisting of kin and affines from rural households who search for work in the eastern and rapidly industrializing provinces, as well as in the major cities. For an excellent recent treatment of this problem, see Li Zhang, Strangers in the City: Reconfigurations of Space, Power, and Social Networks within China's Floating Population (Stanford, Calif.: Stanford University Press, 2001).

55. Bruce Cumings, op. cit.

56. Editorial, "The World's View of Multinationals," Economist, January 29, 2000, 21.

57. Rough estimate based upon the World Bank's report that the world GDP in 1999 was US$30 trillion. See World Development Report, 2000/2001: Attacking Poverty (New York: Oxford University Press, 2001), table 12, 297.

58. Bennett Harrison, Lean and Mean: The Changing Landscape of Corporate Power in the Age of Flexibility (New York: Basic Books, 1994).

59. Dan Roberts and James Kynge, "How Cheap Labour, Foreign Investment and Rapid Industrialisation Are Creating a New Workshop of the World," Financial Times, February 4, 2003, 13.

60. Ibid. According to reporters of the Financial Times story, the Dongguan shoe factory pays the equivalent of US$96 a month, or US$.36 an hour for up to 69 hours a week. The reporters describe the factory and workers' dormitories as well lit and ventilated, and note also that Nike has a full-time monitoring office located at the plant whose job is reportedly to assure satisfactory living and working conditions for the workers. Though a judgment of exploitation with a human face might be fitting, again, there may be others worse or better. It is an empirical circumstance not automatically given by the large size of the endeavor.

61. Gosta Esping-Andersen, *Social Foundations of Postindustrial Economies* (Cambridge, U.K.: Cambridge University Press, 1999).

62. For a complete overview of the role of labor in late-developing countries, see essays collected under the title "Labor Unrest in the World Economy, 1870–1990," *Review of the Fernand Braudel Center* 18, no. 1 (Winter 1995), edited by B. Silver, G. Arrighi, and M. Dubovsky. In particular, consult Beverly Silver, "World Scale Patterns of Labor-Capital Conflict: Labor Unrest, Long Waves, and Cycles of Hegemony," 155–92.

63. Joseph Stiglitz, 2003, op. cit., 230.

CHAPTER TWELVE

Achieving Equality

One of the chilling and disconcerting facts we face in our lives is that we see the pattern of things only as we look back on events. Though living through the last gasps of the Roman Empire was surely mortifying to many of those who did, contemporaries probably had no idea that the Western world was about to tumble into the Dark Ages. Incredible to the modern reader as it may seem, a succession of generations after the fall actually forgot much of the basic know-how that had made living in the Roman world possible and, for some, tolerable. In our time, consider the following experiences. Did anything prepare German people who had lived during World War II for the almost giddying turnabout in their economic fortunes after the death of Hitler? How could the Russian people have predicted the vale of tears that the economic travails of post-Communist society have put upon them? Who indeed expected that a disease like AIDS would arise to destroy the dreams of economic development for hundreds of millions of sub-Saharan Africans?

Do we live in a Hobbesian world? Are we about to enter one? What would it mean to say we are or will be? In the circumstances of today's world, Thomas Hobbes in his magnum opus *Leviathan* (1651) bequeathed a controversial intellectual legacy that is well worth pondering. Hobbes's beliefs about human existence are as caustic to modern ears as they are uncompromising: Humans, while born equal, he believed, soon find themselves at war. It is precisely their natural equality and the equality of their hopes to attain their ends that creates a lack of trust among them. Thus, if two humans desire the same thing:

which nevertheless they cannot both enjoy, they become enemies; and in the way to their end, which is principally their own conservation, and sometimes their delectation only, endeavor to destroy, or subdue one another.[1]

In society, the combination of mistrust and desire, or even just a desire for conquest for reputation's sake, leads to the "war of every one against every one." The consequences of this state of constant war are:

[T]here is no place for industry; because the fruit thereof is uncertain: and consequently no culture of the earth; no navigation, nor use of the commodities that may be imported by sea; no commodious building; no instruments of moving and removing, such things as require much force; no knowledge of the face of the earth; no account of time; no arts; no letters; no society; and which is worst of all, continual fear, and danger of violent death; and the life of man, solitary, poor, nasty, brutish, and short.[2]

Is this where are our world is leading us, to chronic social chaos where one's loss is another's gain, where our lives are lived in continual fear and danger of violent death?

To answer the question, we must consider more closely what Hobbes implies. Like Rousseau, whom we discussed in an earlier chapter, the social calamity Hobbes describes is not a crime of human nature, but a crime against human nature. It occurs as humans seek to satisfy their needs and desires, material and even reputational, at the expense of other humans. For Rousseau, the wresting of surplus from another, the aggregation of riches, and the construction of a legal and social structure that protected this exploitation was in effect a war of the privileged against the powerless. For Hobbes, the struggle was perhaps even more elemental. No one in his war sought justice, and nothing was unjust. Power and advantage become ends in themselves. Only when the fear of death overwhelms all other sensations do humans seek peace. Then, in Hobbes's mind, humans are tamed by setting up a state so powerful as to make all stand in fear.[3]

It could be said that both Hobbes and Rousseau were born into a world used to arguments that contemplated few exclusions, that imagined solutions without the sticky residues of real life. In our age, exceptions and nuance are everything. Perhaps our sensitivity to the great variety of human experience and our ability to express it statistically and in complicated models of human society and behavior ill prepare us for their certainties, their predicating logics of the causes and consequences of human unhappiness. Rousseau's implicit advocacy of revolution and Hobbes's robust rationale for a strong monarchy may seem but interesting anachronisms to the contemporary reader.

Their emphasis on the pursuit of inequality and the social unrest it causes seems quite familiar to our ears. Yet, if something of Rousseau's ardor for equality found its way into the socialist revolutionary experiments of the twentieth century, the impulse for now seems quieted. Instead, it is the Hobbesian vision that comes uncomfortably close to our own experience. Incessant struggles for material goods, power, and domination, conflicts without boundaries and without binding moralities, the rise of obliterating machines of violence and death and, of course, the rise of a kingly nation such as the United States trying to reign above all by making the others stand in fear—these are the portents of a Hobbesian world.

A kind of moral indifference appears ascendant. The human misery, the privation and degradation we have documented here bespeaks the depths to which our economic inequalities, and thereby social and political inequalities, have grown. Ignoring this crime against human nature, to play forward the sense we might attach from the worlds of Hobbes and Rousseau, seems designed only to bring on more of the war of everyone against everyone. Can the monarch who "hath the use of so much power and strength conferred on him, that by terror thereof, he is enabled to form the wills of them all" be far behind?[4]

This chapter seeks to explore how to ease the flow toward reaction, and pursue a politics of equality. We have argued throughout the book that economic equality was first among the other dimensions of equality because without it, both survival and the capacity to successfully wage struggles for social and political equality would be sorely, if not fatally, compromised. We suggested that it would be hard to hold onto strictly political or social gains without the economic equality that provided capacity and fuel for struggle. At the same time, most of the actions that seem to lead to greater economic equality rest upon achieving success in the political arena. Hence, our judgment is that political equality is a necessary, but not a sufficient component of equality. In the pages that follow, we focus on its necessity, as well as its likelihood.

We look first at what can be done to foster greater economic equality in the workplaces of both poor and rich countries. Then we examine the egalitarian import of nongovernmental organizations and social movements, two key sources of activism in global society. Finally, we take a brief look back at our thesis and the arguments for it.

Equality in Workplaces, Poor and Rich

Can there be a version of capitalism that provides greater economic equality? Can firms be organized for the common good and owned collectively rather than being operated in the sole interests of their owners? Can their collectivization increase human sociability and regard? These questions animated Christian socialists, political radicals, workers, and, in the United States, prairie populists to experiment with cooperative economic activities, based upon the search for a common well-being and protection from the predations of capitalist-run economies. Though some parts of the movement shared the English reformer Robert Owen's interest in self-sufficient, autonomous communities, most sought to create an economic environment of equally shared economic burdens and rewards of running a business in mainstream capitalist society. By the middle of the nineteenth century, cooperatives of various sorts had sprung up in the United States, England, and continental Europe. By the end of the nineteenth century, both France and Italy had given legal sanction to cooperatives as special kinds of firms and had granted them several favorable financial concessions.[5] Throughout the United States, farmers after the Civil War built and cooperatively owned grain elevators, feed and seed stores, and even their small-town general stores as a way of reducing the costs of their goods, as well as protecting themselves against the vagaries of markets and the monopoly muscle of the railroad trusts and grain traders.

Though we little note their significance, cooperatives are an important presence in parts of the economies of many countries today. In the United States, for instance, 30 percent of the country's agricultural products are marketed through co-ops. Rural electrical cooperatives provide electricity for 26 million people. Credit unions have 80 million members and assets that exceed US$100 billion. In cooperatives of these sorts, the user is typically an owner whose participation comes via co-op board membership or voting at annual meetings.[6] While workers may be owners, too, they do not solely own the firms, and thus, despite the cooperative settings, the workers may not find themselves much more empowered to set wages and working conditions than they would in ordinary private firms.

Other countries have active cooperative movements. Counting both Eastern and Western Europe, there are some 83,000 cooperative enterprises utilizing the energies of 1.3 million worker-owners.[7] India, for example, boasts of more than 300,000 cooperatives with a remarkable membership of 146 million. Though it should be added that credit cooperatives akin to U.S. credit unions account for about one-third of the number of co-ops and two-thirds of total cooperative membership in India, a majority of the enterprises are industrial and employ 42 million worker-owners. This industrial cooperative sector accounts for 15 percent of India's manufacturing workforce.[8] India's extensive involvement in cooperative schemes owes much to its independence struggle from Britain and to Mohandas K. Gandhi's vision of a self-sufficient "village India." Dairy cooperatives, an outgrowth of the Gandhi-led independence movement, today are the largest rural employers in the country.[9]

In the eyes of many supporters of the worldwide cooperative movement, the collection of worker-owned and -operated enterprises clustered around the Basque town of Mondragon, Spain, are a sort of paragon of co-op success, and an object lesson in how to do it. From modest beginnings in 1956, they have become the eighth-largest industrial group in Spain, with sales of more than US$15 billion a year in industrial goods ranging from machines, tools, robots, and microchips to car parts and kitchen appliances. The 66,000 worker-owners enroll in the Mondragon cooperatives, a collection of 150 businesses, with earnest money amounting to US$10,000 apiece, which entitles them to part ownership in the firm. Every year, they approve the cooperative's business plan, which includes their level of compensation based upon anticipated revenues. A relatively flat skill hierarchy means that managers may make only three to four times what ordinary workers make, though competitive pressures have in some cases been lengthening the gap between the highest and lowest paid.[10] Managers can be dismissed by majority vote of the worker-owners in any Mondragon co-op firm at any time.[11]

Mondragon's success[12] suggests two things. First, cooperative enterprises need not be any less efficient than conventional, private profit-driven firms. In fact, as a comparison of private and cooperative firms performed in mid-1980s Italy shows, co-ops in some cases can have higher worker productivity than private firms.[13] Second, Mondragon's 150 firms are anchored by the cooperative's bank, a nationally prominent institution that enables the cooperative to raise capital and finance its technological upgrading and expansion more easily. Access to capital is generally hard for cooperatives. Conventional banks mistrust co-ops because they account for income, profit, and working capital differently than do private firms, and treat them as greater business risks than other corporate customers to whom they might loan.[14] This suggests that either cooperatives, organizations of cooperatives, or states need to assure that these sorts of firms have good access to capital markets, if they are to serve as important alternative forms of economic activity.

The impact of cooperative enterprises on economic equality in their areas is unknown. The effects are probably quite slight. Except in rare instances— say, the grain elevators of the U.S. Middle West and the countryside dairy co-ops of India, where they may have found unique market niches—they are minor players in a global economy characterized by for-profit enterprise and, most especially, one dominated by transnational firms. Yet within very specific contexts, worker-owned and -operated firms do distribute salaries and surpluses more equally than do for-profit firms—and certainly without the extraordinary salary differentials between top and bottom that one finds in transnational firms. In the case of consumer-oriented cooperatives, the local teachers' credit union, and the like, the financial circuits they use are probably not contributing much to the growth of large transnational banks and other large for-profit firms. To the extent the transnational firms contribute to economic inequality, the cooperatives remain holdouts from the growing consolidation of capital in the hands of the few firms and, finally, their owners.

Co-ops could prove a wedge by which countries, rich and poor, support what Fred Block calls "popular entrepreneurialism." It is a device whereby states could provide partial operating subsidies via tax breaks to cooperatives organized in areas of endeavor useful to society, but where state operation and control were neither wise nor necessary. In the United States, for instance, there is enormous demand for child care services, still unmet despite the efforts of government, nonprofits, and private providers. It is a classic case of market failure, a term of economic art we used in an earlier chapter. It means here that not all of the people needing child care can afford its cost; our inability to provide it has negative consequences for our society, including putting children at risk. Suppose the federal government were to provide a tax break equivalent to 50 percent of a cooperative's cost of providing child care. This would increase the supply of child care, while rewarding people for engaging in socially useful economic activities. Block puts it well when he says:

> the motive behind entrepreneurial effort need not be the search for enrichment; it can just as well be the desire to solve social problems or to provide attractive employment opportunities.[15]

In Sweden, instead of expanding state-run day care centers, the state encouraged the formation through tax incentives in 1988 of co-ops and private firms. By 1994, these co-ops comprised two-thirds of the private child care offered and accounted for a significant portion of the 10 percent of the nation's children who sought day care outside state-run centers. Sweden has begun to sponsor similar cooperative arrangements for the care of elderly, sick, and handicapped persons.[16]

Cooperatives, in sum, are a different kind of economic choice, one in which collective entrepreneurialism can be directly socially useful and lead to more egalitarian salary structures for worker-owners, and indirectly for society as a whole.

No Profit? Nongovernmental Organizations and the Third Sector

We have seen that cooperative enterprises take what a private firm owner calls profit and redefines it as surplus to be shared among worker-owners or saved for the common good. Along with flatter wage differentials, co-ops do make a dent in the everyday inequalities that derive from work life. Thus, they seem like worthwhile ventures for themselves, and are probably capable of absorbing a greater proportion of economic activities than they have in the past.

What if, however, we toss out the concepts of profit, profit sharing, and the like from our affairs? What if we start and/or work for a nonprofit corporation?

We will have joined what people are calling increasingly the "third sector" of the economy: not a state organ, not a private firm for profit, but a nonprofit entity chartered by the state that performs some public service. The nonprofit sector in the United States is immense. Much of our intensive medical care occurs in nonprofit hospitals. Nonprofit providers perform a significant portion of children's and family services, as well as drug, alcohol, and rehabilitative services. Nonprofit groups especially dedicated to people with particular special needs provide services for the blind, deaf, and persons with serious developmental disabilities. Our criminal justice system depends upon the ability of nonprofit providers to provide counseling, training, and postrelease supportive services. Daytime programs for seniors, child care, and early childhood education classes are another several areas of everyday life where nonprofit providers provide crucial services in support of families throughout the United States.

Nonprofit organizations also perform important functions throughout the world. An analysis of nonprofit operations in 22 countries, including Eastern Europe and Latin America as well as Western Europe, Australia, and the United States, shows that, on average, nonprofit workers account for 5 percent of employment in their countries. The distribution of outliers is somewhat predictable: Poorer countries in Latin America and Eastern Europe have smaller nonprofit sectors; richer countries, particularly those with ample welfare states or robust charitable resources, have larger nonprofit sectors. Regarding the latter, both the Netherlands and Belgium have generous welfare states, and each country seeks to solve its cultural pluralism by involving the nonprofit sector of various culturally different groups in their provision. The United States, on the other hand, has persistently sought to subcontract its welfare state to private providers rather than add state employees, which accounts for the fact that the nonprofit sector employs one of every twelve American workers.[17] Some recent estimates suggest that worldwide the sector has more than US$ 1 trillion in economic assets and employs 19 million people.[18]

The third sector includes the nongovernmental organizations (NGOs) that have become such important actors on behalf of poor people since the 1980s. They have started or joined initiatives that try to eliminate poverty and discrimination and bring about, whether in their country of origin or abroad, lasting social improvements in the lives of the world's disadvantaged peoples. There are believed to be at least 37,000 NGOs operating internationally, one-fifth of which were formed in the 1990s. Though no one has a good idea of how many NGOs are operating in each country, their numbers are no doubt vast. Recent tallies for India, for example, placed the number of national NGOs at 1 million; in Brazil the figure was 210,000. The United Nations Development Programme estimates that US$7 billion in development assistance, about one-tenth of the overseas aid of rich countries, is channeled through NGOs.[19]

To be sure, some NGOs do not regard improving the plight of the poor as part of their mission. Greenpeace, for instance, takes direct action against environmental polluters. Others seek to protect tropical rain forest and wildlife heritages.

But fostering economic development is a significant NGO activity. For instance, the Bangladesh Rural Advance Committee (BRAC) runs the largest private school system in the world, educating more than 1.1 million students per year in 34,000 schools throughout Bangladesh. It is particularly successful in getting girls into school; they comprise 70 percent of the school system's enrollment. Like the Grameen Bank, discussed in an earlier chapter on gender, BRAC is a big microlender, reaching 3.5 million women a year. It runs businesses, a university, and provides general health and prenatal care in 2,000 clinics. It gainfully employs 62,000 people in its schools, clinics, and enterprises.[20] BRAC estimates that it is providing gainful employment for 5.5 million persons.[21]

In a sense, BRAC is not simply supporting development; it is helping develop Bangladesh directly by its efforts. It is also filling the void in state actions to provide basic education and health care. BRAC is also acting to provide employment opportunities and banking access in a context where the private sector is either unable or unwilling to do so.

The efforts of NGOs such as BRAC and Grameen probably go further than most to intervene directly in markets in trying to alleviate poverty. Other NGOs provide funds and technical assistance to local groups engaged in specific improvement projects. Craig Warkentin's analysis of the activities of Womankind Worldwide, founded in London in 1989, is suggestive of the way many NGOs work. Womankind first elaborated its goal as helping women to achieve more rights worldwide and to acquire the skills that would enable them to reach their full human potential. The organization provides funds and support for local NGO initiatives. In one case, they supported the efforts of a Ghanaian women's self-help association to improve crop yields so that local women might pay off medical bills brought on by a local attack of cerebrospinal meningitis. In another, they worked with Indian women's NGOs to organize and educate women newly elected to Indian village councils subsequent to a 1993 constitutional amendment mandating women's participation in local elective offices. In sum, NGOs such as Womankind Worldwide supply money and expertise to local NGOs that are committed to their goals.[22]

Though disaster relief and economic development remain key items on many NGO agendas, there has been a noticeable shift over the past several decades toward activities that advocate social justice. Oxfam International, originally Oxford Committee for Famine Relief when it was founded in 1942, describes itself as the United Kingdom's "very first permanent charity shop." After 20 years of short-term relief work, it began undertaking development projects in which it sought to work with poor people "to help them help themselves." Now explicitly dedicated to putting an end to poverty worldwide, it has become a formidable advocacy agency. Its policy papers, many of which have been used in this book, and its constant presence at international organizations and forums, have made Oxfam a major protagonist among NGOs in the struggle for a fairer deal for poor countries in the acrimonious negotiations over trade and aid between North and South.[23]

At the grassroots level, NGOs are often deeply involved by necessity in local and national politics. In many places, service and activism have been fused, either in one organization or by alliances among several different groups. The Bombay political landscape, for instance, includes a broad-based alliance of a social-work-centered NGO concerned with urban poverty, a community organization advocating for slum dwellers, and a women's organization focusing on women's self-help activities. In turn, these three groups have organized pavement dwellers and street children in Bombay's poorest neighborhoods. They share expertise and leverage their popular power to extract resources from a highly politicized city and state apparatus, while refusing to become a part of any political machine. They are particularly keen on developing links across and outside of India with like-minded organizations, building learning and support links as they go.[24]

Though an inadequate "guide" to the scope and variety of efforts that have come in on the high tide of activism represented in the spectacular rise of NGOs throughout the world, the above instances suggest some of its potentials for a politics of equality. In many cases, the connection to inequality is organic: The NGOs are composed of poor and disadvantaged people who have organized themselves. The cases of popular organizations in Bombay and of BRAC in Bangladesh for the most part fit this description. They engage in popular struggle for a greater share of local, regional, and/or national resources. To the extent that they transfer resources to the poor or help trigger the process, they fit into our evolving notion of a politics of equality.

In other cases, NGOs work with and for poor and disadvantaged people, and they also claim to represent them in the global struggles for social justice. We have noted how some NGOs are in fact hybrids, offering care to poor people and engaging in advocacy on their behalf. Oxfam and Womankind Worldwide are exemplars of this kind of organizational mission. Their efforts may indeed diminish equality in locales where they work, provided that they actually transfer resources from rich countries to poor people. Their advocacy on behalf of people in poor countries adds voice of moral concern to the international mix of opinion-making. It must be said, though, that NGO advocacy is no substitute for the participation of poor people in their own politics or that of the world. And it does not solve the most fundamental problem of poor people's political equality.

The growing prominence of NGOs has been highly discomfiting to some. Critics pose two questions. First, aren't NGOs simply filling in for the care and services that states should be providing, and thus relieving states of their responsibilities, as Ronald Dworkin puts it, for "equal concern"? Second, are NGOs becoming, wittingly or unwittingly, agents of a new world order, in which social protections become individual privileges rather than rights, and palliative care is offered the poor to assure political quiescence?

The strongest criticism that the NGOs have fielded is that they are agents of Western imperialism. The belief is that NGOs defuse popular unrest and reorient people in poor countries to the policies and demands of rich countries.[25] It is also argued that otherwise repressive and/or unresponsive poor states use NGOs to perform functions they no longer can or want to perform, especially as many states have been forced to withdraw from providing basic human services under the terms of economic stabilization agreements with the International Monetary Fund. In this case, NGOs help these regimes create an undeserved political consensus.[26]

There is also concern that NGOs are fostering new social inequalities among the poor. When NGOs enter poor areas, they bring financial and political power that few, if any, can rival. Thus, those whom they recruit bene-fit as clients and employees, and the fear expressed by several observers is that they become detached and alienated from their base in poor communi-ties. Moreover, this new local elite's survival depends upon protecting the NGOs' interests, rather than advancing popular struggles for political and economic equality.[27]

This position has merit, even if the claim of imperialism might exceed our empirical capacities for proof. In our earlier discussion of microlending and women, we noted how what can be loosely called the development commu-nity, composed of international organizations, the aid agencies of donor countries, and NGOs, was subject to the changing political winds that em-anate from the capitals of rich countries, and particularly from Washington, D.C. Power politics clearly influences the kinds of projects that NGOs pur-sue. We have seen how an enthusiasm for entrepreneurialism has swept the development community, landing at the top of the policy heap with a blue-ribbon UN commission. While it is true that microlending actually began among poor women in poor countries as their answer to problems of credit scarcity, it became an almost mandatory development device when both Re-publican and Democratic administrations in Washington directed U.S. over-seas development aid into subsidizing NGO start-ups of microcredit circles and banks in poor countries.[28]

To be sure, then, powerful rich country forces intervene to steer the nor-mative policy flow of the development community. But it is also true that this community has developed its own internal system of rewards and incen-tives that, like all normative structures, pushes people to do what everyone whom they consider important says is the thing to do. For instance, if you are an NGO development officer, and all of the conferences you attend, all of your NGO counterparts, and all of the available research suggest that mi-crolending produces good results, you, too, will want to microlend. More-over, your NGO will get access to the system's rewards, such as contracts from international aid agencies, the United States Agency for International De-velopment (USAID), and larger NGOs that also want to show success for their investments. You may believe that imperialism is alive and well in the international system, but you surely don't consider yourself its handmaiden, and you still think that microlending is a policy alternative resulting from the analysis of the best development practices available.

The question does arise: "best practice" by whose standards? And here, then, the problem of political equality is exposed. Working on behalf of poor people is not the same as working with them, their assessments, and their vi-sions of their future. Nor is there any automatic assurance that even a fruitful combination of NGOs and poor people will produce a politics of equality. The first thing to suggest is that collaborations between NGOs and communities need to advance effective democracy both in their operations and in the society at large. In the phrase of the Italian political theorist Norberto Bobbio cited earlier, a process needs to assure "the fullest possible participation of interested parties."[29] It is likely that NGOs can make themselves heard, though they may find themselves in opposition to political regimes of various sorts. But poor people, in relation to all other actors, most often more powerful than they are, are those for whom political equality must be a priority if their well-being, needs, and desires are to count. NGOs must not only be democratic in their processes involving poor and disadvantaged people, but advocate effective democracy for poor and disadvantaged people in all of their programs.

Second, and perhaps more obviously, NGOs must be careful to use economic equality as their guide. Are significant resources being transferred to poor and disadvantaged people? Are some programs more successful in doing it than others? We noted before that programs can be good, or be "best practices," without having a significant impact on inequality. NGOs, no less than anyone else who finds themselves in markets—even if NGOs are nonprofit, they still form a coherent market—become easily preoccupied with the means-ends business logic of efficiency and cost-effectiveness. So, to reprise an earlier argument, microlending to women makes business sense because start-up costs are low, repayment rates are high, and the projects often become self-supporting. We noted, though, that microlending is a nonstarter as regards equality. In all, then, we are insisting on a higher standard: well-being anchored in equality.

Change toward greater equality in NGO processes and programs can occur gradually, and there is no reason why states themselves can't support democratic environments in which NGOs, both local and international, can participate in helping poor people achieve more well-being. The Indian state of Andhra Pradesh (population 80 million) in 2000 began an antipoverty program that looks like and operates as an NGO. With funding from international organizations, the NGO Velugu (meaning "light" in the Telugu language) has targeted the poorest villages in its poorest districts, and offers an array of activities aimed at eliminating the systematic presence of rural poverty. At first blush, the program seems like another microlending program, for the first thing it does in a village is form self-help groups among women in the lowest castes and show them how to save and provide each other with small credits to keep their households going. Realizing, however, the basic paucity of resources in the village, it authorizes the women to offer a limited number of loans with funds provided by the NGO to local endeavors that they believe can improve market access for goods produced by people in the village. For instance, in one village a self-help group decided to organize the marketing and transportation of local grain production. As a collective, they lowered both transaction and transportation costs, made a modest profit, and passed on savings to the local farmers. In another village, a self-help group financed the start-up of a basket-weaving cooperative, once more increasing producers' yields by uniting them and helping them get more out of the market. In these cases, we see that Velugu goes one step beyond microlending as it is traditionally conceived. Women in self-help groups can collectively tap outside monies and make social interventions locally on their own.

Two other features of Velugu add to its equality potential. First, the NGO staff helps villages and their self-help groups do an analysis of the village economy in order to get some idea of its actual basis, as well as its strengths and weaknesses. The assessment is then matched with NGO resources to help villagers plan how they can function economically with greater success in the markets. The basket-weaving co-op and the graining marketing group are examples of the kinds of solutions that arise with study of the local economic appraisal. Second, Velugu provides a centralized training center for turning out "barefoot" (paraprofessional) practitioners in animal husbandry, agriculture, and veterinary medicine, so that the village resource base is enriched.[30]

Local self-determination and greater access to resources mark Velugu as a progressive move in the right direction. In Kerala, India, the state took these notions one step further. The state instituted a planning process whereby it encouraged villages, democratically reconstituted by an Indian federal constitutional amendment into self-governing entities, to assess their needs and submit requests for state government support of local projects aimed at economic development. To fund the process, the state set aside 40 percent of its annual budget for disbursement to village initiatives. Some 100,000 volunteers were trained to support grassroots planning that utilized public assemblies and citizen committees to acquire the necessary local data and draft workable plans. Emphasis was placed on maximum citizen participation.[31]

An analysis of the projects for which requests were sought and monies disbursed provides an interesting window into how poor local communities in Kerala assessed their needs. The biggest share of outlays went into support of agriculture, twice what the state until then had been spending. The village plans called for spending on garden crops rather than paddy production of rice, which had been a long-standing development priority for the state in its drive for self-sufficient agriculture. Local people also invested heavily in animal husbandry, another income aid to small and marginal farmers. Other areas of major expenditure were drinking water and sanitation, housing, roads and bridges.[32]

Effective democracy created by greater political equality makes a difference. "Participatory budgeting," a process whereby citizens shape the priorities of state and local spending through processes not unlike those that take place in Kerala, has also become an important vector of democracy in Brazil. Starting in the city of Porto Alegre in 1989, more than 100 Brazilian cities now engage citizens in budget-making. Again, as in Kerala, people's democratic preferences create priorities different from even those developed by representative government. Porto Alegre citizens put environmental sanitation and street lighting into the city budget. Over seven years, the people's pressure for results in sewage, clean water, and education led to changes in city spending patterns and improved well-being. Thanks to city investment, the portion of households with fresh water rose from 80 percent to 98 percent, with sanitation from 46 percent to 85 percent, and school enrollments doubled. Since 1989, the number of citizens involved in the process has quintupled.[33]

We began this discussion of the third sector and NGOs with care and charity and ended up with popular democracy and political equality for poor people, with states actively encouraging well-being by changing the way they work. It is no paradox. If we keep an egalitarian eye on the well-being of poor and disadvantaged people, then political equality as a process and a demand creates an environment whereby both state and nonprofit sectors can help each other do what they need to be doing.

Moving for Change

Civic life and citizen activity are growing, the World Bank reported in 2003. An international survey of civic participation in eleven countries showed that 25 percent of the population were regular religious congregants, 9 percent were political party members, and 6 percent belonged to environmental groups.[34] For those who believe that we are witnessing an upswing in grassroots democracy around the world, these are reassuring data.

Other data are not. To recall an observation made earlier in this book, democracy flourishes more in name than in deed in a large portion of the world, according to the United Nations Development Programme. The UN survey showed that only 140 out of 200 countries hold multiparty elections, and of these it would characterize only eighty as real democracies. More than half of the total of 200 still abridge their own constitutional rights and guarantees.[35]

Movements for political, social, and economic equality are significant sources of effective democracy. They can aggregate people's interests and passions for dignity and well-being and, by their actions, help bring equality closer to a lived reality. Sometimes they arise like union movements and other organizations of workers in direct confrontation with firms, their managers, and the capital behind them. Other times movements rise up, as David Harvey describes it, because people are being dispossessed of the very conditions of their existence, whether it be land for a peasant, health insurance and retirement benefits to an industrial or service worker, or drinkable water to a city dweller.[36] We have also witnessed in the past century momentous movements against colonialism and dictatorships of various sorts. Many people have been fortunate to act in and share the benefits of movements for equality as regards race, gender, disability, and sexuality. The vast panoply of social and political movements both at home and worldwide, as Marc Edelman points out, come in all sizes, work at many different levels of social life, and, our biases notwithstanding, come in all political persuasions.[37]

Movements for equality are often part and parcel of political and social milieus that also generate activities like cooperatives and NGOs. In some sense, movements are healthier and stronger, in my view, when they can weave themselves into greater swatches of the social fabric that run through workplaces, households, and communities. While some movements are sparked directly by the experience of injustice, others emerge out of searches for personal meaning that bring people together in collective endeavors.

It is important in the midst of this resurgence of citizen activity and, given the limited democratic means available to many around the world, that movements rededicate themselves to equality and that each of us considers our attachments to groups with equality in mind. Given the argument of this book, it would make no sense to argue anything else. What it means is that we apply a simple measure to our commitments: Does the movement or group to which I belong, support, agitate for, and pursue equality in its economic, social, and political dimensions? Are there others more central to the struggle for equality that I should be supporting instead?

This insistence upon equality and a register of intensity in movements may be a bit bracing, even austere, but it puts in bolder relief some choices over others. Labor movements, for instance, acquire an added appeal, for they struggle directly over the distribution of economic surplus, with both firms and states. Battles over worker rights, wages, and welfare states are occurring throughout the industrializing world in nations such as Brazil, Korea, South Africa, Argentina, India, and even China.[38] In the United States, after a fifty-year period when organized labor ignored the needs of new working populations, including women, people of color, and immigrants, and protected its domestic workers by working to shut out the products of workers abroad, the AFL-CIO since the 1990s has evolved in new and positive directions. It now supports immigrant rights at home, organizes women and people of color, and works to support union organizing and worker protection abroad.[39] The AFL-CIO has worked with Mexican trade unions and NGOs in the *maquiladora* assembly districts along the Mexican side of the U.S.-Mexican border to support workers' rights.[40]

This is not to suggest an automatic pass for trade unions onto the "good list" in the politics of equality. It is impossible to know in advance whether a given union or labor struggle advances the cause of equality or not. The checkered career of the AFL-CIO, despite its recent reorientation, suggests caution. Yet in the battles over the economic and social protections provided by states in rich countries such as the United States and the European Union members, unions have been almost uniformly stalwart in their defense, often holding a lonely vigil as old political allies have come to value deregulated labor markets over workers' and old-age security. And in rapidly industrializing countries as well as in poorer countries reliant upon extractive industries like mining, unions find themselves in the thick of fights for equity in the workplace and more equality in their societies.[41]

There are also most likely hundreds of thousands of popular movements throughout the world that are pressing for equality in its several dimensions. They reach out to us for solidarity and support, whether they are a walk away down a city street or in a small town center, or whether they reach us through U.S.-based NGOs, a campus or community meeting, or through the Internet. They are as near to us as we let them be, and I hope that arguments presented here bring them closer still.

Again, the questions for most of us concern how to know we as members or supporters should act, given our beliefs. Participation in or support of movements for equality do not just depend upon us subscribing to "equality." That is a necessary but insufficient condition for intelligent involvement. As we have tried to do throughout this book, we must also develop a sense of what actions, policies, programs, and the like hold some prospect of bringing greater equality, and which among many show more promise than the others.

This last is important because we have incorporated into our analysis here a pragmatic criterion: Since the world, its environment and resources, are limited goods, we need to make the best possible use of them. We need to eliminate the clear nonstarters, those proposals that are equality neutral, and those that create more inequality. But as Amartya Sen pointed out with respect to targeting resources, one does not want to grasp the reins of change so tightly that the needs of many deserving people are set aside in an obsession with a perfectly calculated program. We also need to act cautiously because there are a variety of means that can enhance human well-being. There are many ways to a "good-enough economy," for instance, as we showed in the prior chapter. It is up to people to choose among them democratically, an action and set of actions which themselves enhance well-being. As we have seen just above, people's ideas can be very different from those of their leaders, even if the leadership itself has a strong popular base, as in the cases of Kerala and Porto Alegre.

Practice, experience—these are the things that show us the ways in which we might move toward greater equality. What we can do here is engage in one last thought experiment. Through the brief discussion of one case, the Zapatista movement of the southern region of Chiapas in Mexico, we might explore how and why it is important to keep equality uppermost in the aspirations of movements.

Since their armed uprising on January 1, 1994, the same day that NAFTA was implemented, the Zapatista National Liberation Army (EZLN) has become an international symbol of local resistance to the depredations of global capitalism. The Zapatista advocacy of local indigenous and cultural autonomy has earned them worldwide respect. Their ability to engage the Mexican government directly in negotiations over their demands, culminating in a 1996 accord and a 2001 march on Mexico City to press for changes in national law governing indigenous peoples, has gained the Zapatistas much admiration among those sympathetic to their views.[42] Their degree of success has in part fueled the belief of many, including esteemed anthropologist June Nash, to argue that "indigenous peoples will become the chief protagonists of change in the coming millennium."[43]

There have been many twists and turns of fortune in the protracted conflict between the Mexican government and the Zapatistas, and there will surely be more. One of the most interesting turning points was the San Andres accords, an agreement forged between the government and the movement that was signed in February 1996, and which the Mexican president, eleven months later, subsequently rejected. The accords provide insights into the movement's philosophy and beliefs. The Zapatistas' primary objectives in 1996, a balanced reading of the accords suggests, was to secure regional and indigenous self-determination and autonomy within the state of Mexico. This meant that the state must recognize indigenous peoples' "own internal normative systems," with respect to the administration of justice and respect "the right to free association in municipalities with populations that are predominantly indigenous . . . in order to coordinate their actions as indigenous peoples." The Zapatistas, in turn, recognize that Mexico is a pluricultural society, and thus must guarantee equality for all Mexicans before the law instead of creating "special codes of law that privilege particular people." These issues are taken up and discussed extensively in ten pages of lawyerly prose. With some regret, it must be reported that "the provision of basic needs" and discussions of what the state must do to support them are confined in general language to a clause.[44]

Others have suggested something of the same about the accords. One of the close observers of the Zapatistas commented on this imbalance to political scientist Judith Hellman:

> What I think is needed is not autonomy but a serious redistributive policy. Autonomy would only mean that these impoverished people would even be more enclosed in their misery. What we should be demanding is that the poorest, disadvantaged regions receive a greater proportion of the national wealth. It's little wonder that this proposal on autonomy is the only part of the San Andres agreement that the Mexican state was willing to sign on to. It costs the state nothing if the indigenous people close in on themselves.[45]

This anonymous commentator has captured what needs to be said. The way to equality, in this case economic equality that might facilitate the social equality Zapatistas desire, emanates from involvement and struggle with the Mexican state. The Mexican state, again in the words of that Brooklyn bank robber, is where the money is. Autonomy, perhaps too closely tracking a notion of economic autarky here, does not offer much prospect of creating a politics of equality in Mexico or of improving peoples' lives in Chiapas.

That we could be the flies on the wall in the Zapatista camp and have access to how they might respond! The point, though, for our purposes, is to engage in constructive criticism of the choices they have made, and those that they might make in pursuit of equality. It also gives us some idea of how to engage a world full of possibilities for change, but often not completely focused on what we have argued here is the main event.

As citizens and perhaps as activists, there are many parts we can play, based upon our beliefs in equality. Justice for Janitors, living wage campaigns, campus antisweatshop mobilizations—movements for equality are where you find them. The key is to keep a lookout for the opportunities that movements, voluntary action, and workplace organizations hold for equality, and to measure their prospects against the magnitude of people's needs and the energies particular movements are expending. Some movements have bigger equality payoffs than others.

Rejecting a Hobbesian World: Espousing Equality

We need not live in a Hobbesian world. The specter of one is now apparent. But it is still one of many historical possibilities.

Another possibility is enhancing universal well-being through equality. We have argued that the three dimensions of equality—economic, social, and political—all need tending if well-being is to be secured. However, we have given economic equality priority in the belief that unless it is solved, material life itself for billions can be fatally compromised, and assuredly the other dimensions of equality would not flourish. We have shown how social inequalities that arise from discrimination by race and gender need economic solutions, and suggested as well that political equality could be achieved in any lasting way only if the deficits of economic inequality were erased.

The world as it is will not produce equality. Accelerated economic growth will not do it either. Even the bravest of economic forecasts, we have seen, only envisions halving the poverty rates in poor countries, leaving the question of economic equality completely aside. We have argued that equality of opportunity for disadvantaged people is not enough, and that equality of re-sources offers the only likelihood of achieving equality in its three dimen-sions. Thus we explored how some approaches to the redistribution of re-sources show some promise for achieving equality.

We have argued that capitalism is a crisis-bearing inequality-maker that must be tamed. We have also shown that there are a variety of ways of work-ing within a capitalist world economy that do not cause its collapse. Some provide just as much, and sometimes more well-being than the kind of "Wild West" capitalism that people in the United States often suppose is necessary for capitalism to flourish. Thus, we have set forth some ideas about what a "good-enough" economy would look like, while arguing for redistribution of resources on a significant scale.

In the world as it is, gradual steps toward our goal are more likely than gi-ant steps. Let that be accepted, but not with a kind of Panglossian grace. False reassurance abounds, and mythmaking has become an international pastime. Consider a 2003 version: Rising incomes worldwide, but particularly in Asia, are creating, in the words of the authoritative *Economist* magazine, "a huge middle class." When you consult the *Economist's* accompanying graph and look up the research that supports it, sure enough, you find that the distribution of world income since 1970 shows a growth in the number of persons with an income of US$3,000 or more by 2000. The bulge in the graph at US$3,000 is quite big, but when one consults the scale upon which the data are depicted, the range of population shown on the graph going from

0 to 300 million, one finds a slim victory indeed. Out of the earth's 6 billion, some 250 million now boast an income of US$3,000. This high point on the line graph at US$3,000 amounts roughly to 4 percent of the world's population. To be sure, more people make more money as the slope of the line travels toward US$100,000, but its trajectory is steeply downward. It leaves one wondering how these data confirm the existence of a huge middle class.[46]

We can all be victims of illusions. A towering graph pitched on a small scale, the bustle of cell phones, "McMansions," and lavish weddings in a Bombay, Beijing, or Kuala Lumpur: There is our huge middle class. If we were to put them all in one country, as they are often clustered visibly in one or two of a nation's cities, the impression would grow upon the observer that the world is becoming more middle class. An honest mistake, but we are all finally responsible for our naïveté.

There is nothing wrong with the illusion if it becomes fact. It is our job to make it so. There are many good things in human life as we know it, attributes of life that we deeply enjoy, such as companionship, security, imagination, accomplishment, and the satisfaction involved in enjoying all of these experiences. But there is at base only one great good thing, and that is equality. It is the virtue that assures that all persons have some prospect of enjoying the others.

Pursuing equality in everyday life provides one with a kind of Occam's razor with which to appraise the social consequences of economic and political policies at any level of everyday life, including the homely acts we call our own behavior. It cuts away the array of arguments, rationales, and rationalizations that surround even the simplest of human decisions. It demands an answer to one basic question: Does a policy, does an organization, do my actions advance equality, or not? Of the many questions we can ask of contemplated actions, this is the one that cuts closest to the needs and concerns of human well-being in our world.

If we value well-being for ourselves and all others with whom we share human life, this is the instrument we must use. I hope that this book has convinced you that this is so.

Notes

1. Thomas Hobbes, *Leviathan: On the Matter, Forme and Power of a Commonwealth Ecclelsiasticall and Civil*, edited by M. Oakeshott (New York: Collier Books, 1962), 98–99.

2. Ibid., 100.

3. Ibid., 101–2.

4. Ibid., 132.

5. Robert Oakeshott, *The Case for Workers Co-ops* (London: Routledge, 1978), 148–53. In Italy, cooperative rights were inserted directly into the new, post-Fascist constitution of 1947, and a law passed the same year exempted their capital interest earnings from state tax.

6. National Cooperative Business Association, *Co-op Primer*, available at www.ncba.coop.org/abcoop-stats.cfm, accessed June 15, 2004. See William Greider, *The Soul of Capitalism: Opening Paths to a Moral Economy* (New York: Simon and Schuster, 2003), for highly useful and interesting discussions of how cooperatives and worker buyouts have been working in the United States.

7. European Conference of Workers' Cooperatives, Social Cooperatives, and Participative Enterprises (CECOP), available at www.cecop.org/uk, accessed June 15, 2004.

8. T. M. Thomas Isaac, Richard Franke, Pyaralal Raghavan, *Democracy at Work in an Industrial Cooperative: The Story of Kerala Dinesh Beedi* (Ithaca, N.Y.: Cornell University Press, 1998), 14–15; Richard Franke and Barbara Chasin, "Power to the (Malayalee) People," *Bulletin of Concerned Asian Scholars*, available at www.bcas-net.org/articlesandresources/article2-9.htm, accessed June 15, 2004.

9. Amy Louise Kazmin, "Gandhi and the Milk of Indian Self-Reliance," *Financial Times*, August 24, 2000, 8.

10. Sharryn Kasmir, *The Myth of Mondragon: Cooperatives, Politics, and Working-Class Life in a Basque Town* (Albany: SUNY Press, 1996), finds that management pressure is producing votes to increase manager-worker compensation differentials.

11. William Foote Whyte and Kathleen King Whyte, *Making Mondragon: The Growth and Dynamics of the Worker Cooperative Complex* (Ithaca, N.Y.: Cornell University, 1988); Davydd Greenwood, "Labor-Managed Systems and Industrial Redevelopment: Lessons from the Fagor Cooperative Group of Mondragon," in *Anthropology and the Global Factory: Studies of the New Industrialization in the Late Twentieth Century*, edited by F. Rothstein and M. Blim (New York: Bergin and Garvey, 1992), 177–90.

12. See William Foote Whyte, "The Mondragon Cooperatives in 1976 and 1998," *Industrial and Labor Relations Review* 52, no. 3 (April 1999), 478–81, for a brief review of co-op success over time.

13. Will Bartlett, John Cable, Saul Estrin, Derek Jones, and Stephen Smith, "Labor-Managed Cooperatives and Private Firms in North-Central Italy: An Empirical Comparison," *Industrial and Labor Relations Review* 46, no. 1 (October 1992), 103–18.

14. William Foote Whyte and Kathleen King Whyte, op. cit., 72, 262; Davydd Greenwood, op. cit., 183.

15. Fred Block, *The Vampire State and Other Myths and Fallacies about the U.S. Economy* (New York: The New Press, 1996), 235–40, 236.

16. Victor Pestoff, "Social Enterprises and Civil Democracy in Sweden: Developing a Participatory Welfare Society in the 21st Century," in *21st-Century Economics: Perspectives of Socioeconomics for a Changing World*, edited by W. Halal and K. Taylor (New York: St. Martin's Press, 1999), 307.

17. Edith Archambault, "The Third Sector in France," *German Policy Studies* 1, no. 2 (2000), 189–208, available at www.spaef.com/GPS_PUB/v1n2, accessed June 15, 2004; Marco Revelli, *La Sinistra Sociale: Oltre la civilta del lavoro* (Torino: Bollati Boringhieri, 1997), 168.

18. This estimate is used frequently, though I have been unable to ascertain how it was derived or what organizations were counted as NGOs. Given the big numbers, it almost certainly must include all traditional charities and charitable foundations, as well as the kinds of charitable and politically active hybrids we usually consider as NGOs. Thus, while misleading in accounting for the post–World War II boom in NGOs, it might better capture the dimensions of the third sector. Sources for the estimates include SustainAbility, *The 21st Century NGO: In the Market for Change*, available at www.sustainability.com/programs/pressure-front/ngo-report.asp, accessed August 14, 2003; Quentin Peel, "How Militants Hijacked the NGO Party," *Financial Times*, July 13, 2001, 7.

19. Quentin Peel, ibid.; United Nations Development Programme, *Human Development Report 2002: Deepening Democracy in a Fragmented World* (New York: Oxford University Press, 2002), 5.

20. Amy Waldman, "Helping Hand for Bangladesh's Poor," *New York Times*, April 25, 2003, 7.

21. See www.brac.net/aboutb.htm, accessed August 19, 2003.

22. Craig Warkentin in *Reshaping World Politics: NGOs, the Internet, and Global Civil Society* (Lanham, Md.: Rowman & Littlefield, 2001), 100–104.

23. The Oxfam quotations are taken from Oxfam literature edited and presented by Craig Warkentin, ibid., 116–19, upon which this paragraph's description is based.

24. Arjun Appadurai, "Deep Democracy: Urban Governmentality and the Horizon of Politics," *Public Culture* 14, no. 1 (2002), 21–47.

25. James Petras, "NGOs: In the Service of Imperialism," *Journal of Contemporary Asia* 29, no. 4 (1999), 429–40; see also his "Imperialism and NGOs in Latin America," *Monthly Review* 49, no. 7 (December 1997), 10–27.

26. Lesley Gill, *Teetering on the Rim: Global Restructuring, Daily Life, and the Armed Retreat of the Bolivian State* (New York: Columbia University Press, 2000), 136–38.

27. Lesley Gill, ibid., 155–70; Jeremy Brecher, Tim Costello, Brendan Smith, *Globalization from Below: The Power of Solidarity* (Boston: South End Press, 2000), 86–88.

28. Since 1995, USAID has disbursed US$90 million in aid to microlending agencies. See www.usaid.gov, accessed August 19, 2003.

29. Norberto Bobbio, *The Future of Democracy* (Minneapolis: University of Minnesota Press, 1987), 19.

30. Karen Mason, "Women's Empowerment in Karnataka and Andhra Pradesh: Swa Shakti and the District Poverty Initiative Program," available at www.velugu.org/karen.html, accessed August 21, 2003; Edward Luce, "Hopes Pinned on Poor Women to Alter Economic Landscape of Village India," *Financial Times*, May 2, 2003, 5.

31. T. M. Thomas Isaac with Richard Franke, *Local Democracy and Development: People's Campaign for Decentralized Planning in Kerala* (New Delhi: LeftWord Books, 2000), 7–11.

32. Ibid., 205–8.

33. United Nations Development Programme, op. cit., 80–81.

34. World Bank, *World Development Report 2003, Sustainable Development in a Dynamic World: Transforming Institutions, Growth, and Quality of Life* (New York: Oxford University Press, 2003), 40.

35. United Nations Development Programme, op. cit., 1–2.

36. David Harvey, *The New Imperialism* (New York: Oxford University Press, 2003).

37. Marc Edelman, "Social Movements: Changing Paradigms and Forms of Politics," *Annual Review of Anthropology* 30 (2001), 285–317.

38. Jeremy Brecher, Tim Costello, and Brendan Smith, op. cit., 105.

39. See AFL-CIO website for various policy positions. For immigration, consult www.aflcio.org/issuespolitics/immigration, accessed August 23, 2003; for international position, see "Global Fairness and the Free Trade Area of the Americas (FTAA)," available at www.aflcio.org/aboutaflcio.ecouncil, accessed August 23, 2003.

40. Jane Bayes and Rita Mae Kelly, "Political Spaces, Gender, and NAFTA," in *Gender, Globalization, and Democratization*, edited by R. Kelly, J. Bayes, M. Hawkesworth, and B. Young (Lanham, Md.: Rowman & Littlefield, 2001), 165–66.

41. In a wonderful, though disheartening, set of narratives of the eventual fates of a highly politically mobilized labor movement led by tin miners in Bolivia, see first June Nash, *We Eat the Mines and the Mines Eat Us: Dependency and Exploitation in Bolivia's Tin Mines* (New York: Columbia University Press, 1979). Then read Lesley Gill's portrait of what became of the miners after the mines were shut down and their struggles against the government lost. See Gill, op. cit.

42. There are many, many accounts of the Zapatista movement and of the history of their conflict with the Mexican government. Because of a longstanding interest in the region, anthropologists have produced some of the most interesting and useful accounts of the movement and the context for its development. See George Collier with Elizabeth Quaratiello, *Basta! Land and the Zapatista Rebellion in Chiapas* (Oakland, Calif.: The Institute for Food and Development Policy, 1994); June Nash, *Mayan Visions: The Quest for Autonomy in an Age of Globalization* (New York: Routledge, 2001). For documents and commentaries, consult the collection by Tom Hayden, editor, *The Zapatista Reader* (New York: Nation Books, 2002).

43. June Nash, ibid., 26.

44. "San Andres Accords," translated by Rosalva Bermudez-Ballin, available at http://flag.blackened.net/revolt/mexico/ezln/san_andres.html, accessed June 15, 2004. In the "basic needs" paragraph, health, housing, and nutrition, particularly as regards women and children, are emphasized. Also, women's interventions in these areas are to be given priority.

45. Judith Hellman, "Real and Virtual Chiapas: Magic Realism and the Left," *Socialist Register*, 2000, available at www.yorku.ca/socreg/hellman.txt, accessed August 22, 2003.

46. The data were compiled and analyzed by Xavier Sala-i-Martin and published in a two-page conference summary reported by the International Monetary Fund in *IMF Survey*, March 17, 2003, 74–75, available at www.imf.org, accessed August 13, 2003. Bill Emmott, editor of the *Economist*, used the data and the graph developed by Sala-i-Martin in his 160th *Economist* anniversary focus article, "Radical Thoughts on Our 160th Birthday: A Survey of Capitalism and Democracy," June 28, 2003, 5.

Index

About the Author

Michael Blim teaches anthropology at the Graduate Center of the City University of New York. He is the author of *Made in Italy: Small-Scale Industrialization and Its Consequences* (1990) and coeditor of *Anthropology and the Global Factory* (1992).